Screenwriting in a Digital Era

Palgrave Studies in Screenwriting

Palgrave Studies in Screenwriting is the first book series to focus on the academic study of screenwriting. It seeks to promote an informed and critical account of screenwriting and of the screenplay, looking at the connections between what is produced and how it is produced, with a view to understanding more about the diversity of screenwriting practice and its texts. The scope of the series encompasses a range of study from the creation and recording of the screen idea, to the processes of production, to the structures that form and inform those processes, to the agents, their beliefs and the discourses that create those texts.

Screenwriting in a Digital Era

Kathryn Millard
Macquarie University, Australia

© Kathryn Millard 2014
Softcover reprint of the hardcover 1st edition 2014 978-0-230-34328-3
Corrected Printing 2013

First published 2014 by
PALGRAVE MACMILLAN

Palgrave Macmillan in the UK is an imprint of Macmillan Publishers Limited,
registered in England, company number 785998, of Houndmills, Basingstoke,
Hampshire RG21 6XS.

Palgrave Macmillan in the US is a division of St Martin's Press LLC,
175 Fifth Avenue, New York, NY 10010.

Palgrave Macmillan is the global academic imprint of the above companies
and has companies and representatives throughout the world.

Palgrave® and Macmillan® are registered trademarks in the United States,
the United Kingdom, Europe and other countries.

ISBN 978-1-349-34465-9   ISBN 978-1-137-31910-4 (eBook)
DOI 10.1057/9781137319104

A catalogue record for this book is available from the British Library.

A catalog record for this book is available from the Library of Congress.

Transferred to Digital Printing in 2014

Contents

Figures

Acknowledgements

I am grateful to many for support, encouragement and advice over the last three years. To my colleagues Iqbal Barkat, Maree Delofski, Peter Doyle, Marcus Eckermann, Gill Ellis, Mark Evans, Pat Grant, Bridget Griffith-Foley, Julian Knowles, Tom Murray, John Potts and Kate Rossmanith in the Department of Media, Music, Communications and Cultural Studies at Macquarie University; to Alex Munt at the University of Technology, Sydney; to Paul Wells at Loughborough University; to Adam Ganz at Royal Holloway, University of London and to David Carlin and Leo Berkeley at RMIT, Melbourne. Special thanks to Adrian Martin – whose presentation at the 'Cinematic Scriptwriting' Symposium we organised at the Museum of Sydney proved inspirational – and to screenwriter Keith Thompson from whom I have learnt much over the years in his role as script editor on some of my projects.

Thanks to research assistant Mikael Peck for all his patient work in helping to prepare the manuscript and to Tom Roberts who also contributed to this stage.

Thanks to the Faculty of the Arts at Macquarie University for funding for support for manuscript preparation.

Many thanks to my fellow Series Editors Steven Maras and Ian Macdonald for their support and advice. My sincere thanks to Commissioning Editor Felicity Plester for all her support and advice and to Chris Penfold from Palgrave for his work in helping bring this book to print.

I am especially grateful to Samuel Bollendorff, Guy Maddin, Yaron Shani, Shaun Tan and Au Kin Ye for providing insights into their respective work via email and Skype interviews.

Special thanks to J.J. Murphy, who not only provided excellent advice as editor of this book, but with whom I have maintained a dialogue on 'all things independent screenwriting' since we first encountered each other's work via the Screenwriting Research Network in 2007.

Lastly, special thanks to my partner and fellow writer, Noëlle Janaczewska, for her insightful comments and suggestions on drafts throughout the project.

An earlier version of Chapter 2 'Post Courier 12' was published as 'After the Typewriter: Screenwriting in a Digital Era', Journal of Screenwriting, Volume 1, Number 1, 1 January 2010, pp. 11–25.

Permissions

3.2 Collage by Guy Maddin for his film *Keyhole* (2012) reproduced with kind permission of Guy Maddin.

5.2 Shaun Tan's storyboard sketch for *The Lost Thing* (2010) reproduced by kind permission of Sophie Byrne and Passion Pictures.

6.1 Sophie Toporkoff's production still of the cast of *Putty Hill* (2010) reproduced by kind permission of Matthew Porterfield and the Hamilton Film Group.

8.1, 8.2, 8.3, 8.4 Photographs from *Journey to the End of Coal* (2008) photographed by Samuel Bollendorff and reproduced by kind permission of Samuel Bollendorff.

Introduction

One of my favourite parts of filmmaking is carrying out location 'recces'. Some begin as a door knock in a targeted neighbourhood. That is how the producer and I found the main location for our short feature *Parklands* (1996),[1] set in the suburbs of Adelaide in the mid-1990s. As the thermometer topped 30 degrees Celsius, we walked down street after street in Semaphore, a working-class suburb by the beach, and persuaded people to invite us in and show us through their homes. Eventually, we found a bungalow constructed from red brick in the period of austerity that followed World War Two. Renovated with a layer of pink stucco in the 1970s, it was a perfect fit for one of the film's central characters (Figure 0.1).

Flash-forward nearly a decade. A production designer and I spent day after day driving through expanses of semi-desert saltbush on the edge of Adelaide, looking for a key location for my feature *Travelling Light* (2003).[2] As we drove into the state's scorching, dry interior, the sunlight created a heat haze in the distance. It added to the sense of moving through a timeless, ever-shifting landscape. We eventually settled on a small town called Wild Horse Plains. Although it was close to our production base at the South Australian Film Corporation, it appeared to be in the proverbial 'middle of nowhere'.

It has often been observed that making a film is like going to war, and filmmakers initially borrowed the notion of 'recceing' or *reconnoitring* from their military counterparts. When wars were fought by troops on the ground, small units were sent ahead to check out the lie of the land. Their task was to gather as much information as possible about the terrain ahead and identify any potential obstacles. Smaller units had the advantage of being flexible and fast moving. If the reconnaissance report was favourable, then the military's main forces could be mobilised.

Figure 0.1   Parklands, 1996, Toi-Toi Pictures

This book could be seen as reconnaissance for what lies ahead for the screenplay as cinema is transformed in our digital era. Rather than only looking to the road ahead, however, I have also looked back to the early years of cinema, and to the history of visual media and screen practices more broadly. Just as it was then, cinema is in flux, and there are many resonances between early filmmaking and now. The metaphor of reconnaissance, with its emphasis on the observation of local terrains, seems particularly apt because one of the most pronounced shifts, I believe, is that screen stories are more and more *spatial* stories. Screenwriters and their collaborators create story worlds.

In film production offices, it is usual to have location photographs displayed on a corkboard or electronic whiteboard. Still photographs of possible locations are gradually added to the board as crew members return from reconnaissance trips: images of houses, hotels, bars, streetscapes, stretches of road and airport tarmacs. The potential locations are shot from different angles and at morning, noon or night, depending on the requirements of the script. Some photographs are taken down and replaced as more viable alternatives are found. As the jigsaw takes shape, the creative team walks around it, discussing the film-to-be.

Time-schedule graph

As digital technologies become more sophisticated, there has been a growing interest in analysing screenplays to provide detailed accounts of their structure. It has been suggested that a great deal of time and resources could be saved if data analysis was carried out on scripts before productions were financed and green lit. In the United States, a former statistics professor, Vinny Bruzzese, has established a company called the Worldwide Motion Picture Group to provide script reports based on data from similar films produced in the past. For a fee of as much as $20,000, Worldwide searches its databases and recommends script revisions or rewrites aimed at generating the highest possible box office returns globally.[3] Such services are being aggressively marketed as a means of reducing financial risk. Designed for studio movies, the methodology is gradually filtering down to mid-budget level films.

Regrettably, the search for a reliable way of ensuring box office success is not a new one. In the 1930s, the Hollywood studio RKO went so far as to employ an industrial engineer, M.J. Abbott, as a story analyst. *Popular Science* noted approvingly that making movies had previously been a hit-and-miss affair. RKO, though, now pre-edited their films according to time-tested engineering principles like those used in the construction of buildings, bridges and dams. The mysterious M.J. Abbott was charged with preparing a detailed *time-schedule graph* for each screenplay well in advance of production. All scripts needed to conform to the *units of value* he devised by analysing films that had been particularly successful at the box office. Armed with statistics, Abbott drew up a graph and informed the director of each film where particular scenes should begin and end.[4]

Follow the Fleet (1936),[5] a Fred Astaire and Ginger Rogers vehicle, was broken down into the following time-schedule graph:

- action: 44 and two thirds of a minute;
- dialogue: 21 and two thirds of a minute;
- inserts: eight ninths of a minute;
- titles: two minutes;
- singing: 11 and one third of a minute; and
- dancing: 16 and one third of a minute.

According to Abbott's meticulous and supposedly fail-proof structural calculations, the film would be a box office success if it ran at 96 and eight ninths of a minute. *Follow the Fleet* was indeed a popular success and returned a respectable profit for RKO. It's debatable, however, that this was a result of Abbott's industrial engineering approach to cinematic storytelling. The film featured the same key creatives as the previous year's smash hit, *Top Hat* (1935),[6] which was to be the studio's most profitable film of the 1930s.[7] Like *Top Hat*, *Follow the Fleet* was a loosely constructed screenplay designed to showcase Fred Astaire and Ginger Roger's dance routines and Irving Berlin's chart-topping songs. Despite M.J. Abbott's calculations, the completed film ran considerably over-length, at 110 minutes. In this case, it seems likely that RKO's story analysis, pre-visualisation and editing of the film was more connected to curbing costs than any creative strategies for realising the best possible film.

Over more than 25 years as a writer, director and academic, I have researched and written mid-budget feature films, arts documentaries, essay films and hybrids of fiction and nonfiction. I have assessed hundreds of feature scripts for national screen funding bodies and had both feature and nonfiction scripts and treatments selected for highly competitive pitches in Australia, Europe and the United States. I began to suspect that the endless script development programmes I participated in had remarkably little to do with actually making the best films possible. In recent years, after my essay film *The Boot Cake* (2008)[8] – about Chaplin imitators in India – unexpectedly collapsed at the final financing hurdle, I embraced a new, low-budget way of working, in which scripting and production were more closely intertwined. A semi-improvised soundtrack by composer Elena Kats-Chernin and an ensemble of jazz musicians was a feature of *The Boot Cake* and caused me to rethink the relationship between two practices often seen as belonging at opposite ends of the scale – composition and improvisation.

My next film, *Random 8* (2012)[9] was an experiment in structured improvisation with an ensemble cast. Inspired by a social psychology experiment devised by William Gamson, *Random 8*'s screenplay took the form of a two-page outline and a notebook filled with images and unattributed lines and actions. After a brief studio shoot with two Red high-definition cameras, I wrote another layer of the story in the editing room. I found the process of working with a small team of collaborators and writing between the studio and editing room exhilarating.

Beyond the well-made play

The history of screenwriting has long been dominated by the story of its recent past and, in particular, Hollywood and classical cinema. It is usually considered that the screenplay has a history of around 100 years and can be dated from the beginning of narrative cinema or the story film. The screenplay arrived on the scene in the early twentieth century as the new medium began to mature and narrative asserted its hold on the public imagination – or so we are told. Early studies of writing for the screen treated cinema as an entirely new medium which, emerging in the late nineteenth century, adapted the conventions of European theatre for the 'photoplay'.[10]

Tracing the evolution of the screenplay back further, Ken Dancyger and Jeff Rush proposed that the three-act structure, the dominant model for contemporary mainstream films, was derived from a version of French playwright Eugene Scribe's well-made play.[11] The well-made play, which emerged in the 1820s, emphasised plot and narrative exposition above all else. It is not difficult to see the debt of the contemporary screenwriting manual authors to Scribe's pattern of dramatic construction, which, in its day, was given the authority of a science.[12]

Evolution of screen practice

In recent decades, as we understand more about the prehistory and archaeologies of visual media and screen practice, the evolution of the screenplay begins to look more complex. Historians have traced the emergence of cinema to a much larger spectrum of visual media. Linear histories of progress have given way to more complex narratives of overlapping influences and tendencies. It is generally agreed, for example, that cinema first made its way to audiences in the late nineteenth century. The beginning of cinema is usually considered to be one of two dates: 1894, when the Edison Company held their first public screening of the *Kinetoscope* or, alternatively, 1895 when the Lumière Brothers shot and projected their *Cinèmatographe* films. Screen historians, however, have increasingly challenged the notion that cinema has a history of not much more than a century.

In the mid-1980s, film historian Charles Musser proposed that *cinema* was part of two overlapping forms of visual media. They could be described as *moving pictures*, on the one hand, and *screen practice*, on the other. Cinema could be defined as 'projected *motion* pictures and their sound accompaniment'. Screen practice, however, included *projected* images and their audio complement.[13] This expanded field of screen practice included magic lantern shows and could be traced back to the seventeenth century in Europe. Moving pictures included visual entertainments that did not necessarily involve projection such as peep shows and the mutoscope, a peephole flip-card device.[14]

From magic lanterns to cinema

Cinema was, in part, a transformation of magic lantern shows, in which showmen displayed images on a wall and added voices, music and sound effects. The magic lantern is often thought of as dating back to the 1650s. In the first edition of his *Ars Magna Lucis et Umbrae (Great Art of Light and Shade)* of 1646, Athanasius Kircher described a lamp used to project images onto a wall in a darkened room. Kircher was not the inventor of the magic lantern. The Dutch scientist Christiaan Huygens is usually credited as having invented the device around 1659.[15] As we will discover, the most likely scenario is that the inventors of the magic lantern were from Persia, India or China, where related devices were in use long before Europe. Kircher, however, provided a figure of the device so it could be seen that the images were a result of optics and not magic. For Musser, it was this demystification of the apparatus that marked the beginning of screen practices that continue into the present.[16]

The evolution of cinema from magic lantern shows was made explicit by commentators in the United States who described the new medium as *living pictures*. For Musser, cinema was 'the culmination of long-standing efforts to present ever more lifelike moving images on the screen...Lantern exhibitors had always had an array of procedures for creating movement – whether by projecting shadows of living things or by moving multiple lanterns around behind the screen – but the repertoire of such techniques increased during the nineteenth century'.[17]

Screenwriting beyond the United States

Charles Musser reconnected cinema to an expanded field of screen practice. He emphasised American cinema's debt to the magic lantern showmen of Europe. More recently, media archaeologist Erkki Huhtamo has used the term 'screen media' to consider the connections between contemporary digital screens and earlier versions.[18] Although cinema emerged from a much longer history of *screen practice*, it soon began to dominate as a popular art form of the twentieth century, wrote Musser in the 1980s. In our digital era, of course, that is no longer the case. In the contemporary world, we gaze at various kinds of screens on a daily basis. We move between screens on computers, tablets, televisions and digital camera displays to mobile phones. Screen stories and programmes can be viewed on a myriad of devices – large and small – and watched individually or collectively. Piecing together a history of screens enables us to understand more about forms such as anime, video games, the Internet, transmedia and cross-platform programmes as well as digital cinema.

This opens up the discussion of screenwriting to a far wider range of practices than has previously been considered. In particular, it allows us to more fully consider writing for the screen before the arrival of cinema and its technologies in the late nineteenth century. I would like to look even further afield – beyond the screenwriting practices of the United States and Europe. The arts and literature of India, China and Persia, for example, have been especially influential around the globe, yet are rarely discussed in relationship to screenwriting. Just as cinema itself can be seen as a continuation and transformation of screen practices, including the magic lantern and slide show, screenwriting can be seen as a transformation of earlier modes of writing for screens, performance and visual media.

In our digital world, the boundaries between the once discrete stages of writing, preproduction, production and postproduction are ever more blurred. Digital tools make it easier to cut, shift, morph and reassemble materials throughout the development and production process. The very notion of what it means to write is shifting. But not all of this is new. Alternative models of scripting have existed side by side with the prewritten screenplay. Alternative models in the form of scenarios used as a basis for improvisation, story reels for animation, shot lists and storyboards as scripting tools, and slide shows, trailers or short films as prototypes for feature films.

Practices of screenwriting

Screenwriting in a Digital Era is about how the *practices* of screenwriting are shifting. It builds on the work of writers, filmmakers and critics who have investigated alternative methods of writing for the screen – from Jean-Claude Carrière[19] and Jean Pierre Geuens[20] to J.J. Murphy,[21] Paul Wells,[22] Adam Ganz[23] and Adrian Martin.[24] As Martin wrote recently, 'we are only at the beginning of investigating the various kinds of texts – written, graphic, sonic, and so forth – that filmmakers produce in the pre-elaboration of a film'.[25] I tracked down writers and filmmakers, conducted interviews by Skype and email and followed a trail of critical writing and production accounts. I gradually narrowed my focus to innovative scripting practices on small-scale productions produced in less hierarchical, collaborative modes. In many cases, the writers were also the directors and producers and sometimes even the cinematographers and sound recordists. I zoomed out to consider picture storytelling as part of the prehistory of screenwriting and the new three Rs of digital literacy, and zoomed in to examine the practices of improvising, composing, adapting and collaborating in the work of nonfiction filmmaker Errol Morris, graphic novelist and animator Shaun Tan, essayist Agnès Varda, Hong Kong's Milkyway Image, *Beasts of the Southern Wild's* Court 13, the web documentaries of photographer Samuel Bollendorff and other digital filmmakers around the globe. My focus has been on the conditions and organisational structures within which screen ideas are shaped and realised, rather than simply their expression as scripts or photo-texts or short films.

In order to broaden the discussion of screenwriting and its practices, my approach has been informed by scholarly work and insights gleaned from a number of disciplines – screen history, photography, musicology, design, the visual and performing arts, social psychology, sociology and anthropology. *Screenwriting in a Digital Era* tilts towards the essay form. In part, due to the fact that this book is intended for a dual readership: academics interested in rethinking the screenplay and informed practitioners. The critical essay has a long history of addressing such readers. As a form, the essay aims to ask questions, to probe and test ideas; 'thought does not advance in a single direction, rather aspects of the argument are interwoven as in a carpet'.[26]

One word that strongly resonated while I was researching and writing this book was *constellation*. Since the earliest days of humankind, people have read images whenever they looked to constellations of stars in the sky. In order to tell stories, they traced invisible lines between the stars, drawing on their own experiences and imaginations, says John Berger.[27] Filmmaker Grant Gee has described his writing process as gathering materials until they form a constellation. He looks at them from different directions, seeking patterns and connections.[28] Tracing new pathways in writing for the screen, *Screenwriting in a Digital Era* explores innovative practices across independent and art cinema, nonfiction and animation. In a spirit of reconnaissance, it is my belief that teams devising lower-budget projects for local conditions and specific production paradigms have the most intelligence to offer about the shifting screenwriting ecology. They are the frontline troops of digital screenwriting.

1
The Picture Storytellers:
From Pad to iPad

The history of screenwriting needs to be tackled afresh in our digital era. A media archaeological approach seeks to find the *new* in the *old*, sifting through the evidence and making connections between previously disparate fields. Fractures, or moments of change, are thus especially significant.[1] It is in this spirit that I have approached sketching an expanded history of screenwriting. Digital technologies and frames of mind have fundamentally shifted what we mean by writing. We now write with images, sounds and gestures, as well as text. In addition, the digitisation of books, records, images and sounds allows us more ready access to a wealth of information and ideas. Back through the centuries and in far-flung places around the globe. In our time of flux and change, my aim is to begin to reconnect screenwriting to a long and rich tradition of picture storytelling. Practices of writing with pictures that stretch back to ancient India, China and the Middle East. According to Phillip Pullman, 'Like jazz, storytelling is an art of performance, and writing is performance, too.'[2]

My quest to understand more about digital screenwriting began, paradoxically, with a journey in search of the reincarnations of Charlie Chaplin's Tramp. How had this distinctive screen figure been adapted in different cultures? My search led me to Europe, the United States, Japan, China, South America and finally, India. It led me from the Chaplin fever of the years of the First World War to a small town in the Kutch Desert. In Adipur, in a remote and dusty corner of north-west India, the local Charlie Circle throw a birthday party each year to honour their guru. I wrote and directed an essay film called *The Boot Cake* (2008)[3] about being invited to bring the birthday cake to this party. Later, I realised that I had not travelled far enough. There was much more to discover about why people in cities and small towns around the

Figure 1.1   The Boot Cake, 2008, Charlie Productions

globe were so receptive – not only to Chaplin's Tramp – but to silent cinema. There was much more to discover, too, about screenwriting (Figure 1.1).

Mohammed Charlie

Noor Mohammed Memon is often named as the first comic star of Hindi cinema. He grew up in a village but soon dropped out of school to take a job mending umbrellas. To the despair of his father, Mohammed fell in love with the movies and decided to become an actor. Enthralled by Chaplin's Tramp, Mohammed copied his hero's mannerisms and costume right down to his trademark moustache. Making his way to Bombay, he changed his name to Mohammed Charlie and forged a career in Hindi musicals.

Visiting India's National Film Archive at Pune in 2005, I threaded a reel of brittle celluloid on to a Steinbeck editing bench. I settled in to watch *Sanjog* (1943),[4] one of Mohammed Charlie's early film comedies. The film depicted Mohammed Charlie as an Indian version of the Tramp. A middle-class family welcomes him into their home. They believe he is a wealthy man interested in marrying their daughter. Mistaken identity leads to one comic mishap after another. Mohammed Charlie's performance is particularly expressive. It owes as much to the Hindi musical as Hollywood. In one scene, safely out of the earshot of his potential in-laws, Mohammed Charlie bursts into song. What is he to do? He gazes up at the heavens and wrings his hands. Pigeons on a railing form a kind of poor man's chorus, nodding their heads in time to the music. Eventually, the Tramp is sprung. Denounced as an intruder by the middle-class family, he is turfed out – and into the gutter.

In this film, Mohammed Charlie riffed on Chaplin's *The Idle Class* (1921),[5] embellishing the story with his own observations of 1940s Bombay society. He drew on India's distinctive performance styles, fluidly shifting between drama, dance and song. Amongst the comedian's influences, too, was a long line of *awaara* or drifter characters in Indian drama and literature. Looking even further back, as we shall see, the picture showmen of India who can be traced to the sixth century B.C.[6] Like them, Mohammed Charlie improvised from a situation and a sequence of images. In the process, he adapted a well-known story to local conditions.

In Hindi cinema, story does not necessarily occupy a central position. Rather, song and dance sequences, dialogue, fights and romance all have a part to play. Many scripts give a nod to myths and legends. Writers and filmmakers in India have often successfully incorporated elements from other cinematic traditions into their own freewheeling narratives.[7] Such elements are not always subsumed to the needs of a single overarching story. Instead, balancing different emotions and elements in the mix is considered part of a writer's skill.

Perhaps it is not surprising, then, that screenplay guru Syd Field's visit to Mumbai in 2007 to spread the good news on story and three-act structure was not uniformly well received. Field presented a cut down version of his seminar to an invited audience at the Taj Hotel. It included a number of India's leading directors and filmmakers. The trouble with Bollywood was all those songs and dance sequences which kept getting in the way of the story, said Field. 'What I see here is that...in the middle of something intense that is going on we break into a song and dance which is wonderful and I love it but it does nothing to further the story at all,' he said.[8] Not everyone returned after the lunch break. Had the visiting American even watched any Indian cinema, asked some of the industry representatives? Did he know that Indian filmmakers produced movies for huge local audiences – as well as the Indian diaspora around the globe?

Charles Dickens is sometimes referred to as the 'father of screenwriting'. (In part, due to the wealth of adaptations that his novels inspired in early cinema and the fact that he generated many of his stories as serials.) Charlie Chaplin, who mostly improvised his films (at least, until the coming of sound), could equally be described as one of the founders of screenwriting. While he committed rough versions of his stories to paper, Chaplin *wrote* on film. Until he made *The Great Dictator* (1940),[9] Chaplin worked from story outlines, which were often dictated to a typist. Throughout the production and editing of his films, Chaplin elaborated and embellished on these sketches and ideas. It was not uncommon for him to film individual takes hundreds of times. As the Russian critic Viktor Shklovsky observed, Chaplin's scripts were written in the process of shooting films. 'Chaplin's gestures and films are conceived not in the word, nor in the drawing, but in the flashing of black and white shadows.'[10] The cinematic sequences for which the performer and director is best known, such as the dancing bread rolls in *The Gold Rush* (1925),[11] were generated through extended improvisations on set.

Oral traditions

These two Charlies – Mohammed Charlie and Charlie Chaplin – riffed on the performance and storytelling traditions of Europe and India, respectively. They were both migrants who adapted their stories and performances to meet the needs of the United States' and India's fledgling film industries. Paul Schrader described screenwriting as a part of an oral tradition. Screenplays belong to a storytelling tradition rather than literature. Tracing this lineage, Adam Ganz proposed oral storytelling, and in particular the ballad, as a useful model for screenwriters:

> Oral storytelling not only stretches back much further than a European dramatic literary tradition but it is more improvisatory, adaptable and collaborative as opposed to the model of the screenplay-as-a-text, envisaged as separate from the film which arises from it.[12]

Ultimately, audiences are affected by what they see and what is vivid. It is not especially important whether that vividness is achieved through reenacted drama or narrated drama.[13] The visual component of oral storytelling relies upon the audience to fill in the gaps and reconstruct images for themselves.

Screenwriting, I would like to suggest, is a form of *writing with images*. The proliferation of screens and digital composing practices has made improvisation, adaptation and the hybridisation of art forms and genres even more central to writing. The origins of screenwriting, as we shall discover, can be traced back nearly 3,000 years to the picture storytellers and reciters. Those performers' stories of everyday life, war, news and reportage, strange and wondrous tales share many preoccupations with contemporary screen stories.

Although often reduced to a set of rules, screenwriting is a *living* art constantly in transition. After all, stories serve the needs of individuals and particular communities. As sociologist Arthur Frank says, stories give our lives shape and meaning. The role of stories is to 'give form – temporal and spatial orientation, coherence, meaning and especially boundaries – to lives that inherently lack form'.[14] Stories are not sets of rules. We *live* with stories, adapting them as we go. Stories bring people together – and keep them apart. A renewed engagement with screen stories devised *with* and *for* particular communities is, I believe, one of the defining characteristics of digital cinema. But let me piece together some of the evidence for an expanded notion of writing for the screen.

It begins with a pilgrimage. This particular pilgrimage was undertaken by Victor Mair, a scholar of Chinese language and literature. Mair's story takes us from the sixth century to the present. It takes us from China to Japan, India, the Middle East, Europe and beyond in search of storytellers who used pictures to breathe life into stories. They include picture reciters, shadow playwrights, slide-projection showmen and the writers, performers and directors of early cinema. As Virginia Woolf wrote, 'the present when backed by the past is a thousand times deeper than the present when it presses so close that you can feel nothing else, when the film on the camera reaches only the eye'.[15] In my view, some of the seeds of contemporary digital screenwriting are contained within the many modes of storytelling with pictures that Mair uncovered from the past.

Transformation texts

In the 1950s, Victor Mair set out to trace the evolution of picture recitation in China. Popular stories known as *pien-wen* (or transformation texts) date back to the Tang period (618–907). They were the first vernacular narratives in Chinese literature. Many of the picture storytellers referred to a specific place on their paintings and narrated the events depicted. They said: 'please look at the place where this event occurred and how it goes'.[16] An approach that bears striking similarities to those used today by Court 13, the filmmaking collective responsible for the critical hit *Beasts of the Southern Wild* (2012).[17] But more on that later.

As a popular art, picture storytelling was underrepresented in the Chinese historical records. In the early twentieth century, scholars who discovered a number of *pien-wen* manuscripts believed they were notes used by Buddhist monks for lectures and sermons. More recent research, though, showed them to be the prompts used by lay storytellers who travelled from village to village. The manuscripts developed from an oral version of storytelling with pictures called *chaun-pien*. It drew on both religious and secular tales. Artists painted scenes from the stories to be told on paper, silk or wall-paintings which were then used during performances. The term *chaun-pien* literally meant *transformation*. In part, this referred to the powers of the Buddhist figures that were often represented in the stories. Less literally, though, a *transformation* occurred when the picture reciters brought their stories to life through their performances and the use of images.

In one form of such storytelling that Mair found in the Qing period (1644–1912), picture reciters collected strange tales and created pictures to accompany them. Just as now, war stories were particularly popular. Picture reciters made their way up and down streets, calling out stories and carrying bundles of pictures for residents to buy. This form of storytelling was similar to that practiced by the *bankel-sang*, or bench-singers in Germany at around the same time.[18] Deciding to look further afield, Mair discovered that picture storytelling was not confined to China but also existed in Japan, Iran, Tibet, Turkey, Italy, Germany and other countries. Mair eventually traced the Chinese form of performing with pictures and scrolls back to sixth century B.C. in India. Picture storytelling had gradually spread west from India to Persia and China and north into Europe.[19]

Pao-chuan

On a research trip to Kansu in north-west China in the mid-1980s, Mair discovered, too, that a more recent version of picture storytelling survived there. Prior to the establishment of the People's Republic of China, when *pao-chuan* went underground due to its connections to Buddhism, picture recitation performances were popular during fairs and festivals. The storytellers were often itinerants who travelled from village to village and performed in exchange for food and gifts. Rolling out painted cloths, they pointed to the pictures as they told stories. The multiple versions of *pao-chuan* stories that survive are rarely identical. In a finding that resonates for many forms of picture storytelling around the world, Mair says: 'Each storyteller adapts the story to his own style and the scribes who copy the texts likewise feel free to modify the story....'[20] Stories are not fixed. They are adapted in each new telling. From this perspective, the surge of popularity that improvisation has enjoyed in digital cinema does not look quite so new. Another of the shifts that I would identify in contemporary screenwriting concerns not just how scripts are generated and recorded; but how they are used throughout production. But let's return to the history of screenwriting – in India.

Moving-slide shows in India

The immediate precursors of cinema in India included moving-slide shows known as 'Shambarik Kharolika'. The Patwardhan family in Poona presented some of the more notable shows from the 1890s onwards. From all accounts, the shows were lively entertainments. They featured intricate hand-coloured paintings on glass slides. Two or three slide projectors were used at any one time to create moving pictures.[21] A *sutradhar* (narrator) set the scene and musical numbers were one of the highlights. Some people speculate that the role of the singers and musicians was to drown out the sounds of the far-from silent projectors. The musicians' roles did not stop at playing their instruments. By the time cinema arrived, 'the harmonium and tabla players were expected to use not only their instruments but their feet to stomp, their voices to shout and generally to boost excitement during the fight scenes'.[22]

Living photographic pictures in Mumbai

A Lumière Brothers assistant, who was travelling to Australia, presented the first film screenings in India. An advertisement in *The Times of India* invited residents of Bombay to come and view '*living photographic pictures* in life-sized reproductions'.[23] Continuing the link between photography and cinema, the Madras Photographic Stores advertised some of the first films shown in India as '*animated* photographs'.[24] Audiences greeted the show with 'lusty cheers' and exhibitors were soon showing films in improvised venues such as tin sheds, tents and halls. Cinema was introduced to Calcutta around 1896 with scientific programmes such as 'Living and Moving Pictures of London Life'. The businessman, Jamset Madan, soon established his own film screenings in open-air tents around Calcutta.[25] Most of the Indian population of the time lived in towns and villages and did not have opportunities to visit the tent cinemas in cities. Itinerant showmen therefore played a significant role in bringing cinema to a wider audience, touring around rural India and Asia.

Brightly coloured stories

In India, itinerant picture storytellers of various kinds can be dated back to the sixth century B.C.[26] Painter Amitabh Sengupta suggests that visual narratives played an important role in oral societies in India, bringing diverse groups together around a shared moral code.[27] Showmen known as *mankha* narrated stories with the help of pictures. As in China, they moved from village to village, performing for food. Literature from the third century describes *mankhas* singing as they told their stories: 'One who narrates the story with the help of paintings is a great chitrakathaka.'[28] That is, the picture showman sang without musical accompaniment. Stories were often based on myths. Other *chitrakithi*, professional storytellers, used sets of pictures as prompts. Some led audiences through their sequences of pictures using a peacock feather as a pointer. Performances combined verse, dialogue, song, music and narration. It is not surprising then that the term *chitrakithi* is sometimes translated as *many-coloured* or *bright-coloured* stories.[29] Some of the picture shows could go on all night, accompanied by music and songs. Performances that were especially long were thought to help transport audiences into another realm, far from their daily cares. A square of white cloth borrowed from the local washerwoman often created an impromptu screen on which to project shadows.

The *bhopa* of Rajasthan

In Rajasthan, a local version of the *chitrakithi* performed using a long cloth painted with a story as his script. Performer-narrators (*bhopas*) were expected to be skilled improvisers.[30] Picture the scene. As night descends over the village, people gather. Some walk in for miles. Later, everyone will contribute whatever they can – from a gold coin to a morsel of food. The sound of insects punctuates the night. Anticipation grows. We can glimpse a lamp in the distance. The *bhopa* slowly makes his way towards his audience. He is in costume. Since his story features a battle, the *bhopa* dresses accordingly. His wife, the village's assistant storyteller, holds the lamp high, illuminating his path. We can hear the children's 'oohs' and 'ahhs'. The normally genial man is now a forbidding figure. A wide-eyed boy reaches for his father's hand. The *bhopa* carries a stick. His story-scroll reaches the ground – it looks like an epic.

There had been no need for advance advertising. The *bhopa*, who took on the combined roles of writing, directing and producing, was known to have been preparing a new story. Teams of visual artists had worked under his direction. It often took several months to prepare a picture scroll, which was launched with great festivity. The entertainment begins. Reading from his scroll (*pad bachana*) the *bhopa* brings the story to life through singing, dancing, acting and music.

There were both religious and secular *bhopi* and an important part of their role was to bring the community together. In return, the community supported them. Preparations and performances were often lengthy. When the *pad* became old and torn, or its pictures faded, it was taken to the town of Pushkar and immersed in a kind of 'lake of dead stories' with suitable ceremony.[31] Stories, after all, were simply on loan from the gods. Perhaps this is a practice that usefully could be adapted by Hollywood? Stories that have become old and faded could be given a ritual send-off to make room for new versions?

Just as there are many cinemas in India, many regional variants of picture storytelling still exist. In some, artists paint scrolls, backdrops and cloths for the shows and the performers devise the accompanying stories. In other versions, the picture storyteller is responsible for preparing both the script and images.[32] This long tradition of the picture show in India is perhaps one of the reasons cinema, and especially the Hindi musical, was so enthusiastically embraced in that country. More importantly, the variations of picture storytelling in India demonstrate how living art forms adapt and change to meet the needs of particular communities. After all, change is the natural order of things.

Shadow play

> For in and out, above, about, below,
> 'Tis nothing but a magic shadow-show,
> Play'd in a box whose candle is the sun,
> Round which we phantom figures come and go.
> *Omar Khayyam*[33]

For Shakespeare, life was a stage and humankind its players. For Persian mathematician and poet Omar Khayyam – writing in the eleventh century – life was a magic lantern. People were its phantom shadows who appeared and disappeared. It is widely thought that the first moving images shown on screens were shadows. The origins of the shadow theatre are themselves shadowy. While hand shadows have been around as long as humankind, formal shadow theatre with leather puppets painted in translucent colours and projected onto screens, appear to have originated in China and Japan sometime before the second millennium.[34] There was also an established tradition of shadow play theatre in India long before the coming of cinema. Java later developed its distinct tradition of *wayang* or shadow play, often based around the presentation of mythological stories. In Egypt, *khayal al-zill*, or 'phantoms of the shadow' is one of the oldest forms of drama documented.[35] Performances featured puppets on sticks projected on to a screen and accompanied by music. Most surviving scripts belong to a literary genre known as the 'Alien and Strange'.

The versions of the shadow play developed in Egypt and Turkey eventually made their way to Europe in the seventeenth century. Many featured a version of the Turkish clown, *Karagöz* or Black Eye. In China, it is thought that shadow plays featured glowing translucent colours. Black and white, however, was a better fit with the sensibilities of Europe in that era.

Ibn Daniyal: Shadow playwright

Shadow plays flourished in twelfth-century Egypt. Romance and satire were popular genres and surviving poems suggest that both men and women wrote and performed shadow plays. One of the best-known shadow playwrights was Ibn Daniyal. Born in the area that is now Iraq, he was forced to flee to Cairo when the Mongols invaded his homeland. Daniyal began writing poetry and plays to considerable acclaim. The three of his scripts that survive are all labelled *tayf-al-khayal* or 'phantoms of the shadows'.[36] Daniyal's shadow play scripts incorporated poems, dramatic scenes and practical directions on how the production should be realised. Daniyal typically composed his stage directions in rhyming couplets. It is thought this was so that shadow plays could be read when performance troupes lacked the resources to stage performances.[37] The shadow playwright, it appears, was just as conscious of budgetary limitations as today's independent filmmakers attracted to micro-budget digital methods.

The following is an excerpt from a manifesto that Daniyal wrote. He aimed to reinvigorate what he saw as the art form's stock of tired and over-familiar storylines.[38]

If you sketch the figures, cut them according to their parts, get a quiet place for the crowd and project the figures against a candlelit screen…then Voila! You see, the script is being transformed into animated creatures.[39]

Daniyal's description suggests that paper figures, rather than leather puppets cast the shadows. Audiences were sick of literary topics like religious myths and battles, he wrote. Instead, Daniyal advocated, more shadow play scripts should be based on street life. Sound familiar? Manifestos calling for new storytelling practices in cinema, such as Dogme 95, are hardly new. Even a brief consideration of his work suggests that Ibn Daniyal, as a leading shadow playwright of twelfth century Egypt, has a legitimate claim as one of the founders of writing for the screen.

Shadows of the imagination

Bruce Elder, a Canadian artist and critic, described what is thought to have been a typical scene in twelfth-century Cairo during Ramadan. As the sun went down, crowds gathered in city streets and squares in search of a meal to break their fast. Feasting was followed by entertainment. Performances featuring tumblers, gymnasts, magicians and storytellers were all on offer. The *khayal-al-zill*, sometimes called 'shadows of the imagination', though, were the most popular entertainments. While the stories presented varied in subject matter, they invariably followed a set sequence. The shadow-master appeared on stage with a stick with which to attract the audience's attention. Rather like the Japanese *benshi* and film explainers of silent cinema, he narrated the story, introducing the characters and making asides to the audience. The performance ended with a song and dance or news of a battle that demanded a sequel. In an epilogue, the shadow-master presented the names of everyone who had contributed to the production and thanked the audience.[40] By all accounts, these sequences went on almost as long as contemporary feature film credits.

Lotte Reiniger goes to Athens

Lotte Reiniger undertook a pilgrimage of her own. In the 1930s, the renowned animator and filmmaker travelled to Athens to view a *karaghiozis* performance or shadow play. Reiniger's research into the art, performance and music of Asia, the Middle East and Europe inspired her distinctive visual storytelling. It was especially influenced by the two folk art forms of paper cutting in Poland and shadow play in China. Reiniger traced three major traditions of shadow play theatre; in China, in India and Java and in the Middle East, Turkey and Greece. What were the origins of the art form? According to popular myth, a Chinese emperor was grief-stricken after his mistress died. He took no interest in life. In an attempt to comfort him, an artist put up a silk screen, lit it from behind and imitated the movements of the dead woman.

Reiniger observed that there may be a more practical explanation for the evolution of shadow play. Long ago, Chinese women were not allowed to attend live performances. Consequently, many plays were converted into shadow shows, which could be performed in the women's private quarters.[41] Chinese shadow plays were performed against a silk or linen screen and lit by an oil lamp. Curtains masked the manipulation of the figures for the audience. Shadow players told stories with figures made from animal skin, which was treated and painted with colours.

In both Greece and Turkey, shadow plays were associated with entertainment rather than religious practices. The most popular stories were usually comedies and the storylines sometimes provided an outlet for political expression. The *karaghiozis*, or central figure, was typically a penniless character who earned his daily bread through treachery, thievery and even robbing the graves of the dead.[42] Like Charlie Chaplin's Tramp, the character eventually became a symbol of protest for those seeking freedom. In Turkey and Greece, shadow play stories were both handed down orally and written down.

Working on her own silhouette films, Reiniger constantly struggled with the objections of distributors. Her films were works of art and not suitable for popular audiences, they said. Hearing that crowds flocked to shadow plays in Athens, Reiniger decided to go and see a performance. On arrival in Athens, Reiniger was directed to an open-air café with a white screen under a midnight blue sky. As a fellow professional, the troupe invited Reiniger to watch the performance from behind the screen.

Picture the scene. The musicians tune their instruments. A stout middle-aged man struggles into a white suit. The murmur of voices as hundreds of people wait for the show to begin. They sip coffee or throw back shots of ouzo. A waiter offers a tray. Thrilled with the spectacle, the warm evening and her own daring (she had been warned against attending such a disreputable and vulgar entertainment), Reiniger accepts a glass of ouzo herself. Five musicians take their places in front of the screen. The shadow-master takes his place behind it. Buttoning his jacket, he clamps a straw hat on his head.[43] The orchestra begins playing. The screen lights up. To the crowd's cheers, the *karaghiozis* appears and begins a lively dance. His transformation is nothing short of astonishing. As the *karaghiozis* tells his tale, he manipulates the silhouette figures with rods. They cast shadows onto the screen.

Reiniger wrote that she was transfixed by the shadow play's richness of colour, movement and gesture. One man – the *karaghiozis* – was responsible for writing, orchestrating and performing the play, Reiniger discovered. The range of skills involved could easily make many hyphenated filmmakers (who combine writing and directing or producing and directing) look like under-achievers. Lotte Reiniger described her films made afterwards as an attempt to recreate that one magical evening early in her career.

The screen performances that Reiniger described sound far from 'primitive' entertainments. Yet shadow plays are often dismissed as such by writers tracing the history of screen media. So I was fascinated to discover that Turkish shadow plays of the nineteenth century introduced a new stock character: the bumbling European visitor.

Cinema as shadow play

Cinema in Iran is thought to have emerged from a popular form called *pardeh-khani* which shares some of the attributes of picture-storytelling in India and China. A *pardeh-khan* (narrator) gradually uncovered a painting as he told a story. In a similar art form, *nagali* performances were often staged in coffee houses. The *naqal* improvised stories that were inspired by images painted on glass and hung from the walls.[44] In Turkey, cinema was strongly influenced by the variant of shadow play popular there. The first public film screenings in Istanbul were held in 1896. A year later, the first films were shown in a coffee house in the Muslim section of Istanbul. The two screen practices, one thousands of years old and the other in its infancy, met as motion pictures were projected on to the white *karagöz* (or shadow play) screen.[45] A similar scenario played out in China and other countries around the globe as films were projected on to shadow play screens in coffee palaces, teahouses, fairgrounds and marketplaces.

American shadow play

Introduced by French showmen, cinema made its way to China only months after the Lumière Brothers' first screenings in Paris. Films were projected alongside live entertainment such as opera, magic, firecrackers and acrobat shows. But not everyone agreed that cinema was a new medium. The 'American shadow play' was a local variant of an art form based on projected light that originated in China, said some. 'What we should keep in mind is that five hundred years before the invention of film in the West, this kind of motion shadow play, which used light to project images on screen, already existed in China.'[46] Other art critics believed that motion shadow plays had existed in China for much longer. They included the two filmmakers and critics who launched China's first screenwriting correspondence course in 1924. Students from China, Japan and the Philippines soon signed up.[47]

'Introduction to the Shadow-play' was broken down into eight lessons. Its teachers advocated use of the term *yingxi* (or shadow play), rather than *moving pictures*. Shadow play linked cinema to drama, they said. Further, the term *yingxi* acknowledged China's 3,000-year history of the performing and expressive arts that had led to cinema. Such art forms included dance, drama, lantern-shadow play, idea-sketching, painting, photography and slide shows. Shadow play was especially important as a form of drama that represented life.[48]

In the mid-1920s, two influential Chinese filmmakers and critics published books about writing the new variant on the Chinese shadow play. Huo You, author of *Techniques of Writing Shadowplay Scripts* (1925) was a filmmaker associated with the Great Wall Picture Company. Yao began his career as a screenwriter by adapting his theatre script *A Forsaken Woman* which was one of Great Wall's first productions He insisted on the centrality of the script. 'The film script is the soul of the film.'[49] Xu Zhuodai, a comedian and popular entertainer who migrated to the new medium, published *The Science of Shadowplay*. For Xu, the soul of cinema was its use of moving shadows. An admirer of German expressionist cinema, Xu wrote a sample script for his book adapted from *The Good Student of Prague*. His version – *Shadow: A Thought Drama* – downplayed conflict. In the original script, the poor student Balduin sold his shadow for gold sovereigns. It haunted his every move. Eventually, Balduin was forced to kill his shadow to take back his former carefree life. In Xu's retelling of the story, the student reconciled with his shadow to create harmony.[50]

As in India, Chinese cinema built on the many different versions of shadow play, which varied from region to region. In the early twentieth century Beijing, for example, there were two major forms of the entertainment. In a theme that seems to be echoed in practices of writing for screens the world over, one version relied on scripts while the other made use of remembered texts and improvisation.[51]

Kamishibai

In 2005, in a cafe in bustling downtown Tokyo, a collector of film memorabilia showed me his prized set of picture cards featuring Charlie Chaplin's Tramp – or Professor Alcohol as the character was initially known in Japan – in his early short comedies. As we sipped green tea, the collector laid his picture cards on the table. I was in the early stages of researching my documentary about Chaplin's Tramp. *Kamishibai*, the picture-card show, was still popular in the Japanese countryside in the mid-1950s, when it was estimated that there were still 25,000 storytellers roaming the villages of Japan. The storyteller carried several sets of pictures, each typically containing around ten figures. He went from place to place, hitting a wooden clapper or beating a drum to attract attention. As an audience gathered around, the storyteller inserted the sequence of pictures into a large fixed-frame aperture and recited his tale. His script was usually in the form of a text written on the back of each picture.[52] At the height of *kamishibai's* popularity in the 1930s, the storytellers acted as combined reporters and entertainers. Their tales ranged from westerns, historical stories, folktales and melodramas, to nightly news reporting on World War Two in the early 1940s.[53]

The *uncle kamishibai,* as the storytellers were known, made their living by selling sweets and trinkets. Audience members who bought snacks were given a prime viewing and listening spot at the front of the crowd.[54] The stories were told as one never-ending tale with each instalment ending on a cliffhanger. 'To be continued' the *kamibashai* performer would announce, as he packed up his storyboards and rode off on his bicycle. Writers tracing the evolution of manga, graphic novels and comics have emphasised *kamishibai* as an important antecedent.[55] Itself adapted from a number of sources, *kamishibai* is equally part of the lineage of screenwriting.

Magic lantern shows in Japan

Another strong link to the cinema in Japan was the *utsushi-e*, a magic lantern show performed indoors in the dark in the late nineteenth century. 'Images were projected on a white-cloth screen, manually operated by a master-artist, who also designed and painted the narrative lenses and directed the theatrical performance.'[56] The scenes were lit by a candle, which created an eerie atmosphere. Perhaps not surprisingly, ghost stories and samurai adventures were especially popular. The performances were usually accompanied by music. The skill with which the master-artist manipulated the transitions between scenes was considered a test of his art. Although the magic lantern device was imported from the west, Japanese craftsmen soon devised their own wooden versions. Show boxes allowed viewers to look at scenes of distant lands through smudged glass.

From pulling pictures to peep media

Peepshows, known as *pulling pictures*, were also popular in China in the nineteenth century and the first half of the twentieth century, as they were in the United States and Europe. The operator provided minimal information about his scenes and attracted customers by yelling. Sound is an important part of peep media and plays a significant role in pulling in customers. As the viewer pressed his or her eye against the glass, the operator attached an image to a string and pulled it through the frame. Chinese peepshows were given names like 'Western Scenes' and 'Pulling Foreign Picture Cards'.[57]

Improvised from pictures

Reflecting on forms of picture storytelling, from *etoki*[58] to *kamishibai*, Victor Mair noted that it was common for pictures to have their accompanying texts written on the back. It would have been relatively easy for experienced performers to memorise their texts. Therefore, he speculated, the texts may have been there to remind the storytellers which sections should remain unchanged in order to provide the structure of the story.[59] Sometimes, there were no texts to accompany the cards and stories were improvised directly in response to the pictures. Picture storytelling often combined prepared material with improvisation. Jacob Riis, a prominent photographer and social reformer in the United States on the cusp of the nineteenth and early twentieth centuries presented slide shows without scripts. A handwritten note on his only known surviving script reads 'As I speak without notes, from memory and to the pictures, the result is according to how I feel.'[60]

Another echo that strongly resonates from the past to the present concerns the *open-structure* of many shadow plays. Writing about shadow plays in Turkey, performance historian Stanley Hochman said an important structural element of their plots was that that they were 'open form' or 'flexible form'.[61] That is, the plots consisted of independent elements that could be rearranged differently from performance to performance. Similar dramatic structures are now often referred to as 'modular scripts' or 'open texts'. It is not difficult to see how such structures help writers adapt stories to local circumstances and contexts. Open forms – currently enjoying a resurgence of interest amongst performance writers, screenwriters and filmmakers – are just one of the ways that stories remain alive.

Words and pictures

In the contemporary industrial screenplay, derived from the classic period of Hollywood, writers are often discouraged from using images. The pre-written screenplay is expected to proceed in a series of stages, from outline to treatment to a series of fully written drafts. Each stage involves a series of readers' notes and formal approvals. It is often only after the screenplay has been fully scripted that images come more fully into play in the form of storyboards, design sketches and other means of pre-visualisation. The animation screenplay is a notable exception, employing story reels and beat boards from relatively early in the process and, for this reason alone, it provides an alternative model for contemporary screenwriters. Implicit in the industrial model is the separation of words and pictures. Yet writers, performers and filmmakers have long explored their ideas using both words and images. Indeed, the insistence on separating words and images may be a relatively recent phenomenon, primarily suited to the needs of Hollywood studios.

Anne-Marie Christin, a French historian of writing, sees no reason to distinguish between text and images. Historically, images precede the development of writing systems. Images can be seen as a form of writing since they create meaningful relationships between elements within a frame. Since the earliest days of humankind, people have been reading images whenever they looked to constellations of stars in the sky. In medieval Europe, too, the term *pictura* simply meant 'to bring to mind'. Writers are frequently advised to imagine sitting around the campfire, spinning a yarn. Challenging this model of storytelling, Christin says that campfire scene emphasises words.[62] By contrast, looking to the sky puts a greater emphasis on images. That campfire scene is one of the founding myths of screenwriting. Perhaps we could instead imagine ourselves gazing at a star-strewn sky on a clear night? Watching shadows and colours projected on a white screen? Scrolling down an iPad or mobile phone screen?

Cinema is connected to a rich history of picture storytelling around the globe. It made use of painted scrolls called *pads*, cloths, boards, cards, puppets, light boxes, shadow boxes, peep boxes, magic lanterns and many other devices. Cinema is connected to a myriad of art forms, which draw on images, projections, performance and sound. Art forms which bring images to life. In our digital era, too, the previous divisions between live action and animation, the real and the illusionary, are increasingly blurred. Neurologist and writer, Oliver Sacks, observed that 'the history of science was anything but a linear story. Instead, it leapt about, split, took off at tangents and repeated itself.' The same could be said of screenwriting.

Screenwriting, as we know it today, is part of a long history of writing for various kinds of screens. The practice stretches back thousands of years and forward to encompass an ever-increasing range of digital screens, large and small, fixed and mobile. A news agency in Japan recently reported that tablet computers such as the iPad were giving the *kamishibai* a new lease of life. A veteran storyteller had incorporated the device into his performances. He displayed pictures on his iPad and accompanied them with a live narration. The example of the *kamishibai* alone demonstrates how picture storytelling forms evolve and adapt, constantly incorporating new elements.

Echoes of picture storytelling can be found throughout contemporary digital cinema. From the picture showmen of ancient India – where screenwriting may well have begun – to the shadow playwrights of Egypt. Whether working with shadow entertainments, story paintings and scrolls, magic lantern shows or cinema the world over, the task of these writers and performers was to provide the basis of *living* or *animated* picture stories. Stories themselves breathe life into individuals and communities.

Stories, of course, are never completely new. Like mosaics, stories are assembled from pre-existing fragments. They are made afresh in each telling and viewing. Nevertheless, in *Screenwriting in a Digital Era*, my aim is to tell some new stories about screenwriting. Where have we come from? Where are we headed? Are visual storytelling, improvisation and voiceover (often disparaged by the authors of screenwriting manuals) actually foundational practices of screenwriting? Should design, music and composition all be more regularly introduced into the development phase of screen ideas? Unlike Victor Mair and Lotte Reiniger,

I did my sleuthing via libraries, database and internet searches; via email and Skype conversations. For many of the writers and filmmakers whose scripting processes I explored, I discovered that dissatisfaction with conventional ways of writing and making cinema was a significant impetus in trying to do things differently. Time after time, they expressed a desire to make their stories *live*. But how?

2
Post Courier 12

In 2003, I directed a feature film called *Travelling Light* which was loosely inspired by Allen Ginsberg's visit to Australia to participate in Adelaide Writers' Week in the 1960s.[1] The script, which was in development for approximately six years, was funded draft by draft through the Australian Film Commission, the national film-funding agency then responsible for script development. The project was conceived as a multi-stranded narrative with an ensemble of characters at pivotal moments in their lives, all connected via their relationship to television: in particular, to a fictional 1970s variety show called *Adelaide Tonight*, hosted by the equally fictional Ray Sugars. The screenplay utilised motifs of light and electricity to be played out across the film's image and soundtrack. As is so often the case, as the project progressed down the financing route, there came increased pressure for the screenplay to conform to a more classic protagonist-driven, three-act structure. Myself, the script editor and producer were repeatedly advised by assessors and readers that we should complete the set-up more quickly; snip out those scenes about early television they deemed unnecessary; focus more on a central character, thereby ensuring sufficient screen time to retain the prominent young Australian actress who was attached to the project. We were also encouraged to fill out the soundtrack with hit songs of the 1970s to ensure audience accessibility. These pressures did not come from the film distributors who were providing a distribution guarantee, but from the public broadcaster and government screen-funding agencies that would form a vital piece of the financing jigsaw if the script was to make it to the screen. Needless to say, my talk of independent cinema with its ambiguity, internalised character conflict and visual motifs as structuring devices did not go down well.[2]

Over the third, fourth and fifth drafts, the film was restructured and pruned to fit a template more closely aligned to those promoted by the screenwriting manuals. In the process, temporal, stylistic and thematic complexities were significantly minimised. Finally, I made enough changes to steer the film through the two state agencies, Australian theatrical distributor, Australian public broadcaster, Australian pay-TV broadcaster and European-based sales agent all needed to attract the balance in federal film funding. The additional plot, included at the last moment to provide the narrative closure demanded, was undoubtedly the most 'undercooked' aspect of the script, introducing a false note to the characterisation of Lou, our beat poet/trickster character. Despite a number of nominations, awards and enthusiastic responses, critical reactions to the film were sharply divided, and *Travelling Light* had difficulty finding its cinema audience in the narrow time-span within which even specialised, limited release films are expected to perform.

While the claim is frequently made that Australian feature screenplays are underdeveloped, I would argue the opposite: my experience with *Travelling Light* and my background as a script reader and assessor for various funding bodies leads me to the conclusion that many scripts are *over-* rather than *under*developed. The handful of screenplays and film projects chosen for development through government programmes all too often lose momentum and energy as a consequence of this selection. A selection which almost invariably subjects them to drawn-out rounds of assessment, reports, required revisions and yet more revisions – all justified in the name of critical rigour and industry imperatives. Along the way, screenwriters and their collaborators struggle to retain, or reinject into their screen ideas, what social psychologist Abraham Maslow called a quality of 'aliveness'.[3] An attribute that Maslow considered fundamental to works of art if they were to connect with their intended audiences (Figure 2.1).

Early in his career, Atom Egoyan observed that many script development and film-funding mechanisms seem to aim at delaying the production of the film as long as possible in the belief that this was a good thing.[4] In all the many and various deliberations about *Travelling Light*, it was invariably words on a page that were discussed, dissected and analysed, rather than images, sounds, gestures, rhythm or the cinematic qualities of the script. The work of many innovative screenwriters and filmmakers has long favoured audio and visual expressivity over plot and narrative drive and provides a wealth of alternative scripting methodologies and structures for analysis. Scripts can be inspired by still photographs, visual art, sense memories, location pictures, video footage, or popular songs. Acclaimed writers and filmmakers including Gus Van Sant, Jim Jarmusch, Tony Grisoni and Michael Winterbottom,

Figure 2.1   Travelling Light, 2003, Toi-Toi Pictures

Wong Kar-wai, Wim Wenders and Chantal Akerman have all developed methods of shifting between writing and production, working with both words and images. These writers and filmmakers embrace *cinematic* scriptwriting. Some of the terms used to describe the resulting story designs include: the road map, the open screenplay, the visual scenario and the *ars combinatoria* screenplay.[5] As filmmaker and screenwriting theorist J.J. Murphy suggests: 'Real innovation in screenwriting...comes not from ignorance of narrative film conventions but from being able to see beyond their limitations.'[6]

Script development as a process, not an end in itself

Increasingly, I find myself interested in screenwriting and development processes aimed at realising films within *specific* production contexts and parameters, rather than free-floating script development programmes that can so easily become ends in themselves. As Australian playwright and dramaturg Noëlle Janaczewska notes in her blog entry *The Development Sceptic*, the most useful development of new play scripts is undertaken in contexts where the writer works with the company and collaborators who are committed to producing the play. Janaczewska is particularly wary of development programmes influenced by the development practices of film. She argues:

> Film has a whole host of development initiatives, most of which seem to exist to (a). provide an income stream for assessors, script editors,

programme directors, administrators and others, presumably while they try to get their own projects up, (b). generate activity and create the illusion that your project/screenplay is progressing, and (c). to explain why things can't or won't happen.[7]

Many development processes simply shape screenplays to pre-existing templates, so that the distinctiveness of works can be gradually eroded, assessment-by-assessment, draft-by-draft. As Ian Macdonald observed at a European script development workshop:

> The screen idea was being shaped, altered and drawn towards what the professionals thought of as right, based on internalised experience and expressed as craft or lore.[8]

Although this workshop was specifically aimed at screenwriters collaborating with directors and producers as part of their studies at film school, the methods used were modelled on those used within the subsidised sectors of the film industry. That is, screenplays and projects are often selected on the basis of attributes such as originality and innovation, only to have these very qualities systematically minimised through the workshopping and script development process. As Lewis Hyde suggests in his book about the archetypes of creativity: 'Works proceed according to their own logic ... Premature evaluation cuts off the flow.'[9]

Beyond the blueprint

The screenplay is often referred to as a 'blueprint' for the film to come, but perhaps it is time to reconsider this term? After all, blueprints derive their name from the cyanotype photographic process developed by John Herschel in the 1840s.[10] Herschel coated paper with photosensitive compounds and then exposed it to strong light. In the process, areas of paper were converted to Prussian blue. The cyanotype, one of the tantalising byways of early photography, did not find wide acceptance because many viewers were unable to accept the world rendered in shades of blue and white. The process, however, was widely used to reproduce architectural and engineering technical drawings until replaced by less expensive printing methods in the 1940s and 1950s, and more recently, by digital displays. Given the term 'blueprint' still carries with it this residue of technical drawing and specifications rather than fluidity and flux, it seems a less than ideal metaphor for the screenplay.[11] The development of the screen idea, too, inevitably involves collaboration.

> Collaboration involves reading and re-reading, notes, discussion
> and redrafting, creating and recreating something that represents a
> common understanding. The reader(s) of the screenplay and other
> documents inevitably construct a version of the screen idea in
> their heads which (unlike readers of novels) they then have to
> contribute to…[12]

This process has only intensified with the proliferation of digital technologies and the working methods they enable. In our era of digital
cinema, previously discrete stages of preproduction, production and
postproduction tend to get collapsed into a single, more fluid stage, in
which images and sounds can be reworked to a much greater degree.
Increasingly, elements of postproduction and preproduction can be happening simultaneously. Surely then, more than ever, the screenplay
needs to be a flexible document? Film editor, Walter Murch observes:
'Digital technologies naturally tend to integrate with one another.'[13]
Surely in this environment it is more appropriate to consider the
screenplay as an open text that sketches possibilities and remains fluid
through the filmmaking process?

Courier and the screenplay

> The screenplay … is the record of an idea for a screenwork, writ-
> ten in a highly stylised form. It is constrained by the rules of its
> form on the page, and is the subject of industrial norms and
> conventions.[14]

When I began writing screenplays in the 1980s (assembling images
and text with scissors, paste and colour Xeroxes to construct the
treatment for my first production), I was astonished to discover the
degree to which scriptwriting formats were rigidly prescribed. Even now,
the Nicholl Fellowships Guidelines, sponsored by the US Academy of
Motion Picture Arts and Sciences, warn that you can create a negative impression of your script through the following list of foibles and
indiscretions: 'Art on the script cover … Hard, slick Acco covers (i.e.,
plastic spine binding) … Commercial, "college paper" covers … Wimpy
brads … Long "dangerous" brads … . Cut "dangerous" brads.' Reading
this list, a trip to the local stationery shop begins to sound surprisingly complex. The pitfalls awaiting the writer seeking professional
acceptance and eventual production are many. The Nicholl guidelines
go on to advise against: 'A "clipped" or "rubber-banded" script on

non-three hole paper... Overly thick scripts... Thin scripts... Three-ring binding... Color [sic] of card stock cover that inadvertently bugs a reader.'[15]

The number one convention, however, is that the screenplay MUST be presented in Courier 12 font. Similar advice can be found in screenwriting training manuals and submission guidelines around the world. Why? Is it because the font conveys a sense of timelessness, thanks to its association with the typewriter? Yet the Courier font was designed not in the early twentieth century along with the first mass-produced typewriters, but much later, in the 1950s Populuxe era. It rapidly became one of the most popular fonts around, with versions available for almost every typewriter on the market. The font's inventor claimed: 'A letter can be just an ordinary messenger, or it can be the courier which radiates dignity, prestige and stability.'[16]

Of course, this message is exactly what many screenwriting manuals and funding guidelines have long been trying to drum into aspiring screenwriters. Present your scripts in the approved formatting, and you not only imbue your work with 'Dignity, Prestige and Stability' but announce your status as an insider in the film industry. In *What Happens Next: A History of American Screenwriting*, Marc Norman reports that Preston Sturges was initially hired to write dialogue in 1930s Hollywood on the basis of his stage plays. Producer Jesse Lasky initially dismissed Sturges as an amateur when he offered to take an idea that he had pitched him, straight to first draft, bypassing the conventional ten-page treatment common at the time. When a month later, Sturges turned in a script, Lasky was forced to eat his words:

> [It was] a complete screenplay of proper length, complete to every word of dialogue, the action of every scene blueprinted for the direc-tor, and including special instructions for the cameraman and all the departments... I was astounded. It was the most perfect script I'd ever seen... I wouldn't let anyone touch a word of it.[17]

There are several ways to read this, but it is hard to go past the view that in Lasky's eyes, it was Sturges's command of screenplay formatting that accorded him the status of the true professional.

The personal computer and the rise and fall of Courier

One of the main reasons that Courier was able to migrate successfully from the typewriter to the first personal computers in the 1980s was that it did not require much memory. This is because Courier is a fixed pitch font, in which every character has the same width, and therefore requires no kerning. Although perhaps even more important to note is that the packaging of Courier with the first PCs ensured that users would be able to replicate typewriter-looking documents, enabling a smooth transition to the new era of word processing and personal computing. By 2004, however, *Slate* writer Tom Vanderbilt reported that the United States State Department was replacing Courier 12 as its official font-in-residence:

> Courier 12, created in 1955 by IBM, is perhaps the most recognizable typeface of the twentieth century – a visual symbol of typewritten bureaucratic anonymity, the widespread dissemination of information (and a classification of documents), stark factuality, and streamlined efficiency.[18]

Exiled from bureaucracies, the film industry remains one of Courier's last strongholds. But for how much longer?

Conventional wisdom in the film and television industries suggests that the screenplay is not only a creative document, but also one that encompasses production planning, providing information about locations, actors, sets, props, time of day and, most vital of all, programme timing. If the usual formatting conventions are followed, then a page of screenplay equals one minute of screen time. I suspect, however, that the equation has never been as easily calculated as this convention might imply. Different genres and styles of filmmaking, as well as individual director's preferred patterns of coverage, are likely to result in a much greater range of page to screen ratios than the idealised one minute of screen time per page of screenplay. Moreover, one can't help but wonder if the enforcement of this equation doesn't nudge the screenplay towards more of a production and budgeting document rather than a creative record of a screen idea? An idea in flux and transition: an idea on the way to becoming a film. Indeed, the insistence on a single method of writing and presenting a range of screen ideas across genres may primarily owe its existence to the need to process efficiently large numbers of speculatively written screenplays. It may be a response to the growing numbers of screenplays (fuelled in part at least, by the growing number of screenwriting manuals and workshops), rather than a response to the needs of the development process.[19]

Fluidity: Improvising the screenplay

Cognitive psychologist David Perkins notes that 'a lively interplay between the developing work and the mind of the artist' is an important factor in crafting large writing projects. Novelist Anthony Burgess, for example, described the early stages of new work: 'I chart a little at first...lists of names, rough synopses of chapters, and so on. But one doesn't over-plan; so many things are generated by the sheer act of writing.' Nelson Algren also spoke of a book finding its own shape in the process of creation.[20] Wong Kar-wai 'typically allows his stories to evolve as he films them; he simply sketches an outline of the story, finds locations, and begins shooting'. As Wong puts it, he doesn't really know what he wants at the writing stage, thus 'making the film is actually a way for me to find all the answers'. There is a particularly liquid dynamic between Wong's writing and films. 'He never writes a script with the intention of turning that exact script into a film. The script is just one interpretation of the story he wants to tell. He gets a lot of feedback from his actors,' comments Wong's cinematographer, Chris Doyle.[21]

The evolving systems theory of creativity proposes that major innovations across the arts and sciences are usually the result of extended periods of focused work on multiple, overlapping projects. Howard Gruber terms this the *network of enterprises*, arguing that such a way of working increases the likelihood of cross-fertilisation across projects.[22] Canadian filmmaker, Guy Maddin, uses just such a process. He describes the genesis of his mockumentary *Brand upon the Brain!* (2006), explaining that he was approached by Seattle's not-for-profit The Film Company. They were willing to fund a low-budget feature providing that it was an original idea. Or as Maddin explains it: 'You can't use an old pre-existing script that's got the producer's breath all over the title page.'[23] He was asked to write something new within a month. Since Maddin's films typically revisit his autobiography, it was a given some such scenes would be included.

> I didn't have time to make up a lot of stuff, so I took some episodes from my childhood, one key sort of pivotal coming-together. I knew I didn't have time to write dialogue, but I knew I had time to wing a film poem together...especially if I started writing it later in the editing process, using title cards or narration.[24]

In fact, his script never really existed as a traditionally presented and formatted screenplay. Instead, Maddin and his collaborators worked from a story outline with lists of sets and props. He also describes gradually introducing other elements into the mix. Fascinated by sound postproduction, he invited the film's team of Foley artists to contribute to a live performance, and his narration was partly inspired by *benshi*, the film explainers of Japanese silent cinema. Because of his insistence on working with cinematic elements from early in the process, Maddin's work presents one possible model for opening up the screenplay.

Maddin and Wong's methodologies also have parallels with the improvisational processes that some performers and musicians utilise. Social psychologist and creativity theorist Keith Sawyer observes that improvisational theatre groups that do 'long form improvisation' almost always prepare a *loose structure* in advance. 'Good jazz improvisers have years of experience...they build a repertoire of phrases, overall forms, and memories of other musicians' famous solos and recordings...When improvising, they draw on this material.'[25] In other words, they draw on these phrases and forms, modifying and embellishing them to suit the demands of specific situations. Yet in the film and television industries, it is usually only actors who are given the latitude to improvise. Research conducted in the IT industries also suggests that successful innovators build on limited structures. 'The critical balance for innovation is at the edge of chaos; not too rigid to prevent emergent innovation, but not too loose to result in total chaos.'[26]

Comics and graphic novels

Screenwriter Jim Taylor (*Election*, 1999 and *Sideways*, 2004) argues that screenplays could draw more on comics and the graphic novel in their formatting and layout. 'I'm hoping to figure out a new way to make screenplays more expressive,' he says.[27] Taylor points to the work of comic artist Chris Ware as one of his own inspirations for experimenting with the look of screenplays, since in Ware's comics text is often more prominent than pictures. Taylor's own experiments in creating visual interest include using a number of fonts and letterforms. In a sample page from *Sideways*, he delineated characters with the use of different fonts and typefaces, formatting all of the Miles character's lines in Comic Sans, and all of Jack's in Chalkboard.[28]

One of the most thoughtful recent publications on writing for the screen is Paul Well's *Scriptwriting* in the *Basic Animation* series, due in large part to its focus on the role of narrative forms and concepts, images, sounds and music in the development of screen ideas. Well's wealth of examples for generating audiovisual narratives include story friezes and story ladders which combine sketches and hand-drawn text.[29] In *This Book Contains Graphic Language: Comics as Literature*, Rocco Versaci notes that comics of all kinds are increasingly being adapted into films. While mainstream superhero films have long drawn on comics, less well-known and edgy material has successfully been adapted into high profile films too. Versaci cites Frank Miller's *Sin City* and Alan Moore's *V for Vendetta* as examples.[30] His analysis of comics suggests that the form has considerably more to offer cinema than simply a stockpile of stories ripe for adaptation. For Versaci, they are a form of graphic language that operates within a unique poetics:

> Comic narration blends and modifies features shared by other art forms – especially literature, painting, photography and film. Like literature, comics contain written narrative and dialogue, and they employ devices such as characterisation, conflict and plot... Comics blend words and pictures... Unlike film, the images in comics are 'read' more like paintings and photographs rather than 'watched' like movies.[31]

Versaci contends that reading the interplay between the written and the visual is complex and that comics *do not happen* in the *words* or the *pictures* but 'somewhere in between', in a process that requires the active participation of the reader to fill in the details between the panels. It is this *filling in the space between the words and the pictures*, he suggests, that fosters an intimacy between creator and audience.[32] For me, it is this dynamic mix of words and images, the fact that both images and words (and the relationship between the two) take centre stage from the beginning, which makes comics and graphic novels one particularly apt model for the screenplay.

One artist/illustrator whose work I have found especially inspiring is Jon J. Muth. In his graphic novel *M*, Muth restaged Fritz Lang's film about the investigation of a child murder with a neighbourhood cast and a collection of borrowed costumes. He then produced watercolours based on stills from these reenactments. His blurred, unfocused images of his characters help convey the sense of an everyman's version of *M*. His graphic novel juxtaposes stills of dramatic action and evidence from the investigation – maps, memos, bars of haunting music and dialogue bubbles. *M* suggests yet another possible pathway for the screenplay, perhaps with collected and assembled images for those of us who do not have Muth's skills as a visual artist.[33]

In her account of breakthrough thinking across the arts and sciences, *Notebooks of the Mind*, cognitive psychologist Vera John-Steiner argues that images are a more nuanced form of representing ideas than words.[34] This is not to suggest, of course, that words such as the scene description within a screenplay cannot evoke images for readers. Indeed, in his discussion of the evolution of screenplay, Kevin Boon argues that the trend towards less technical information within screenplays and a more distilled, literary style has been particularly pronounced over the last 30 years. Boon describes this transition as cinema and television shaking off the influences of staged theatre and developing its own distinct literary form. He regards Robert Towne's influential 1974 screenplay for *Chinatown* as a significant marker in this evolution. For Boon, though, the object of screenplay analysis is always this written documentation rather than the processes and collaborations that are part of both the development of the screen idea and its transformation into the screen work. Perhaps this arises from the fact that in charting the transitions in the formatting of the screenplay over the last century and more, Boon is primarily concerned with making a case for the film script as a distinct literary form?[35]

Just add words: Formats

Andrew Gay observes that although technology seems to have changed the format of the screenplay very little for writers, how everyone else deals with the screenplay has changed dramatically. The script has gone paperless, he suggests. 'People are reading screenplays on a screen: on their laptops, iPads, Nooks, and Kindles. Production managers are breaking down the script through automated processes using software like Scenechronize and Tagger.'[36] On set, script revisions are now routinely issued to casts and crews via files to be read on iPads and tablet computers. Given this, a broader range of script formats could easily be accommodated.

PowerPoint, one of the most maligned software packages of our age, offers many possibilities for digital screenwriters, suggests writer and screen theorist, Adam Ganz. It is readily available. As the world's most ubiquitous audiovisual media, PowerPoint is installed in more than one billion computers around the world. Requiring only a laptop computer, the software and a projector, it can be beamed onto almost any surface. A sequential narrative medium, in which a performer projects slides while talking to an audience in situ, PowerPoint is essentially an event media. It offers one means of reinventing oral storytelling for a

Figure 2.2   District 9, 2009, Tri-Star Pictures

digital era. Indeed, there is no reason scripts could not be generated in PowerPoint, asserts Ganz (Figure 2.2).[37]

We live in an era of maps and all stories are maps of a kind. Writers and filmmakers Tony Grisoni and Michael Winterbottom (*In This World*, 2002), Gus Van Sant (*Elephant*, 2003) and Christopher Nolan (*Inception*, 2010) are just some of those who have used maps as part of their scripting process. *In This World* and *Elephant* were both produced with the small flexible teams that make looser script structures possible. By contrast, *Inception* was a much larger scale production and so Nolan used a map at an earlier stage of thinking through his film and its structure. Another viable alternative to the industrial screenplay was produced by writer and director Neill Blomkamp for his feature film *District 9* (2009). Blomkamp's package of script materials included the short film that inspired his project, a graphic novel-style presentation of his script and production design and a ten-minute test scene shot on location. This package played a significant role in attracting investment, furthering the project's creative preproduction and laying the groundwork for *District 9*'s highly effective viral marketing campaign. Again, due to the scale of the production, it was unlikely to have been the sole document used on set.[38]

For many years, the film industry's standard software for screenwriting has been the *Final Draft* computer programme, marketed with the slogan: 'Just add words.' While *Final Draft*'s main function is to assist writers in formatting screenplays to industry standards, it also contains an expert problem-solver, based on Syd Field's three-act structural paradigm. This generates reports and suggestions about how the screenplay could more closely fit Field's model. Other software programmes for writing screenplays, such as *Dramatica, Montage* and *Story,* have similar features. Ironically, just as digital technologies and networked media are opening up new methods of sketching screen ideas and collaborating with others, much of the scriptwriting software may be serving to restrict the range of possible storytelling strategies on offer. Too many story templates from the likes of Syd Field, Christopher Vogler and Robert McKee have migrated across to digital platforms, along with *Final Draft* and its Courier font. On the other hand, some individuals and communities are developing shareware computer programmes like Celtx, which allows writers to add 'assets' to conventional script layouts. These 'assets' can include video, stills, music and sound. Plus Celtx aims to build online communities who can respond to each other's work. The potential source of innovation is when these features are seen as aids to screenwriting as well as preproduction and production. While programmes like Celtx still have a long way to go in enabling a more fluid use of imagery, sounds and words in the development of screen works and ideas, they do perhaps point towards one new set of possibilities for the screenplay.

Cross-platform writing

'Want some screenwriting advice? Add drawings to your script. And then put your dialogue in bubbles. If recent studio acquisitions are any evidence, then the fastest way to get a movie deal these days may just be to turn your next Big Idea into a graphic novel', wrote Jay Fernandez in *The Hollywood Reporter*.[39] A new generation of screenwriters who have grown up in a networked world saturated with YouTube, TiVo, instant messaging, MP3s and cell phones as well as graphic novels are abandoning the idea of writing only for the movies. Instead they are embracing a more elastic, cross-platform approach. Perhaps the era of the speculative script with its armies of gatekeepers has passed? The United States-based manager/producer Paul Young, for example, encourages his comedy clients to film excerpts from their speculative scripts and post them online. He sees producers, studios and distributors looking beyond the printed page for material to film. Many people are now used to watching material online and do not expect it to have high production values, Young suggests.[40]

We are all subject to what Susan Stewart calls the 'constant self-periodization of popular culture', to the ways in which shifts in technologies and viewing platforms shape our experiences of viewing and watching.[41] Courier, a product of the 1950s, could perhaps be regarded as the film industry equivalent of the Ploughman's Lunch. If the Ploughman's Lunch was a fake heritage item devised in the 1980s to bolster lunchtime trade in British pubs, then might we see Courier as a font maintained by a nostalgic film industry keen to keep itself aligned with the era of classic Hollywood?

Media theorists Henry Jenkins and David Thornburn challenge the assumption that new technologies displace older systems with decisive suddenness. Instead, they view 'media change as an accretive, gradual process, always a mix of tradition and innovation, in which emerging and established systems interact, shift and collude with each other.'[42] So much of cinema did not begin with film, but migrated across from earlier art forms and entertainments. Consequently, its histories can be found in photography, painting, portraiture, music, the fairground, the peep show, picture palaces, vaudeville, theatre, the nickelodeon, magic shows, travelogues, the illustrated lecture, the public science experiment, the book, the typewriter and the architectural sketch. Digital cinema will continue to transform, to adapt and reconfigure itself. So much of the current era, with its proliferation of digital technologies, returns us to the beginnings of cinema, and creates spaces to investigate the paths that were not followed, the possibilities not explored. The branching lines and loops, or the byways of cinema, as Guy Maddin describes them. Film theorist, Robert Stam notes: 'Pre-cinema and post-cinema have come to resemble each other. Then, as now, everything seems possible.' I think the same is true for the screenplay. As Lawrence Lessig argues, the more interesting ways to write are increasingly with images and sounds in addition to text.[43] The processes of screenwriting and filmmaking have been separated since the early years of cinema when Thomas Harper Ince, Hollywood's answer to Henry Ford, devised his industrial system of the continuity script as a basis for pre-planned productions.[44] Over 90 years later, the digital era offers the possibility of reuniting screenplay and film production in an expanded notion of the screenplay.

3
The New Three Rs of Digital Writing: Record, Reenact and Remix

The three Rs for schoolchildren were once thought to be reading, writing, and 'rithmetic. These were considered foundation skills for literacy, generally understood as the ability to read, write and interpret information using the tools of the time. According to some media scholars, we now require multiple literacies. Douglas Kellner suggests that 'we need to learn to think dialectically, to read text and image, to decipher sight and sound...to develop forms of computer literacy'.[1] While typewriters and biros were once key technologies of literacy, networked computers now play the central role.

I would like to consider the innovative writing practices of several writer/directors whose work falls on the cusp of fiction and nonfiction. The methods they employ to shape their screen ideas have all been developed over significant bodies of work. The practices central to their respective work are recording, in the case of Lucien Castaing-Taylor, based in the United States; reenacting, in the case of Thai filmmaker Uruphong Raksasad; reenacting and remixing, in the case of Grant Gee, based in the United Kingdom; and remixing, in the work of Canadian filmmaker Guy Maddin. Their hybrid screen works convey a sense of immediacy and intimacy enhanced by the fluidity of digital tools and processes. In our digital landscape, the writing spaces of pages and screens are coming to resemble each other. What insights about writing for the screen can we glean from the processes of Castaing-Taylor, Raksasad, Gee and Maddin? During the history of cinema, filmmakers such as Dziga Vertov, Alexandre Astruc and Jean-Luc Godard have weighed in on debates about writing with words, images and sounds. How do their insights on writing for, with and on screens resonate in the digital landscape?

Writing in the digital landscape

What *is* writing? While the complexities of this question are beyond the scope of this discussion, contemporary shifts in our understanding of literacy underpin any discussion of screenwriting in the digital space. As has often been observed, the word text derives from the Latin word *textus*, to weave.[2] Roland Barthes drew attention to the collective aspect of text making, proposing that texts are like 'a tissue of quotations' drawn from those common to a particular culture.[3] In the early 1990s, Jay David Bolter, imagining writing in an electronic space, suggested that more and more we focus on the communicative function of writing rather than any particular system of representation such as words or images.[4] I find the work of media theorists Gunther Kress and Theo van Leeuwen insightful and persuasive. They have identified a drift towards multimodal texts, stressing how 'most texts now involve a complex interplay of written text, images and other graphic or sound elements designed as *coherent . . .* entities'.[5] More recently, Kress suggests that the trend towards multimodal texts has intensified; we are in the midst of a major shift from books to screens and from written words to images as the dominant forms and spaces of public communication. The new media 'make it easy to use a multiplicity of modes, and in particular the mode of image – still *or* moving – as well as other modes such as music and sound'.[6] In our new media environment, decisions about which combinations of text, images and sound best represent the ideas to be communicated have taken on a more central significance. Since not everything can be said in any medium, it always matters which of these modes are being used.[7] Kress considers that visual language, in particular, has been neglected in western culture and accorded less value than written language. This is not true, of course, of all cultures; many cultures value visual means of communication more highly – indigenous Australians being a notable example. In the digital environment, it is not simply that screens are replacing pages. Rather, both pages and screens are being transformed.

*   *   *

Patrice Pavis, writing about drama, suggests that almost anything can be a dramatic text so long as it used on the stage.[8] (Or, I would add – since not all drama is staged in theatres, a performing space.) While a dramatic situation, plot, conflict and characters were once considered essential to the construction of a dramatic text, that has not been the case since the twentieth century; even a telephone book can be a dramatic text if it forms the basis of a dramatisation. Although running with this notion, we could come up against the difficulty that I have already identified; everything is writing. Pavis, however, proposes that writing a dramatic text involves a *search for coherence*.[9] A significant part of this search involves generating structures and considering the relationship of the parts of the text to the whole. I find this concept especially helpful in considering writing for the screen because it captures the thinking processes involved in writing a screen text, rather than simply the technologies or modes of communication. At the core of these two definitions then – of multimodal texts and writing dramatic texts, respectively – is the notion of *coherence*.

Recording as writing

One trend in digital cinema has been a radical reclaiming of the term 'recordist'. Writer, producer, director and screen theorist Lucien Castaing-Taylor has claimed his work on *Sweetgrass* (2009)[10] as that of a recordist. That is, he considers the central act of composition for his film, which chronicled the lives of sheep and ranchers over more than a year, took place while recording on location. Castaing-Taylor wore a camera harness every day for an extended period in order that human and animal characters alike could become accustomed to his presence.[11] Discussing the development of his idea, Castaing-Taylor said 'I foreswore interviews, scripting and re-enactments, as I was more concerned, as James Agee famously put it, "to perceive simply the cruel radiance of what is" than to listen to people interpreting their lives after the fact, with all of the attenuation and affectation that allows.'[12] While Castaing-Taylor's decision to privilege observational filming over interviews is, of course, a legitimate choice about his project's creative methodology, there are number of assumptions implicit in his statement about eschewing any kind of scripting. Is this simply a re-versioning of observational documentary's often-stated claim of a privileged relationship to 'the real' due to the adoption of a particular mode of filmmaking? Is he claiming that notes or written texts did not play any part in the elaboration of his screen idea?

Cinéma vérité and the caméra-stylo

Castaing-Taylor and his co-filmmaker Ilisa Barbash work within a cinema vérité or observational tradition of nonfiction filmmaking. Cinéma vérité is often used as a broad term for the cinema of the 1950s and 1960s, which favoured the spontaneous observation of everyday life over reenactment or retelling. Variants such as direct cinema, observational cinema and candid eye are often included under this umbrella term, emphasising a shared interest in spontaneous observation.[13] Like their contemporary counterparts, the inventors of cinéma vérité rejected advance planning, scripting and staging, typically shooting large volumes of material and finding the film's structure in the editing room. Typically, cinéma vérité made use of lightweight, portable film cameras, high-speed film stocks that allowed filming in low light, synchronised sound and small crews. Ironically, these new technologies which – initially developed by the military – fostered a more grassroots and less authoritarian form of filmmaking. Documentary theorist Patricia Aufderheide, however, suggests that the impulse towards cinéma vérité actually pre-dated these technologies, emerging with the British Free Cinema movement of the late 1950s.[14] Free Cinema's manifesto drew attention to the 'significance of the everyday' and asserted that 'No film can be too personal.'[15]

Joram ten Brink, discussing the work of Jean Rouch, author of *Chronique d'un* été (1953), one of cinéma vérité's seminal films, suggests that Alexandre Astruc's idea of the 'Caméra-Stylo' had considerable impact not only on French fiction filmmaking, but on the practices of nonfiction filmmakers.[16] The French cinema of the period, claimed Astruc, over-relied on literature and professional scriptwriters. There was no need for so many films to be based on novels. Coining the term 'Caméra-Stylo', or camera-pen, Astruc advocated that filmmakers should instead work directly with the tools of cinema. Jean Rouch, whose body of work can be seen as a response to this idea, aimed to create the world in front of his film camera, describing his camera and microphone 'as indispensible as a notepad and pencil'.[17] Cinéma vérité and observational filmmaking placed a renewed emphasis on sound and its role in creating meaning. Working with what were then new sound recording technologies, Rouch claimed to produce scripts 'in the oral tradition'.[18] That is, his audio interviews with participants acted as an initial recording of the screen idea, which remained open to new input throughout the production. Since the films of cinéma vérité and direct cinema required some kind of organising principle, a crisis structure was common: filmmakers selected subjects tackling significant personal challenges and structured a crisis narrative in the editing room. In recent years, the claims to the truth made by cinéma vérité filmmakers have been strongly contested; notably by Errol Morris who said 'the truth isn't guaranteed by style or any means of expression...or anything'.[19]

Anna Grimshaw is more sympathetic to the aims of cinéma vérité and observational cinema, taking its claims to represent the real rather less literally. Observational filmmakers attempted to witness the lives they encountered and the aesthetic qualities of the films often lay in their distinctive found rhythms.[20] In Grimshaw's view, the films of contemporary observational cinema practitioners, such as David and Judith MacDougall, attempt to ' "render peoples" lives more fully – not in the sense of more accurately or completely but *existentially.'*[21]

Reinventing the pastoral

Castaing-Taylor described the impetus for *Sweetgrass.* 'I grew up in Liverpool, but my grandmother was from the Lake District – Wordsworth country, and about as rural and remote as could be.'[22] He stayed with his grandmother on weekends and vividly recalls the sense of freedom he felt each weekend, escaping the postindustrial Merseyside and approaching her cottage. His fantasies of the countryside as a rural paradise, though, were the projections of a child who knew nothing of what it was like for humans and animals alike to inhabit this particular landscape. Decades later, living in Colorado, Taylor and his co-filmmaker Ilisa Barbash heard about a family of Norwegian-American sheepherders in nearby Montana. They were one of the last families to herd their sheep long distances, leading them by foot to the mountains each summer towards new pastures.[23] The pair arranged to meet the herders. Over a ten-day period, Castaing-Taylor made preliminary recordings with a consumer camera to explore what kind of film might be possible. Fundamental to the initial concept for *Sweetgrass* was that the film would seek to portray people living their lives rather than interpreting them after the fact. Many of the people and animals featured in the film were fitted with wireless microphones, and this sensory overload, with sound coming from all directions, is one of the features of *Sweetgrass.*

While describing *Sweetgrass* as being a western played out in sheep country, Castaing-Taylor acknowledges notions of the pastoral as highly influential. 'My immediate reference...was the pastoral, from poetry and painting. Typically, an outsider's rhapsody or evocation of a bucolian, arcadian idyll – from Theocritus, in Greek, Vergil, in Latin, all the way up to Marlowe and Spenser and Wordsworth.'[24] Rereading Wordsworth, though, Castaing-Taylor realised that his work made a significant break with the past; the poet was not the unbridled romantic he had imagined. Shepherds were depicted tending their flock but snoring, pissing or performing other bodily functions. After a lengthy shoot, *Sweetgrass* proceeded to postproduction. For eight years. On completion of the film, Castaing-Taylor reflected on the refocusing of the material that took place during this extended editing period. 'I was aware of a shift in the film from culture to nature, humans to animals, as the piece evolved during editing, and once we became aware of it, we worked it quite deliberately.'[25] That is, *Sweetgrass* gradually became more about the sheep and less about their human minders.

Rewriting the pastoral

Robert Koehler observes that *Sweetgrass*'s structure, which its filmmakers discovered in the editing room, is symphonic. Although the film does not use music on its soundtrack, its structure is organised around four movements – like a symphony. Specifically, Koehler compares the structure of *Sweetgrass* to Beethoven's *Sixth Symphony*.[26] According to literary critic Charles Mahoney, pastoral poetry (named for the Latin word *pastor* for shepherd) does not conform to a set of formal rules but simply depicts rural life. As a mode, it is thus constantly being reinvented. Wordsworth, for example, embedded the counting rhymes of shepherds – surviving fragments of everyday speech that pre-dated English and varied from county to county – within some of his own poems capturing rural life in the mid-nineteenth century.[27] Fast-forwarding to the early twenty-first century, a rich vein of ideas and images drawn from the pastoral tradition in western poetry, painting and music runs through *Sweetgrass*'s hyper-real depiction of rural life in the mid-west of America. Indeed, these texts form such a significant part of the inner structure of *Sweetgrass*, that there is a case for considering the film as a loose adaptation of these pastoral texts transposed to contemporary mid-west America.

Like much of the output of cinéma vérité and observational cinema, the editing process clearly contributed as much to the writing as the recording. Arguably, the search for the film's inner structure encompassed both the preliminary and principal shooting periods and the editing as well as the poetry of Wordsworth and others. While in comparison to digital cameras and microphones, words on the page may have played a relatively small part in the 'writing' of *Sweetgrass*, they are implicit to the weave of cultural references embedded in the film via Castaing-Taylor's extensive research.

Recording the avant text

On *Leviathan* (2013),[28] an aesthetic collage about deep-sea industrial fishing, Castaing-Taylor took his methodology one step further by eschewing not only formal scripting, but also any research and preparation before shooting.

> We did our research *with* and *through* the camera…Journalists and broadcast documentarians might come in and do all this preproduction and interviews and have all this knowledge before they start filming, but the first trip we ever went out on, we went with cameras so we were filming from the get go.[29]

One way to make sense of Castaing-Taylor's claim for recording as an act of both preparation and composition of the film-to-be is that it provides an *avant text*, which is further elaborated in the editing process through the selection and arrangement of material. Digital technologies and processes make it easier to continue researching throughout the life of a project. Writing inevitably involves choices about the arrangement, juxtaposition and the structuring of material. It involves a search for coherence and the generation of structures that relate the parts to the whole. The collage structure of *Leviathan* also points to the significant part editing plays in the writing process of films that may not have formal prewritten scripts.

Reenacting memory

Robert Koehler coined the term 'the cinema of in-between-ness' to describe films such as *Sweetgrass* and *Leviathan* that blur the lines between narrative and documentary.[30] While films documenting the rhythms of everyday life in particular communities are one of the staples of nonfiction cinema (and especially visual anthropology), Koehler observed an increasing trend towards the introduction of elements from other genres. The 'cinema of in-between-ness' encompassed films that slipped back and forth from drama to document or fused the hyper-real with elements drawn from poetry or the courtroom drama.[31] It is in this space between fiction and nonfiction; the cinema of in-between, that reenactment is flourishing.

The term reenactment literally means 'to enter amongst the public record' and criminal investigators, archeologists, historians and documentary filmmakers are just some of those who have reconstructed events in order to flush out new evidence. Reenactments are often used to fill gaps in the audiovisual record and, at its most fundamental level, documentary reenactment aims to visualise historical events and bring them to life. The method can be used to move beyond presentation and rethink the event.[32] Cinema has made use of reenactment as a technique since its beginnings. Documentary filmmaker, Robert Flaherty, for example, asked people to reenact building an igloo and harpooning a seal for *Nanook of the North* (1922).[33] While cinéma vérité and observational filmmakers insisted that only unscripted, unplanned and unrehearsed events were legitimate in nonfiction cinema, this view has been increasingly challenged. Digital cinema, and its recent shift towards more hybrid forms, has seen a renewed interest in reenactment. Scripting practices for reenactments can be placed along a continuum, with some heavily pre-scripted, and others based on a loose structure or an image. While many reenactments draw on authorised accounts of events, Thai filmmaker Uruphong Raksasad reenacts his personal memories of life in the village in which he grew up. Written texts do not form part of his process; instead Raksasad translates his memories into vignettes or dramatic scenarios staged for the camera.

Recording my happiness

Raksasad's feature-length film *Stories from the North* (2006)[34] combines nine short films made separately but thematically connected. The world of work is prominent. Like the work of Castaing-Taylor and Barbash, Raksasad's films could be seen as reinventing the pastoral tradition. Rather than recording rural life in northern Thailand, however, Raksasad employs nonprofessional actors to reenact key memories and records them. 'My idea is to tell the stories of my home village in Chiang Rai, the stories and images that I remember from my childhood. The scenery, the people, the way of life.'[35]

Beginning work on *Stories from the North*, Raksasad's script idea was simply this: to reenact and record a fast-disappearing way of life he called 'my happiness'. Some screen ideas are described by financiers and funding bodies as 'execution-dependent'. More common in art cinema than the output of studios, they are typically more difficult to finance than ideas that feature plot and action. A plan to record 'my happiness' is certainly at the more execution-dependent end of the spectrum of screen ideas. Raksasad had grown up in Chiang Rai in Thailand, where the villagers grew rice as a staple crop and recalled a time in which the rhythms of the natural world were paramount. People and animals lived side-by-side. In particular, the spark for Raksasad's project was a memory of harvest time when his whole village worked in the fields together.

> The fields were in yellow and gold. A mango would fall from the branch when a gush of wind swept past. And at night when the moon was full I would sit in front of my house listening to my uncle play his *sueng* (northern mandolin). We would see a man bicycling home after visiting his girlfriend in another village. And we shouted "Who's that? Who's that?" but it was dark and sometimes there was no answer.[36]

This evocative scene from Raksasad's childhood illustrates many aspects of what psychologists term *episodic memory*. In the early 1990s, memory researcher Endel Tulving proposed a distinction between two forms of autobiographical memory: *semantic* memory, which consists of working knowledge and *episodic* memory, which preserves significant personal experiences. According to Tulving, episodic memories are encoded so that aspects of the initial space and time with which they are associated are embedded in our consciousness. The visual, acoustic and sensory dimensions of our personal experiences, too, are encoded within these memory traces. Significantly, when we retrieve episodic memories, we do not simply locate and replay them but retrieve and actively reassemble fragments and impressions.[37] Building on Tulving's model of autobiographical memory, others have proposed that episodic memories can be reconstructed from a number of entry points; via timelines, maps or a series of tags.

From chapbook films to song cycles

Traditional script development processes emphasise the pitch in which the writer communicates the screen idea to backers in a brief, punchy verbal presentation. She or he talks *about* the idea, emphasising the storyline and its narrative hook, the potential market and its similarity to successful films that have already been produced. Trailers and audiovisual materials are usually supporting players for this verbal pitch. Yet the shift towards writing as an activity that can encompass the use of text, images and sounds and the interplay between them allows for the possibility of incorporating audio recordings alongside more familiar screenplay elements. The memory narrative Raksasad calls 'my happiness' could, for example, have been expressed as a sound recording of this fragment of memory, aimed at evoking its distinctive imagery and rhythms. That is, a variation on what Jean Rouch calls 'the oral tradition of screenplay'.[38]

Raksasad's innovative films have been likened to many other art forms such as chapbooks – small booklets of writing, unified around a theme or place. While the term is now mostly applied to poetry collections, it once referred to all kinds of ephemeral writing. The structures of his films have also been compared to series of paintings depicting rural landscapes, such as those of Gustave Courbet. For me, the notion of the song cycle is equally relevant. This form, which became popular in classical music from the beginning of the nineteenth century, brought together individual songs around a theme. The works within a song cycle were typically intimate and small-scale. According to Laura Tunbridge, song cycles were often based on seasons or months of the year, collections of flowers or colours, the expression of wonder, a series of emotional states or the exploration of an image or place. The song cycle's scale made it an especially suitable site for experimentation.[39]

Raksasad's evocative script idea for *Songs of the North,* which used very little dialogue, could have been expressed on the page in poetic form like the scripts of early German expressionist cinema. This form found its way to Hollywood when renowned German screenwriter Carl Mayer wrote the script for expatriate director F.W. Murnau's Academy Award-winning *Sunrise: A Song of Two Humans* (1927). Now:

> The Vamp walks into picture
> In very short negligee, with limbs exposed
> A typical creature from a big city.
> Beautiful.
> Racy.
> Coquettish?
> Just lighting a cigarette at the burning candle.
> Now smiling and looking around.
> What should she wear?[40]

One of the advantages of Mayer's poetry-like screenplay format is that it provides readers with the interpretative space that enable us to visualise each scene. Filmmaker and screen theorist, Jean Pierre Geuens, notes that Mayer found a form that read like poetry yet could still specify concrete dramatic actions. As Mayer's title *Sunrise: A Song of Two Humans* suggests, he may have been drawing on the song cycle as well as poetry.[41] His particular take on the screenplay is especially successful in capturing the rhythms of the film-to-be. Reading Mayer's atmospheric script, I wonder whether the screenplay as a written text did not reach its heights in the silent cinema of Germany. The current shift towards multimodal texts, incorporating written texts alongside images and sound, provides a significant opportunity to reclaim and explore the possibilities of the screenplay as poetry or song. The chapbook, painting series and song cycle provide ideas and possibilities about ways in which screenplays for works based on episodic memory might be structured and presented.

As it happens, Raksasad's memories found their way to the screen as *Songs of the North* without the need for a written script, each fragment leading him to recall the next fragment to be reenacted and recorded. This web of memory traces and associations might be termed the 'ghost text' that encapsulated the project's inner structure.

Over time, Raksasad has increased the scale of events depicted in his films from vignettes based on autobiographical memories through to reenacting life on the land for a group of villagers over a year. For *Agrarian Utopia* (2011),[42] the filmmaker rented land in the province he grew up in, hired farmers and helped them to grow rice there. In so doing, Raksasad aimed 'to capture moments that will soon be swept away by urbanization and mechanization'.[43] He said of his own family's situation:

> We can no longer farm for two reasons: one is that the bank has already taken almost all our lands. And second, farming won't help us pay off all our debts in this lifetime. We are not able to live the idealistic Utopian life. We can only do the best we can to get by, that's all.[44]

Raksasad began filming without a written script. His films are insider's accounts that capture the rhythms of everyday life. Raksasad is often described as a subsistence filmmaker since he makes films for minimal budgets, recording images and sound himself. Far from exercises in nostalgia, his films invite reflection on the plight of farmers around the globe and what has been lost in the shift to industrialised agriculture.

Collaged landscapes

Another minimalist filmmaker whose use of reenactment as a writing methodology I would like to consider is music video documentary director, Grant Gee, who is based in the United Kingdom. Gee, whose films have focused on the creative process of musicians and writers in particular, is unusually articulate about his work. His 2012 project, *Patience (After Sebald)*[45] involved reenacting the walk that underpins the narrative of W.G. Sebald's book *The Rings of Saturn*.[46] Producer Gareth Evans proposed a series of projects based on artists' responses to the British landscape and approached Gee to participate. After some discussion, Gee came up with the idea of tracing Sebald's walk. This was a formal device of the kind favoured by contemporary British artist Richard Long, who set himself tasks such as picking up a stone and walking with it for 400 miles across the country. According to Gee, if he had begun the project by considering how he might inhabit Sebald's literary world and translate it to the cinema, his imagination would have been crippled. Gee decided on a literary pilgrimage. His reenactment of Sebald's walk forms the spine of his film, in keeping with his notion that 'a script is something like an *itinerary* of a film rather than the content of a film'.[47]

'I filmed the walk first – I did it myself with a Bolex and God knows how many rolls of 16 mm film stock, and I did it all in one hit. It was a self-contained event for me.'[48] He then edited the footage into a sequence. Increasingly, even modestly budgeted digital projects generate an enormous amount of footage without the economic constraints of developing and printing film stock. Thus, one of the consequences of Gee shooting his micro-budget project on film was there were only around 100 minutes of footage and he thus had a rough outline of his film within four hours of editing. He then added layers of material, including archival footage, interviews, graphics and music (Figure 3.1).

Patience begins with a voice in the darkness: 'I set out to take a walk through Suffolk, to escape that sense of emptiness that can overtake one.'[49] Gee's film juxtaposes melancholy black and white compositions of landscapes, processed colour images, sound recordings of Sebald, excerpts from the book, interviews, music and text on screen. This rich layering creates a sense that we are moving not just in and out of the landscape, but consciousness itself. The film has an essayistic quality; it is preoccupied with the 'continual asking of questions' that Phillip Lopate suggests is one of the key characteristics of the essay.[50] A recurring image features the boots of a walker and helps the film's diverse elements cohere. Both reenactment and the remix are integral to Gee's method of composing his film ideas: 'I conceive of various elements of documentary, or film, as separate instruments, which then play at the same time – the voiceover, the soundtrack, the wild track from a piece of archive film, and treating it as a multi-layered thing.'[51]

Figure 3.1   Patience (After Sebald), 2012, Illumination Films

Sebald saw photographs as an essential part of his writing. Typically, he began writing by collecting images in a deliberately nonsystematic manner, rummaging through collections of photographs, postcards and ephemera in thrift shops in what he described as 'the dead of day'. These images became the springboard for his distinctive books. 'When writing you recognise possibilities: to start by drawing out stories from the images, to walk into these images through the telling of stories'.[52] Alongside their written texts, Sebald's books incorporated a vast array of these visual materials: photographs, children's drawings, newspaper clippings, postcards, ticket stubs, visiting cards, pages torn from day planners and film stills.[53] They provide inspiring examples of the way that the printed page has come more closely to resemble screens.

Gee describes his own scripts as constellations. The word captures something of the way he arranges ideas and images:

I'm captivated by the idea of arranging something in a form. Thinking about the constellations of the stars, they are only perceived in this form from a certain perspective. But then, you can rotate them and get another perspective and the form of the thing can change.[54]

Gunther Kress suggests that in the shift towards multimodal texts, design and the arrangement of individual elements on the page or screen has become a more significant part of writing. I would describe

Patience as an essay written on the screen, combining iconic moving and still images, interviews, music and text.

Remix

The last of the new three new Rs that I would like to consider is the remix. The term was initially used to refer to mixing alternative versions of music recordings but has broadened to include many kinds of media formats and ideas. Cultural theorist Lawrence Lessig suggests that all culture is remixed. According to Lessig, at its most basic level, the remix is the idea of someone mixing things together and then someone else coming along and remixing by adding something new. He divides culture into RO (Read-Only) and RW (Read-Write). In the Read-Write culture enabled by digital technologies and processes, we can more easily add new elements. For Lessig, too, writing has moved beyond words. For most adults, a concept of writing primarily involves working with text but increasingly we use video and sound to write. Words themselves need no longer be read in a linear way. Instead, remixed media 'may quote sounds over images, or video over text, or text over sounds'.[55]

It is in this context that I would like to examine how the inventive Canadian writer, filmmaker and artist Guy Maddin utilises the remix aesthetic that is central to his work. In particular, through the scripting process for his accomplished feature-length *My Winnipeg* (2008).[56]

My Winnipeg: The script idea

Guy Maddin is a man who finds inspiration everywhere – or so it seems: even in contemplating his hometown of Winnipeg, not exactly renowned for its big city atmosphere. *My Winnipeg* had an unusual history, says Maddin. Canada's Documentary Channel commissioned him to make a long-form project on the basis of his previous work. It was agreed that the documentary would be in a nontraditional form, most likely what Maddin terms a docu-fantasia. At the time of the commission, the project was simply called 'Trains' or 'Winnipeg'. At a screening of Maddin's film, *The Saddest Music in the World* in 2005, an audience member asked Maddin how Winnipeg had inspired him to produce such a unique body of work. Maddin improvised what he later realised was a parallel history of his hometown. At his hotel, he wrote the material in the form of an email to his commissioning editor. This email was his first script outline. Later, he wondered how he would be able to connect all the myths about Winnipeg that he would like to recount in his film. After watching a movie set on a train one night, Maddin decided to shoot some scenes involving trains with his lead actress. Although he had hoped to avoid the long development process typical of his films and simply shoot a pre-scripted film, a more organic process gradually evolved. Ultimately, the production of *My Winnipeg* involved only ten days shooting spread out over a year, hence there was considerable time to daydream about the project and where it might go.[57]

Walking and city films

Amongst his many cinematic inspirations, Maddin credited not only the films of Fellini but travelogues, city symphony films and the Oskar Fischinger three-minute short *Walking From Munich to Berlin* (1927).[58] Fischinger packed a 16 mm camera and walked from Munich to Berlin, taking a series of one-second shots along the way. Like W.G. Sebald setting out to walk around the coast of Suffolk, Fischinger was motivated by a longing for freedom. He wanted to break the ties that bound him.[59] Fischinger added that he took back roads wherever possible throughout his more than 1,000 mile journey on foot. This resonated for Maddin, whose influences are always the byways of cinema history rather than the main route. Maddin described W.G. Sebald's book, *The Rings of Saturn*, also Grant Gee's source material for *Patience*, as perhaps the most significant creative spur because it was an extended meditation on walking. Maddin finds that 'with the structure a walking book suggests, you can have digressions upon digressions and always still be going somewhere'.[60] He stressed that since he was incapable of copying a writer as accomplished as Sebald, there was little danger that the film would not be in his own voice. A related influence was the city symphony film. Such films are usually about significant places like Berlin, New York and Tokyo and so placing Winnipeg at the centre of the universe would inevitably introduce a comic element.

Script as record of a search

In his published, annotated screenplay for *My Winnipeg*, Maddin layers text, research material, photographs, animation frames and still photographs alongside notes on the making of his film. The material includes poems, myths, historical accounts of Winnipeg, dream-diaries, stories, narration and excerpts of rejected narration. Rather than a transcription of the final version of the completed film, Maddin's postproduction script is the record of a search, a creative process that captures some of Maddin's collage method. The cover of Guy Maddin's script notebook for this project reads 'Winnipeg, Outline/Script, 20th February 2006.' The following note is underlined for emphasis: 'Give the film a unified look – including limited palette, limited locations: the alleys, the snow, coziness, old, dark, palimpestly, peeling, railways and fog, frosty, ENCHANTED SOMEHOW! Limit the geography. Keep the film thematically focused! Or else Winnipeg will simply look like every other North American mid-western city!!!!!'[61] Maddin's use of underlining, of different fonts, sizes, capitals and bold, visually creates a sense of the cut-and-paste aesthetic of *My Winnipeg*. It conveys a sense of the tone of the film: irreverent and freewheeling. Who knows where exactly this story will take us? Maddin recalls the initial idea: 'The film starts with a brisk narrated introduction to my hometown and my discomfort with it, my perceived need to leave it once and for all.'[62] Significantly, his Outline/Script is written in the first person singular rather than the more orthodox first person plural. Indeed, this may be one of the emerging features of the digital screenplay. It is a more intimate form, using first person and addresses its readers and audience singly, each gazing into our individual screens or mobile devices, rather than gathered together.

The next section of Maddin's Notebook suggests a brief look at Winnipeg's location and history, riffing on ideas and story fragments from Arthur Conan Doyle on psychic phenomenon, the influences of the *aurora borealis* and the trains that dominate this particular part of the Canadian landscape. Maddin recalls that once he had decided to make a film about Winnipeg, friends and colleagues kept telling him facts about his hometown. The first page of Maddin's Notebook Script/Outline thus conveys a great deal of information about the film that the writer/director envisages; from its style, tone, themes and imagery through to the key locations of Maddin's film-to-be. *My Winnipeg's* Scenario/Script page bears the usual marks of production: handwritten notes, doodles and coffee stains. Like most screenplays, it had a dual function as a container of creative ideas and a production-planning document. In scrawled notes, Maddin reminds himself to check the sources for some archival material, read a *Storyboard Frieze* article and consider the character of Winnipeg as a city. On the cover of his 'My Winnipeg Notebook', Maddin penned the word 'Emblematic'. Rather like an entry in an adolescent's diary, the word is surrounded by stars to indicate how important this idea was to him. 'For all movies, there must be a scene, an image, an idea that stays in the mind long after the movie's end,' musing that, 'from the beginning, there must be an emblematic idea that will make the poster design easy'. If there is a prototype for what a multimodal screenplay might look like on the page, I believe that prototype is Guy Maddin's postproduction script for *My Winnipeg*.

Keyhole

Maddin took his preoccupation with finding an emblematic image further in the development of his next feature project. While *Keyhole* (2011)[63] is arguably not as strong a film as the sublime *My Winnipeg*, its methodology offers significant insights into Maddin's evolving writing process. 'I promised myself I would start my next script, not with so many words, but with images – strong, original compositions – instead.'[64] Maddin enlisted Paul Butler to help develop the idea for his project. A visual artist, Butler founded the Collage Party, an experimental nomadic studio that incubates ideas. A number of visual artists were invited to join Maddin and Butler in a series of studio sessions in which they worked with paper, scissors and glue to generate images for Maddin's new film. Maddin kick-started the process with a two-line prompt which read something like 'Two gangs holed up in a house, one all women, one all men, an electric chair in the living room.' The collage parties Maddin and Butler hosted in Toronto, Winnipeg, New York and Oakland produced more than 100 collages, some of which went directly into the film. The source material Maddin provided in the form of old books, magazines and pornography helped steer the resulting artworks. 'I wanted the project to be born out of images rather than words, so tried this experiment of harvesting images from other artists.' The key image he had been seeking was that of the keyhole. 'Keyhole images ... are old school, melodramatic. I liked the idea of kneeling and looking through them.'[65] (Figure 3.2).

Living spaces

Fittingly for a screen story about childhood houses and memory, Maddin claims French phenomenologist Gaston Bachelard's *The Poetics of Space*[66] as another key inspiration for his project. Indeed, his initial intention was to take this dense philosophical work and adapt it for the screen. Maddin soon rejected this as an impossible task. Instead, he looked for a story in the public domain about a haunted house around which he could build his own narrative. He decided on Homer's *Odyssey*, about a man returning to his home and wife and sons after a 19-year absence, as a suitable starting point.

WONDER CITY

Figure 3.2   Keyhole collage, Guy Maddin

Unusually, his preferred version of *Odyssey* was filtered through its retelling online in Wikipedia. Reading the Wikipedia entry, he understood *Odyssey* as 'the ultimate downbeat dad story' about a father who abandoned his children. This echoed some of his own experience. Many other writers, Maddin noted in his usual irreverent style, acknowledged having structured their scripts on *Odyssey* and thus it was probably a durable enough structure from which to borrow. He constructed his version by having Ulysses wander through the house, one room at a time.

Many films that utilise less traditional scripting processes are envisaged with specific locations in mind. In Maddin's case, an old asbestos and pesticide warehouse in Winnipeg has become a key location for staging his films. He has been using this warehouse as a makeshift studio for more than 20 years, regarding it as a 'living space' and therefore preferable to a professional studio. A distinctive feature of Maddin's approach is that he is unusually collaborative – even with the past. 'I often think of myself as collaborating with the past, or stealing from it.'[67] While the visual style and narration style of silent cinema formed an important part of his inspiration for *My Winnipeg* and *Keyhole*, his enthusiasm also extends to early Hollywood films, horror films from the 1930s to 1960s, film noir and trash cinema. He is just as enthusiastic about literature. By attempting to copy or plagiarise books and films that have been lost or forgotten, Maddin claims to find himself ending up with scripts and films that barely resemble his initial sources of inspiration.

A bag of marbles

While Grant Gee compares writing films to arranging a constellation, Guy Maddin compares his process to playing with marbles. He described writing his short film *Brand Upon the Brain* (2005):

> I was acting very impulsively and just grabbing things and writing things down and just trying to find a place for them. So even the finished script, which was about forty-five pages long of prose never really had a proper order. I would sort of cut and paste on my computer.[68]

He compared his story structure to a bag of marbles, a sprawling structure in which marble-like memories rolled around.[69] Maddin claims that he is currently switching his attention to the world of art galleries and museums since he can no longer finance his work via film.[70]

Maddin's films lie at the intersection of past and present, documentary and fantasy, fiction and dreams, the visual arts and film. They are about the way more than a century of moving images haunts the present, how old movies with their tonal shifts and jumps inhabit our dreams. While *Keyhole* has been less successfully received than

My Winnipeg, Maddin thrives on experimentation and testing new models of creating work. Indeed, I think his body of work could be seen as a catalogue of cinematic experiments that, for all their irreverence, are deeply informed by knowledge of screen history and the visual arts.

The image-music collage

Some of these ideas and practices concerning writing with images, sound and text are, of course, not new. Jean-Luc Godard is one of a number of filmmakers who view collage as central to their work. Godard sees cinema itself as montage, arguing that this is what distinguishes the medium from painting and the novel. For him, montage is not the act of physically gluing pieces of film together but a principle of combining events, facts or objects drawn from across the arts. Godard has described himself as a *combiner,* putting 'Raymond Chandler in contact with Fyodor Dostoevsky in a restaurant on a particular day with well and lesser known actors'.[71]

In the early twentieth century, renowned Russian director and screen theorist Dziga Vertov described himself as a cine-poet. 'I write not on paper but on film. Like any writer, I must have a creative stockpile. Recorded observations. Rough drafts. But not on paper, on film.'[72] Vertov preferred to only write events as they were unfolding. Yet his methodology could not have been more different from the practitioners of cinéma vérité. To explain how he had arrived at this methodology, Vertov described his difficulties attempting to prepare a script for *Three Songs of Lenin* (1934),[73] a film inspired by folk images. He tried to draft a script in many forms; from poems and short stories, accounts and travel sketches through to diagrams and schemata. None of these methods, however, 'helped one to see, hear and feel this film before it was edited and screened'.[74] In an address, 'I Wish to Share My Experience', he reiterated his observations about the various forms of writing that had not adequately expressed his ideas for *Three Songs of Lenin*.[75] This time he added a term for a new form of writing: the 'image-music-collage'. An alternative mode for exploring the idea for a screen-work that sounds rather like what Gunter Kress terms a multimodal text.

Vertov's image-music collage did not include words. Yet, by his own account, while shooting and editing *Three Songs of Lenin,* he filled thousands of pages with notes. He rejected the idea that these notes were his blueprints, since they did not provide a structural underpinning for his film. They were simply a means of recording his initial ideas and discarded as he made discoveries in the process of shooting and editing. Although the different elements were not all united in one text, Vertov's writing process clearly encompassed working with images, sounds and words. His illuminating discussion of the methods he trialled as he shaped *Three Songs of Lenin* provides another example of the search for coherence that is fundamental to the role of the screenwriter. Working from what he termed his Script Laboratory, Vertov sought a uniquely cinematic method of composing a screen idea, a method in which writing and production merged.

The fourth R

Tracing the development of the screen idea in these selected works, I wondered if there was not a fourth 'R'? Another key element of literacy in our digital screenwriting ecology? I would nominate that fourth 'R' as research. Far from being confined to the preparatory stage of a screen idea, writers increasingly carry out research throughout the scripting and shooting stages of their production. While that has long been the practice within nonfiction filmmaking, the technologies and processes of digital filmmaking have made research more central to fiction and hybrid screen works, too. As remix becomes a more significant aspect of writing, the ability to 'write back' involves not just being conversant with new technologies but deeply versed in the world of ideas and art. To use Guy Maddin's evocative phrase, writers and filmmakers 'collaborate with the past' as they develop ideas for their screen works.

Kress proposes that in our new media environment, interactivity comprises two key things. Firstly, the interplay between words, images and sounds in multimodal texts. Secondly, the ability to 'write back'. As we become more conversant with multimodal texts, which combine words, images and sounds that interact with each other, some films can be written directly onto screens rather than pages. Indeed, progressing the screen idea will increasingly involve shifts between different kinds of screen texts, rather than the translation of an idea from page to screen. This is not to suggest that written text cannot form an important part of the writer's search for coherence. Not all modes of communication can do all things. Written text has historically had an important role, not only as a means of recording verbal language but in expressing abstract thought. Film ideas that are directly written onto screens via the processes of recording, reenactment, remixing and research nearly always rely on written texts alongside visual and aural modes of communications to structure their ideas and stories.

4

14 Lessons on Screenwriting from Errol Morris

Philosopher-turned-private detective-turned-director Errol Morris has long claimed it was his inability to write that led to his particular brand of investigative nonfiction filmmaking. 'I became a documentary filmmaker because I couldn't write. And it was all that was open to me for artistic expression.'[1] In the 1980s, Morris wrote scripts for a number of projects, from films about a highway to adaptations of Stephen King novels. He was unable to secure funding for any of them. It is presumably this experience Morris has in mind when he calls himself a failed writer. 'I had all these projects. I would submit proposals routinely. They would be rejected.'[2] Yet over the past four decades Morris has written and directed a vast body of influential work for advertising, film and television. It includes the feature documentary *The Thin Blue Line* (1988),[3] the Academy Award-winning *Fog of War: Eleven Lessons from Robert S. McNamara* (2003)[4] and *Standard Operating Procedure* (2008),[5] awarded one of the Berlin Film Festival's major prizes. Plus, the documentary series *First Person* (2000) and hundreds of acclaimed television advertisements in the form of micro-documentaries.

In recent years, Morris has also migrated to online platforms, publishing investigative essays and video documentaries via *The New York Times* website. More and more, Morris's work takes issues of photography, truth and the nature of visual evidence as its central subject. The opportunity to write *with* words, *with* sounds and *with* pictures, both still and moving, has led Morris to an outpouring of work across platforms. Blogs. Films. Books. From essays to dramatic features. Reviewing this groundbreaking body of work, Morris hardly seems to fit the profile of someone who has difficulty with writing. Did he ever really have difficulty writing and structuring his screen ideas? Or has the rest of the world simply caught up? Have digital technologies finally allowed Errol

Morris to write and structure stories in the more fluid way he has long employed? I would suggest the latter, and to this end, examine his back catalogue for some lessons on screenwriting. Fundamental to a consideration of Morris's work as a writer is the fact that in a digital era we increasingly write with images and sounds as much as text.[6]

Opening shot

If this were a film, Errol Morris would look to camera. A man in his 60s with close-cut grey hair. A man with a habitual air of slight bemusement. In interviews Morris often wears a long-sleeved white shirt, open at the collar. As if, at any moment, the writer/director could roll those sleeves up, pitch in and do whatever might be required. He smiles often and speaks with great enthusiasm. So much so that his collaborators and media minders frequently have to remind him to stay on topic. But his interests are diverse and a huge array of things *is* on topic for Morris. Here are just some of them: the nature of truth, insurance fraud, pet cemeteries, photographic evidence, film noir, the cello, murder investigations, war, politics, eccentric characters, philosophy, robots, gardeners, lion tamers and tabloid storytelling.

One method of tracking the evolution of projects generated by creative thinkers is especially relevant to considering the work of Errol Morris. In the 1970s, cognitive psychologist Howard Gruber set out to shed light on the work of creative people.[7] He chose scientists and writers – including Charles Darwin and Jean Piaget – as subjects and traced the evolution of their ideas through notebooks, jottings and sketches over lengthy periods. Surprisingly, this approach was relatively new. An earlier generation of philosophers of science, for example, was more concerned with how theories were constructed. They therefore focused attention on their subjects' correspondence with other eminent people in their fields rather than laboratory notebooks or notes taken in the field. But Gruber's aim was to understand how key generative ideas evolved into *networks of projects* over the work of a lifetime. He called his method the 'evolving systems theory'. Although underutilised in the arts, Gruber's methodology is applicable to many areas of creative endeavour.

Howard Gruber identified a number of significant aspects of the work of creative thinkers. Most of them can easily be applied to Errol Morris. This is a snapshot. It is usual to have a number of projects on the go at any one time. This network of enterprises is shaped by the creative individual's evolving sense of purpose. When one project grinds to a halt, he or she moves on to another. This allows the person some sense of control over the rhythm and ordering of their work. It also provides opportunities to work with a range of collaborators, exchange ideas and learn techniques from many others. Ambitious ideas often take a long time to be realised. Not only insights but also obstacles can lead to articulating new problems and tasks. Periods of downtime allow the creative thinker to distance himself or herself from their projects and cast their net wider, thus increasing the likelihood of the work benefitting from chance and serendipity.[8] As an individual's work progresses, a constellation of separate but related projects gradually comes into focus. At any given time, some projects shine more brightly. Others, barely visible, eventually make their way to the centre frame.

The copious interviews to which Errol Morris cheerfully subjects himself provide a trail of evidence that allows us to track the evolution of his film ideas. He is an unusually articulate subject. Watching him on YouTube or listening to him on podcasts, there is a sense that the writer/director relishes opportunities to talk about his work. The would-be filmmaker studied music and history before dropping out of graduate studies in the philosophy of science. Twice. Before abandoning his graduate studies at Berkeley in the 1970s, Morris became a habitué of screenings at the Pacific Film Archive. He found himself more and more drawn to the film medium – especially documentary art films and noir. High on his list of personal favourites were Vertov's *Man with A Movie Camera* (1929),[9] Buñuel's *Land Without Bread* (1933)[10] and Hitchcock's *Psycho* (1960).[11] The archive's director, Tom Luddy, asked Morris to programme a season. 'He was a film noir nut. He claimed we weren't showing the real film noir. So I challenged him to write the program notes.'[12] As Morris tells it, inspired by his love of *Psycho*, he set off to make a film or a book – he was not entirely sure which – about the murderer Ed Gein whose real-life crime inspired Hitchcock's film. He spent a year conducting hundreds of hours of interviews before shelving the project. Much later, he realised that the real story was his own obsession with Ed Gein. Two critically well-received documentaries followed in the meantime: *Gates of Heaven*[13] and *Vermont, Florida*.[14] Morris still faced difficulties getting projects into production. Unable to make a living from film, Morris began working as a private investigator. He was hired by a Wall Street detective agency specialising in jobs for law firms. Later, he returned to the subject of murder investigation for his 1988 breakthrough film *The Thin Blue Line*.

* * *

'Our vision is partial and incomplete.'[15] Morris is preoccupied with how we fill in the gaps in the evidence and tell ourselves stories.[16] And more and more, it seems that seeing, imagining and remembering all have far more in common than previously thought. This, for example, is how Simon Ings describes the act of seeing; 'Our eyes bring little bits of the visual world to our attention, and from these shards we build our world.'[17] Where does seeing end and thinking begin? For Morris, the voice we all have in our heads, that original unreliable narrator, spins stories in pictures.

1. Branching trees and flying milkshakes

Images are fundamental to creative thought. According to Howard Gruber, one of the characteristics of generative ideas likely to sustain a cluster of related projects over some decades was that they initially appear as *wide scope* images. 'An image is "wide" when it functions as a schema capable of assimilating itself to a wide range of perceptions, actions, ideas.'[18] Gruber's best-known example was Darwin's sketch of a branching tree – one of a number of key visual metaphors that Darwin sketched and re-sketched over many years. *Wide scope* images play a role in allowing creative thinkers to track an idea as it unfolds. They were not always recorded visually. Virginia Woolf, for example, captured key images in phrases in her notebooks. Phrases that often read like telegrams.[19]

Not surprisingly for someone who thinks with a camera, Errol Morris's key images are recorded on film or video rather than in a notebook. One of them, Morris's version of Darwin's branching trees, if you like, is the three shots that make up the spilt milkshake sequence in *The Thin Blue Line* (1988).[20] It provides visual shorthand for the writer/director's musings on evidence and the nature of truth throughout his subsequent work. Those three shots of a malted milkshake have triggered a myriad of visual experiments. Let me explain.

The Thin Blue Line is the story of the arrest and conviction of Randall Adams for the murder of a Dallas policeman in 1976. Billed as 'the first movie mystery to actually solve a murder', the film is credited with overturning the conviction of Adams for the murder of officer Robert Wood.[21] As Morris says, 'I investigated a murder with a camera – an oddity in and of itself, it was not telling a story about a murder investigation, it *was* the investigation – and evidence was accumulated with that camera.'[22]

It was a bitterly cold night on 28 November 1976. Two Dallas police officers – Robert Wood and Teresa Turko – stopped at a Burger King in a deserted area of the city. They pulled out of the parking lot. They noticed a blue car on the road, its headlights off. They turned on their red flashing police lights and directed the car to pull over. Shortly afterwards, the car sped off and Wood was dead at the scene – shot at close range. Randall Adams was charged with murder. But for Errol Morris something did not quite add up. Who was really responsible? And how did a routine warning turn into a murder investigation? Morris's investigation began with an interview. As he says, his films nearly always start out as something else. In this case, he initially planned a film about a psychiatrist whose expert testimony had contributed to a number of convicted murderers being given the death sentence. Morris interviewed a number of the prisoners. One of them was Randall Adams, who insisted that he did not murder Wood. Morris was inclined to believe him.

Morris began reviewing the evidence and, in particular, the conflicts between the accounts of eyewitnesses. A police crime scene diagram alerted him to the fact that Turko's account may not have been reliable. For Morris, the telling detail was where Turko's milkshake landed. It demonstrated that she could not have been where she said she was. He reconstructed the flying milkshake moment in slow motion. 'Why does the milkshake matter? Because we assemble our picture of reality from details. We don't take in reality whole. Our ideas about reality come from bits and pieces of experience. We try to assemble them into something that has a consistent narrative.'[23] He's been on the lookout for those telling details in people's accounts of events ever since. The flying milkshakes.

2. Look for the unknown in the familiar

On the topic of finding subjects for films, Morris advises 'look for the unknown in the familiar'.[24] In the early 1980s, Morris set out for Vernon, Florida, to research insurance fraud for a proposed fictional film called *Nub City*. (The town had earned the nickname because a number of residents deliberately sacrificed an arm or a leg in order to collect the insurance payout.) After several months of work, Morris abandoned the project. If there is a pattern that emerges over time, it is that Morris gained a lot of practice at immersing himself in things and then either abandoning them or allowing them to shift course. This has been a surprisingly useful skill. A headline in a San Francisco newspaper grabbed his attention: '450 dead pets going to Napa Valley'. He drove there, tracked down pet owners and interviewed them. The research formed the basis of his first feature film *Gates of Heaven* and defined Morris's method of finding film subjects. He has since discovered most of his stories – murder inquiries, war, and photographs of Abu Ghraib – on the front pages of newspapers. Literally. He then conducts exhaustive research to find the story behind the story. For writers working to predetermined briefs, such a time-consuming and high-risk method is unlikely to be an option. But it may be that drift is a crucial element in the writing process.

3. History is a crime scene

History is a crime scene and you're the detective; film can be tool to solve the mystery, says Morris.[25] He cites historian Carlo Ginzburg, one of the architects of micro-history, as an influence. In his essay 'Clues', Ginzburg speculated that following a trail and connecting bits of evidence may go back to humankind's early history as hunters. 'We learned to sniff out, record, interpret, and classify such infinitesimal traces as trails of spittle.'[26] Following a pathway of evidence is itself a form of narrative.

4. A film should not be able to be summed up in a topic sentence

In composition, journalism and media classes, people are often advised to begin each paragraph or sequence with a topic sentence that briefly sums up the main idea. None of Morris's films could be described in a topic sentence. Indeed, according to Morris, if your film can be summed up in a topic sentence it's probably not a film idea. A sense of discovery is critical to the filmmaking process.

5. The shut-up-and-listen school of interviewing

'My movies start from interviews… *The Thin Blue Line* started from bizarre, odd interviews.'[27] Over the course of his career, Errol Morris has developed a method of using interviews as scripts. 'In lieu of being able to write, I became obsessively interested in interviewing.'[28] He began developing his distinctive 'shut-up-and-listen' school of interviewing in the 1970s. Interviews, he felt, should be investigations in their own right. Conducting interviews for a proposed book on convicted killers, he provided himself with a challenge: to speak as little as possible. The tapes got longer and longer, going from 30 minutes to 60 minutes and then 120. Morris spoke less and less. He noticed that people revealed themselves: 'if you just shut up and let someone talk, within three minutes they will show you how crazy they really are'.[29] His lengthy interviews gradually became a method of scripting documentary films. 'I'd have people write these scripts for me in the forms of interviews, and then I would create a movie out of the material.'[30]

While the filmmaker and his team now carry out extensive research about each subject, Errol Morris prefers not to do preliminary interviews or even meet his subjects in advance. It is critical that there is an element of surprise and discovery. 'You can't go into an interview already knowing where you're headed. I need to explore and investigate and discover as I go along.'[31] He deplores the adversarial interview favoured by many television current affairs programmes. Instead, he aims to provide a space for interview subjects to present themselves to camera in their own words. As the subjects drop their inhibitions, interviews gradually morph into first person monologues. Morris describes his interview technique as an 'obsession with unconstrained monologue, of putting people in a place where they are trying to tell you who they are and how they should be understood in their own words'.[32] Over time, interviews have come to assume more and more importance in Morris's films. After all, what are portraits but pictures of someone's head?

6. Technology matters

In discussions of Morris's distinctive interview style, much has been made of his use of a device he calls the Interrotron inspired by the Teleprompter. He describes his invention like this: 'The Interrotron...removes me from the area around the camera. Instead, there's just a half silvered mirror, an image of me floating in front of the lens. It allows for direct eye contact with me, and out at the audience at the same time.'[33] Essentially, interviewees address Morris's image on the mirror while looking at the monitor. The device fosters a sense of intimacy between audience and subject. Like so much of Morris's filmmaking practice, it violates one of the fundamental conventions of documentary filmmaking: the subject should not look at the camera. Morris is of the view that the emphasis on technology in his writing and filmmaking process is a positive rather than a negative.

As new technologies become available, Morris puts them at the service of his cinematic investigations. New recording technologies are used to create visual texture and layer stories. *Standard Operating Procedure,* for example, incorporates video footage from mobile phones to evoke the perspective of the American soldiers. Even the aspect ratio of mobile phone footage becomes a metaphor for experience in *Standard Operating Procedure*. Typically, mobile phone images were three by four. Vertical strips surrounded by a black frame. Morris and cinematographer Robert Richardson panned the image in black from left to right to evoke the feeling of looking at the world through that tiny slot in a mobile phone. *Standard Operating Procedure* used one set, an endless ghostlike corridor, to look like 50 or 60 rooms and superimposed images of people. According to cinematographer Robert Richardson, 'We made the hallway look like it goes on forever as part of the story of the endless parade of military factions passing through the prison.'[34] As Howard Gruber has observed, creative thinkers are constantly beginning again. A series of new starting points allows them to keep their ideas fresh and alive. Invariably, problems are solved not with one tool but a collection of tools.

7. Look outside the frame...

Standard Operating Procedure began with the widely published photographs of prisoner abuse at Abu Ghraib taken by American soldiers. Were they evidence of systematic abuse of Iraqi detainees? Or did they simply document the behaviour of the proverbial few 'bad apples'? Morris was thinking about a new way of telling history on film. 'What if we could enter history through a photograph?'[35] The photographs themselves formed the basis of Morris's investigation. Why were they taken? What was happening outside the frame? As the film's press kit proclaimed, a two-year investigation, a million and a half words of interview transcripts and hundreds of photographs later, the story began to emerge.[36]

Morris interviewed those who 'could inform the story around the pictures'.[37] He initially spent more than a year trying to track down Gilligan, the hooded man on the box depicted in one of Abu Ghraib's best-known images. Without success. He decided to begin instead by interviewing Janis Karpinski, the head of the military prison in Iraq who had since been demoted. Morris filmed a 17-hour interview over two days. Karpinski was angry; she clearly had a lot to get off her chest and Morris was convinced that he had some valuable material. He consequently decided to interview as many of the military identified by the media as 'bad apples' as possible.[38] Along the way, he pieced together a counter-narrative about some of the world's most viewed photographs.

8. I don't know where to start …

Errol Morris always begins his interviews with the same prompt: 'I don't know where to start.'[39] It seems to work.

9. Look for metaphors

In 2008, Morris devoted an entire essay to his chocolate milkshake sequence from *The Thin Blue Line*. 'The three slow-motion shots of the milkshake – the milkshake being thrown, its parabolic trajectory through the night sky and its unceremonious landing in the dirt at the side of the road – are designed to emphasize a detail that might otherwise be overlooked … '.[40] Flying objects in slow motion – malted milks, bullets, ashtrays – have become one of Morris's key storytelling devices. At the conclusion of his interviews with subjects, Morris scans the transcripts for metaphors that will form the project's visual lexicon. The imagery specific to each film aims to 'take you into the mystery and drama of what people are saying. It's expressionistic rather than realistic. Images work in the service of ideas rather than facts.'[41] This relates back to his interviewing technique. 'If the person you're interviewing is telling you the details of the story, it's by and large useable. I try to focus on certain details that interest me … '[42] He keeps clarifying details. If someone mentions a fridge, for example, what kind of food did it contain? The story is *always* in the details, he insists.

Morris is just one of many contemporary filmmakers who reject the traditional fiction and nonfiction divide. He prefers to think that there are films that are 'in control' and films that are 'out of control'.[43] This questioning of the boundaries between documentary and drama is, of course, not confined to cinema. In 2010, David Shields appropriated and assembled quotes from writers, artists and filmmakers to devise a manifesto he called *Reality Hunger*.[44] An *ars poetica* for those working across writing, the visual arts, graphic novels, film, television and performance who shared an interest in introducing chunks of reality into their work. He struck a chord. In Morris's worldview, though, reality and fantasy blur just as much as fiction and nonfiction.

10. Everything is a reenactment

It is not simply that Morris's films make use of reenactments, but that the whole process of scripting and producing his films could be described as investigative reenactments. Just as detectives recreate crime scenes, Morris stages experiments with a camera. He uses the camera to get inside people's heads. His films are dreamscapes. They explore what might have happened.

Errol Morris was initially uneasy with the term 'reenactment' but has increasingly come to accept it, pointing out that consciousness itself is a reenactment. 'Everything is a reenactment. We are reenacting the world in the mind.'[45] The reenactments in *The Thin Blue Line* were in conflict with each other. They were reenactments of what people believed they had seen rather than what the filmmaker thought they had seen. '[T]he purpose of them was to bring you deeper and deeper and deeper into the mystery of what actually happened. And to heighten the conflict between the claims made by the various witnesses and the reality of that world out there.'[46]

As memory researcher Elizabeth Loftus discovered, the legal system's rules of evidence rely on outdated notions of visual memory.[47] We do not record our experiences in the way that a camera does. Instead, we save key elements of our experiences. In order to remember, we retrieve these stored impressions and process the event anew. Along the way, new feelings and thoughts are added – as filters are added to mobile phone shots via camera applications. I recall, for example, the first time I saw *The Thin Blue Line* at the Sydney Film Festival. Sitting in the dress circle, high above the screen. The thick red velvet curtains and their gold tassel caught in the beam of the projector. Philip Glass's mesmerising score. Rich colours. Red. Gold. Blue. Spirals and spools of music.

Why do I remember the soundtrack so strongly? Then I recall that Glass's score was part of a boxed set of his soundtrack CDs I bought before travelling in Japan and Korea for several months in the early 1990s. I listened to them incessantly on my Walkman and have performed a kind of interior remix of the composer's soundtracks. How could I possibly have known that the film was to top my personal playlist of influential films? (Along with Chaplin's *Modern Times* and Altman's *Nashville*. I don't think I can choose between the three of them.) Like seeing, memory is an act of imaginative reconstruction. It is a dynamic process. Memories are constantly in the process of being assembled and reassembled as they are retrieved.

11. Editing is writing, too

'My movies are made – not entirely, but to a large degree – in postproduction and editing. It's just not something you can slap together as a script (and then follow that script). You are actually writing the script while editing.'[48] This approach extends to the use of music. Although Morris abandoned his formal study of classical music, his musical training and sensibilities have arguably been extremely important to his writing and filmmaking practice. Composers drawn from classical music and jazz have been some of his key collaborators. John Kusiak, a contributing composer to *The Fog of War* (2003) and composer for films including *Fast, Cheap and Out of Control* (1997), *First Person* (2000) and *Tabloid* (2010), described Errol's approach in an interview for Radiolab. 'He likes to have the music early in the process. And he likes to edit the film to the music rather than the traditional Hollywood approach in which the film is edited completely to temp music and then given to the composer to complete.'[49] It is not unusual for Morris to shift a musical cue to somewhere it was not intended in order to bring out the subtext of a particular scene. Or to reject a number of musical cues for a particular sequence in pursuit of the right feel and rhythm. Morris's films are structured musically: after all, stories are patterns.

12. Flip things

On his first film, *Gates of Heaven* (1978), Morris took the prevailing ideas about documentary films and how they should be made and flipped them. These rules were primarily drawn from cinéma vérité. Since filmmakers should be unobtrusive, it was best to use the newly available lightweight film cameras. Morris chose heavier equipment, which suited both his budget and his inclinations. Documentaries should use available light. He lit everything possible. The subject should never look directly to camera. Subjects looking straight to camera have become Morris's trademark.[50]

There is another sense, though, in which Morris flips things. Those interested in psychobiography have noted that Morris is blind in one eye as the result of a botched childhood operation for a 'lazy eye'. (I have a 'lazy eye' too. But I managed to avoid the recommended surgery.) He cannot rely on the stereoscopic vision that most of us take for granted. This may even have been one factor in his interest in the mechanics of vision. In an essay for *The New York Times*, Morris compared two photographs taken of the Crimean War by Roger Fenton in 1855.[51] They are some of the earliest photographs of war. One image depicted the dirt road through the Valley of the Shadow of Death. The scene is as dusty and desolate as that name suggests. A second image depicted the same road with one significant difference. It was littered with cannonballs. Was it a fake? And which image was taken first? Morris's investigative skills kicked in. He tracked down diaries, journals and letters from the photographer and soldiers. There were no fresh leads. He interviewed five historians with expertise in the field. They were divided on whether the cannonball photograph was a fake. Next he travelled to Crimea, found the location and calculated the movement of the shadows on that day in history. His results were inconclusive. He placed the photographs down and flipped between them: A, B, A, B. Still musing, Morris took the photographs to Dennis Purcell, an expert in digital photography and fraud. Purcell ran the images through his computer. Still nothing. He then did something suggested by Morris. Purcell flipped between the two photographs: A, B, A, B. Over and over again. Eventually, he noticed a new detail. There were rocks in the foreground on the first photograph, which had been removed by the time of the second photograph. Purcell magnified the images and found evidence that the second photograph was doctored. But the bigger question of truth and authenticity was still not resolved. The truth was somewhere between the two pictures, said Morris. You needed to step between them: A, B, A, – B, A, B.[52]

13.   Forget script development. Research. Produce. Release

For many screenwriters, yet-to-be-realised projects take the form of filing cabinets overflowing with research materials and drafts of screenplays. This is not the case for Errol Morris. Yes, he keeps research materials. But his unrealised projects are far more likely to take the form of videotapes of lengthy interviews. A six-hour interview with philosopher-turned-private investigator-and-writer Josiah 'Tink' Thompson, for example, was the point of departure for Morris's six-minute film *The Umbrella Man* (2011).[53]

Wide shot. A man in black walks across an emerald green lawn holding a black umbrella. We hear voiceover narration. This is Josiah Thompson. We cut to interview footage. Widescreen again. Thompson, a man in his 70s, is pictured against a grey background. He is relaxed yet energised. Thompson speculates that there may be a phenomenon in historical research similar to quantum theory's explanation of physical reality. 'If you put any event under a microscope, you will find a whole dimension of completely weird, incredible things going on. It's as if there is a macro level of historical research and a micro level that do not conform to our expectations.' He should know. Thompson, a former university professor, spent years of his life researching a fragment of film. His 1967 book, *Six Seconds in Dallas: A Micro-Study of the*

Kennedy Assassination, analysed the 40 frames of amateur super eight footage shot by a Dallas dressmaker, Abraham Zapruder.[54]

It remains the most complete visual record of the Kennedy shooting. It was a beautiful day in Dallas, on the day of Kennedy's assassination, says Thompson. Why was this one man carrying an umbrella? Off camera, we hear Morris echoing the thought. 'It was a beautiful day in the neighbourhood'. The black umbrella becomes the detail through which we enter Morris's reopening of the Kennedy assassination.

The Umbrella Man was published via *The New York Times'* video column 'Op Docs' to coincide with the 48th anniversary of the assassination. The series aims to extend the opinion piece column to the audiovisual medium. Each video is accompanied by a column that is usually written by the project's director. On the site, documentary and journalism, essays and animation, still and moving pictures all blur. *The Umbrella Man*, running at six minutes, is effectively the screenplay for Morris's proposed feature documentary on the Kennedy assassination.

As with many of Morris's projects, the initial shooting provided a framework for the film. New material was incorporated in response to that footage. Writing thus becomes a process of layering and adding new strands of material rather than fully planning the project from beginning to end.

14. The short film is the new screenplay

It has become common wisdom that in our new media landscape, early iterations of projects circulate to build audiences. Jim Jarmusch's *Stranger Than Paradise* (1984)[55] extended his 30 minute short film of the same name. Neill Blomkamp's acclaimed feature *District 9* (2009)[56] scaled up his short film *Alive in Joburg* (2006).[57] Ridley Scott has produced a number of series of short films for online viewing. In 2013, Scott announced he was collaborating with entertainment company Machinima to produce a series of 12 science fiction short films to be released online. The most successful would be considered for expansion to feature-length. Morris has taken an even more direct route, releasing *The Umbrella Man* online. In a digital era, it seems, short films are increasingly the new documentary screenplay – or, at least, one form of the digital screenplay. Rather than packaging written proposals with throwaway-teasers of prospective programmes for commissioning editors, more and more filmmakers are simply producing work and getting it out to audiences. Longer versions follow.

Closing shot

Here is Errol Morris on stories, a topic on which he maintains a healthy cynicism. In his view, investigation and storytelling are at opposite ends of the spectrum. He prefers to look behind the curtains to see how stories are constructed. 'Stories are so powerful that we exclude informational evidence because it doesn't conform to the story that we have in mind, the story that we feel most comfortable with, the story that we wish to believe.'[58] Morris imagines film as an experiment. 'I have my own laboratory of filmmaking – and I love it.' I would add that he has a laboratory of writing.

5
Adaptation: Writing as Rewriting and *The Lost Thing*

From the moment I saw writer, artist and filmmaker Shaun Tan's evocative and moving animated short *The Lost Thing* (2010), I wanted to know more. It is a film that is tonally assured. You might even say pitch perfect. How did Tan create *The Lost Thing's* distinctive and meticulously thought-through story world, transposing it from an award-winning children's picture book (with more than its share of adult admirers) to an Academy Award-winning short animation?[1] How do you adapt what filmmaker Raúl Ruiz called 'an atmosphere of story'?[2] In the past, notions of what may have been lost along the way dominated much discussion of adaptation from books to screen. Yet, as Salman Rushdie wrote in his own allegorical children's book, *Haroun and the Sea of Stories*, 'No story comes from nowhere, New stories are born from old – It is the new combinations that make then new.'[3] Shaun Tan's process in writing and rewriting *The Lost Thing* across multiple media provides an illuminating example of the role of improvisation in adaptation. But, firstly, let's consider the some of the backstory and state of play on adaptation.

Adaptation: Beyond fidelity

The screen industries usually distinguish between adapted and original screenplays. As a screenwriter, I wrote my own feature films from a mix of personal memory, detailed research and character observation. That is, until recently, when I made a low-budget digital feature adapted from a social psychology experiment.[4] For most of my career, I saw myself as firmly on the original side of the screenplay landscape. I took pride in the fact that I was not one of those writer/directors who made a habit of buying up novels and plays to adapt to the screen. Instead, I wanted to use the medium of cinema to explore lived experience. Some years

ago, I made two fiction films set primarily in suburbia: the short feature *Parklands* (1999)[5] and *Travelling Light* (2003).[6] While both films had
their genesis in moments of autobiographical memory, I think it's more
accurate to view them as what Tennessee Williams would term *emotionally autobiographical*, rather than literally based on the events of my own
life-story.[7] In addition to the acts of imagination and invention that
screenwriting involves, research into the eras and places depicted in the
two films played a strong part in shaping their fictional textures and
trajectories (Figure 5.1).

Parklands is the story of Rosie (played by Cate Blanchett), who returns
to Adelaide and its suburbs after the death of her father Cliff (played
by Tony Martin), a Drugs Squad policeman. Mystery surrounds the last
year of his life. Was his car sold? Or, for some unexplained reason, set
alight? Why, out of the blue, did he suddenly leave his wife of many
years for another woman? Was he a cop on the take? Or an honest
man who unwittingly found himself in the shadow lands of police
corruption? Prompted by her father's diaries, Rosie begins her own
investigation. As her inquiries proceed, however, she finds herself drawn
to the textures and silences of her childhood. Her personal memories are

Figure 5.1   Parklands, 1996, Toi-Toi pictures

more and more at odds with the brightly coloured images of Adelaide's civic pride. As the story of Rosie's investigation, *Parklands'* narrative is structured around a number of timeframes or strands of memory. *Parklands* intercuts Rosie's investigation with archival films of civic life from Adelaide in the 1950s and 1960s. Looking back, I wonder whether its story was not a retelling of the accounts of suburban life and progress promoted in sponsored documentaries like *A Place to Grow* or *The World of Tomorrow*?[8] Weren't these films the particular myths that accompanied my childhood and adolescence? Weren't the source texts these Kodachrome documentaries? Is the divide between original and adapted stories quite as clear-cut as I once believed?

Adaptation is an increasingly dominant trend in popular culture as fictional and nonfictional worlds can be dispersed across ever more media and platforms. Transmedia projects and franchises that include both movie and game versions of a screen idea are increasingly common. Often versions destined for different media are developed and produced side by side. The stories of such projects are designed to form macro-worlds more like soap operas than novels. The suitability of the core narrative for expansion is more significant than issues of characterisation and plotting.[9] Increasingly, we adapt *story-worlds* rather than stories.

Not all of this is new, of course. It is sometimes said that film and screen media have relied on adaptation more than any other art form, drawing on source material from folktales, poems, stage plays and novels to feature articles, comics and computer games. Literary theorist Linda Hutcheon suggests that adaptation is central to western culture. The Victorians adapted everything from poems, novels, plays, operas, paintings and songs, to scientific papers and exhibits. The cycle of adaptation did not flow in any particular order, and stories were freely adapted back and forth, from one medium to another. Adaptation is itself a process of creation, writes Hutcheon. It always involves reinterpretation and recreation.[10] As Arthur Frank argues in his 'socio-narratology' of stories: 'If, according to Heraclitus's maxim, a person can never step into the same river twice, so also the same story is never told twice, no matter how many times it is told.'[11] For audiences, part of the appeal of adaptations is that familiar stories are reiterated – with variations.

Until recently, notions of fidelity dominated discussion of screen adaptation – with source-texts on the one hand and their usually inferior adaptations on the other. Increasingly, however, we question the very notion of originals and copies. In our digital era, novels are increasingly adapted to participatory video games, fan fiction, graphic novels and blogs rather than to film and television. Conversely, all of these media can be source texts for film. To a degree, all films are adaptations, functioning as texts translated by various specialists including directors, producers, actors, designers and cinematographers. Films originate from ideas and stories that are written or sketched in a condensed form and then elaborated through one of two methods. In the industrial method of screen production, films are adapted from prewritten screenplays while art-house and independent films are adapted from a wide range of materials (including notes and sketches) via a process of improvisation during production. These two methods are not mutually exclusive but borrow from each other. Digital processes fundamentally challenge the formerly discrete boundaries between stages of production within the industrial model of screen production. Stages of production are increasingly fluid and elastic. Soundtrack design and special effects, for example, may be explored as part of the scripting stage rather than in postproduction. Once considered solely the province of art-house and independent cinema, scripting as *a process of adaptation through improvisation in production* is now more and more relevant to a broader range of screen media production.

Adaptation expanded

I would like to make the case for an expanded notion of adaptation. Screen media themselves are in the process of adaptation as they overlap and borrow – from each other and from forms such as reportage, the blog, email and Twitter. Television is reinventing itself through more complex storytelling, web series and experiments with hybrid forms such as 'emergent drama'. The latter combines elements of video games and virtual reality environments as artificially intelligent characters improvise their own storylines. In Channel 4 Education's online drama series *SuperMes*, developer Somethin' Else 'programmed the game's AI characters with a set of disparate behaviours and characteristics and then let them loose, filming the resulting interactions and building a narrative around them.' Production and scripting proceeded hand-in-hand.[12] Writer Ben Lerner says that the novel, too, is being adapted and reinvented in a digital era rather than being simply replaced by newer forms. Novels are elastic, he says. They have the ability to absorb and constellate other modes and forms of writing.[13] Screen media potentially have a far greater elasticity since they incorporate images, sound, text and characters into their story worlds.

Retelling epic stories

Adaptation is an enormous topic and the subject of considerable contemporary debate. In keeping with my focus on shifts in screenwriting practices, I am going to consider screen adaptations that involve working with both images and text from the beginning. But first, let's rewind to the early twentieth century in India and another story brought to life on film from performance and paintings. Perhaps adaptation as a writing practice is just as significant in nonwestern cultures? Some of India's first narrative films were based on legends. They were drawn from epics such as the *Mahabharata* and *Ramayana* and typically featured battles between gods and demons. As explored in Chapter 1, these mythological stories had long been presented by picture storytellers, folk theatres, singers and dancers and were well known to the audiences of early cinema. In 2009, India's official entry for 'Best Foreign Language Film' at the Academy Awards, *Harishchandrachi Factory* (2009)[14] was a fictional account of the making of *Raja Harishchandra* (1913).[15] The silent film, *Raja Harishchandra*, was itself adapted from the epic *Ramayana*, which began as an oral storytelling practice in northeast India. It took the form of songs, verbal prose narratives, myths, legends, mantra, proverbs and riddles. Poets are thought to have been the first to write these stories down. As Jaydipsinh Dodiya observed in his study of this particular collection of myths and legends, oral and literary traditions coexist and intermingle. Each transforms the other and, over the centuries, ever more stories have been grafted onto the *Ramayana*.[16] In recent times, some of them, I imagine, will have derived from screen adaptations and retellings. Stories are always in the process of adaptation.

Raja Harishchandra was written, directed and produced by Dadasaheb Phalke – a photographer, magic lantern showman, printer and filmmaker. I watch *Harishchandrachi Factory* (2009), the tale of its making, on my computer screen. I become absorbed in a Bombay brought to life in the colours of hand-painted slides. Lead actor, Nandu Madhav draws, in part, on Charlie Chaplin-style slapstick for his screen portrait of Phalke. The showman and his son find themselves in Bombay. Phalke stumbles across a tent cinema. He wants to see the show. A poster advertises Alice Guy Blaché's *La Vie du Christ* (1906) as the feature film. Some documentary shorts on the theme of 'animal stories' are on the bill, too. Phalke, sporting a moustache and a version of the magician's customary top hat, leads his son into the makeshift theatre. They slowly adjust to the dim lighting. In front of the screen, a woman plays violin. An audience member demands that Phalke remove his hat. The show begins.

We see black-and-white pictures of a matador waving his cape at a bull fill the screen. We hear the audience's sharp intake of breath. There are cries of fear. Some patrons flee.

The scene echoes Maxim Gorky's famous report on watching an early Lumière Brothers' *actualitié* in Paris. 'Yesterday I was in the kingdom of the shadows,' he wrote. 'If only you knew how strange it is to be there. There are no sounds, no colours...Suddenly a strange flicker passes across the screen and the picture comes to life...It is terrifying to watch but it is the movement of shadows, mere shadows.'[17] Far from being terrified by the moving pictures of the matador and his quarry, though, Phalke was enchanted.

Phalke recalled that after watching *La Vie du Christ* he mentally scrolled through images of Indian gods and goddesses. He soon decided to make his own feature film based on the story of Harishchandra from the *Ramayana*. A noble king, Harishchandra was tested by the gods. He was asked to relinquish his wealth, family – and finally, his wife. The former king ultimately found himself living alone and as a commoner. As in real life, Harashchandra's difficulties appeared randomly and seemingly without rhyme or reason. The gods were impressed with the sacrifices that Harishchandra was prepared to make in his quest for a noble life. They relented and returned the king's good fortune.

Preparing to make his version of Harishchandra on screen, Phalke imported a camera and began learning how to operate it. One of his first tests was a time-lapse sequence documenting the growth of a seed sprouting into a plant. He was especially interested in depicting miracles on screen and so began with one – albeit on a minor scale. The resulting educational film *Growth of a Pea Plant* (1912) helped Phalke secure backing for his first feature.[18] He wrote the scenario as an episodic narrative. It brought to life the story of Harishchandra through paintings by Ravi Varma. Both the legend and the paintings were likely to be known by audiences. Images devised from Varma's richly coloured paintings and prints of gods and goddesses continued to feature in Phalke's films. He went on to make 100 or so more films in the genre he invented – *mythologicals*.[19]

Phalke later introduced material about the making of films into some of his features and produced a short documentary called *How Films Are Made* (1917).[20] This gave his films an added resonance and topicality. Phalke's films were stories about the potential of cinema as much as the myths they depicted. The audiences who flocked to see his films came to see a retelling of familiar stories in a relatively new medium.

Adaptation as a creative process

A key aspect of our digital era is that we can access the past more easily. A wealth of material can form the basis of adaptations. One of the ways that we now participate in digital culture is through translating our favourite texts. 'Rather than develop wholly new works, audiences take ownership over existing media, adapting stories and films they most identify with.'[21] In another sense, too, *all* screenplays are adaptations. They serve as source materials to be adapted by teams of specialists including directors, producers, actors, designers and cinematographers.

In their call for a new approach to thinking about adaptation, Christina Albrecht-Crane and others suggest a renewed focus on 'how texts form and *in-form* each other'.[22] After all, works of art are essentially responses to other works of art. As Derrida observed, in the act of reading we take certain paths. Yet there are always other possible pathways contained in the works we read – or view and hear. We might consider the following questions in examining a work of art across media: What is the path taken by the writer of this adaptation? Why did this screenplay take this particular path?[23] Such questions place an emphasis on adaptation as a creative process.

Remembered films

Pierre Bayard, who combines the roles of literary critic and psychoanalyst, uses the term 'inner library' to characterise 'that set of books – a subset of the collective library – around which every personality is constructed, and which then shapes each person's individual relationship to books and other people'.[24] Our inner libraries are mostly composed from fragments of long-forgotten and imagined books. We are the sum of these fragments of texts and stories. This is how we understand the world, says Bayard. Can our inner libraries include films? Does the flashlight of memory make its way along both library shelves and vaults filled with celluloid, video cassettes, DVDs and hard drives? Do we mentally illuminate fragments of words, images and sounds as we assemble the narratives that are most resonant for us? Victor Burgin, a photographer and writer, suggests something like this with his idea of 'remembered films'. We often discuss films as complete narratives, says Burgin. But at an individual level, what we remember is a kaleidoscope of film fragments drawn from the media, the Internet, memory and fantasy.[25]

My own archive of remembered films includes fragments of everything from Robert Altman's *Nashville* (1975) to Michael Winterbottom's *In This World* (2002). From Charlie Chaplin's *Kid Auto Races at Venice* (1914) to Bertrand Tavernier's *Round Midnight* (1986). It even includes a fragment of *Soldiers of the Cross* (1900), produced by the Salvation Army, which some people believe was Australia's first feature film.[26] In Australia, as in India, stories adapted from religious myths and folktales were popular in early cinema. *Soldiers of the Cross* intercut slides with film sequences and music with spoken word.

A homegrown western, *The Story of the Kelly Gang* (1906) is more often recognised as Australia's first feature film. It tells the story of Ned Kelly, a real-life bushranger and folk hero. Kelly and his gang were on the run from the police in Victoria's high country from 1878 to 1880. They were finally captured in what has become known as 'Kelly's last stand' at Glenrowan. The story has inspired countless nonfiction books, plays and films, and performers from Mick Jagger to Heath Ledger have taken their turn at playing the folk hero. I have never personally found the Ned Kelly story especially resonant; perhaps, in part, due to the fact that women are primarily restricted to supporting roles as mothers, wives and girlfriends. Some stories simply get under our skins more than others.

I found my own preferred version of the Ned Kelly story in the vaults of Australia's National Film and Sound Archive. It featured in a locally produced advertisement for a Kodak film stock made in the 1970s. John Waters, playing the ironclad bushranger, enters a chemist's shop and demands supplies for his camera. The shaking proprietor hands over some film cartridges. 'I wouldn't shoot with anything else', says Kelly, taking out his gun and coolly firing off a few rounds. The advertisement is predicated upon public knowledge of the basics of the Ned Kelly story and the acknowledgement of its multiple screen versions. Its hero is now even demanding a say about the film's shooting stock and colour palette.

But let's go back to *'Round Midnight*. Set in the smoke-filled jazz clubs of 1950s Paris, the film was adapted from a nonfiction book. Its central character, an American jazz player trying to make it in Paris, was a composite of two real-life musicians. Saxophonist Dexter Gordon played the lead. It is appropriate that images and riffs from *'Round Midnight* should have made their way into my own 'remembered films', since jazz is one of the most resonant metaphors for the creative process. Organisational theorist Karl Weick proposed the jazz band as a prototype organisation and Frank Barrett extended and embellished this idea. As Barrett, an accomplished pianist who toured with the Tommy

Dorsey Band, observes, jazz players invent 'novel responses without a pre-scripted plan and without certainty of outcomes; discovering the future that their action creates as it unfolds.'[27]

Jazz ensembles challenge traditional divisions between planning and execution that are fundamental to the many modes of organising creative work. The insights of organisational theorists are especially relevant to screenwriting, I believe, and the jazz metaphor provides one significant alternative model to the notion of the screenplay as a blueprint.

The Lost Thing

Tan's *The Lost Thing* was published as a book in 2000.[28] It was favourably received at the Frankfurt Book Fair that year, where it won an Award of Merit. London-based Passion Pictures approached Tan with a view to adapting the book into film. Almost a decade later, after many versions of various synopses, scripts and storyboards, *The Lost Thing* was realised on screen. The film won an Academy Award for Best Short Animation (Adapted) in 2010. Shaun Tan and his collaborators' process, I believe, could serve as a model for other teams whether working in animation or live action. I would like to trace the pathways taken in the screen adaptation of *The Lost Thing* with this jazz metaphor in mind. Firstly, Tan worked with both images and text from the outset. Secondly, various forms of improvisation were central to the working methodologies of both Tan and his film collaborators, Andrew Ruhemann and Sophie Byrne, as they translated the picture book for the screen. The writing and rewriting of *The Lost Thing* over a nine-year period provides an unusually rich case study of an adapted screenplay. Both book and film versions of *The Lost Thing* were well received by readers, audiences and critics. Far from being an inferior version of a source text, the film version of *The Lost Thing* amplified and expanded elements implicit in the book, such as the story's acoustic environment. Yet, as we shall see, the development process was not without its challenges and difficulties. As many paths were rejected as were embraced. Why? (Figure 5.2).

It began with a doodle

This is how Shaun Tan describes the story and themes of *The Lost Thing:*

> The story is about a fairly introverted boy who discovers a strange creature on the beach, one that nobody else seems to notice... Is the

lost thing metaphor for nature, childhood, art, disability or something political? Or is it simply about finding a lost animal, and the dilemma of being unable to just walk away?[29]

Nine years after writing and illustrating the first draft of *The Lost Thing*, Tan was still speculating about what his story might mean. It began with a doodle. Tan draws hundreds of sketches each year. But this one made him ask a whole lot of questions. As jazz bass player and composer Charles Mingus observed, 'you can't improvise on nothing; you've gotta improvise on something'.[30] Tan recalled that 'the doodle was of a man apparently talking to a crab on a beach, which came about from looking at a photo of a little blue pebble crab on a nature magazine cover and simply imagining it was enormous, rather than tiny'.[31] Why was the man talking to the crab? What would Tan do in his position? 'Writing and painting is very much about trying different things based on hunches and intuition, often in a silly and playful way, and then looking at them critically to see if they make any kind of sense when cast against the backdrop of lived experience.'[32]

Tan has described his preferred method of starting projects. He writes down all his ideas about a given subject, incorporating political, social and personal perspectives. This list forms Tan's 'brief' to himself. These ideas, he says, create scaffolding for the project. A year after the crab doodle – many sketches, paintings, designs and notes later – Tan had written and illustrated his picture book *The Lost Thing*. The story seemed to take on a life of its own and raised a lot of questions for the children and adults who read it. It was a book, said Tan, which could be

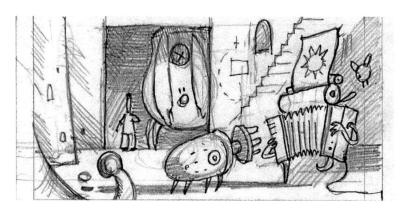

Figure 5.2   The Lost Thing (storyboard sketch), Passion Pictures

read at different levels of complexity. The story encouraged readers to make their own interpretations. Many people had experienced losing a pet and perhaps his story tapped into those experiences and feelings? The lost thing was not just lost; it was out of place. It was large and strange looking and difficult to ignore. Yet, in the story, most people did ignore the lost thing. Many cultures have myths and legends about people's life-changing encounters with strange creatures from the ocean, the forest, or a distant region. The *Lost Thing* is likely to have resonated with these myths and folktales. Not only the creature but the world of the story, too, was puzzling. Its colour palette was mostly restricted to industrial greys and browns. The houses were all the same. Mathematic formulae written on scraps of paper appeared everywhere. Why?

Shaun Tan continued to find his own new meanings in the story as he wrote and illustrated his book. In 2002, he listed some of the possible themes:

> It could be read as a critique of economic rationalism, for instance, or the transition from childhood to adulthood; about the value of whimsy, our obsession with categories and bureaucracy, about alienation, claustrophobia, altruism, disability, entropy and the possibility of joy in places where this has been extinguished.[33]

It could also be a story about visual literacy, he mused. One kind of literacy focused on recognising the familiar and rejecting everything that did not have a place. Another kind of visual literacy was playful and worked through questions and enigmas. The lost creature perhaps represented the world of imagination. As the narrator tells us, though, it is difficult to know what the moral of this story might be. In his study of the contemporary appeal of Indian theatre, Ralph Yarrow noted that the picture storytellers of the past adapted epics to local circumstances. The performer was at liberty 'to improvise, weave in contemporary references, use and interact with the audience'.[34]

Art and literature, says Tan, always encourage us to answer questions about what we think we know. The process of making any kind of art involves 'assessing a series of often accidental and mysterious ideas'.[35] Organisational psychologist Karl Weick described improvising as a kind of *sense making* that happens in retrospect. Jazz musicians arrive at their musical compositions note by note, one riff upon another. They feel their way in the dark.[36] This is a surprisingly accurate description of the process of writing and rewriting *The Lost Thing*.

The atmosphere of story

Not surprisingly, given the organic nature of his writing and illustrating process, Tan was initially sceptical about the idea of adapting *The Lost Thing* for the screen. He was disappointed with the results of a number of book-to-film projects that he had seen. Moreover, he had no experience in filmmaking and Andrew Ruhemann was proposing that the two of them co-direct. When he viewed the work of his potential collaborators, though, Tan was impressed by its sophistication. He had always seen the book as a condensed film idea. 'I had always envisioned the original illustrations as "stills" from an imaginary film, hence a certain cinematic or theatrical quality to the way the characters and landscapes are framed, illuminated and laid out upon the page,' he said.[37]

Tan and his collaborators recognised from the outset that *The Lost Thing* was not a dynamic story. Tan described the story's setting as an unemotional world; 'It's a static and desolate city, much like the paintings of Edward Hopper, steeped in a kind of a post-industrial boredom.'[38] Consequently, there were limited possibilities for the project's central, non-human character to express itself emotionally. Tan and Ruhemann wondered how to keep audiences engaged. A particular atmosphere was at the heart of *The Lost Thing*. How could they translate that atmosphere from page to screen? As they began to adapt the book, the creative team constantly sought to find the right balance between distance and intimacy. They applied this idea to every element of the production: design, animation, lighting, sound, voice and music.[39]

Scripting interpretative space

'At every step, my concern is to involve the reader by the use of their own imagination, in trying to make sense of the "unfinished" stories that I'm presenting to them,' Tan said in 2002.[40] I asked him how he went about creating that interpretative space in film, given the pressure that screenwriters experience to spell everything out? Film was generally a more literal medium than writing or illustration, he replied. The medium relied on consecutive action and did not allow much time for audiences to examine a scene in a leisurely way, as they might do with a painting. Film often involved more commercial pressure, too. The work was expected to have broad appeal and immediately make sense to viewers. 'All these conditions make it more difficult to open an interpretative space of the kind I enjoy with picture books, where you show things in quiet fragments, and can draw heavily on a reader's imagination.'[41] Tan attempted to resist these pressures by keeping *The Lost Thing's* dialogue and narration sparse. There was little camera movement and, in comparison to many other animated films, the action unfolded at a languid pace. Little context was provided about the strange creatures and world depicted, so that viewers had to actively interpret what was going on. The meaning of the story was derived primarily from the visuals and *The Lost Thing* invited multiple viewings. The filmmakers hoped that would allow audiences to pick up on subtexts and details they may have missed the first time around. As Arthur Frank suggests, 'The value of stories is to offer sufficient clarity without betraying the complexity of life-in-flux.'[42]

Script development in reverse

The Lost Thing adaptation began its life as a more traditional film script and went into production on the basis of a synopsis and storyboards. That is, the creative team reversed the usual script development process by beginning with a detailed draft and gradually moving towards a more open script. In interviews, Tan has referred to making the film from a two-page outline and storyboards. The outline, says producer Sophie Byrne, was probably the three versions of the synopsis required by Screen Australia, the government-funding body that was a major investor. Screen Australia's application for production investment required a one-sentence, one-paragraph and one-page synopsis of the film. Such documents would usually emphasise plot and storyline.

Given the project's long and complex development process, dozens of different documents recording the screen idea were developed along the way. One of the most intriguing of these is a pre-storyboard script that combined the proposed film's key locations with the narration of the central character, Boy. Here is an excerpt:

The Lost Thing Pre-Storyboard Script: Excerpt 1

1. Int. Tram – Day

So you want to hear a story? Well I used to know a whole lot of interesting ones. Some of them so funny you'd laugh yourself unconscious, others so terrible you'd never want to repeat them.

But I can't remember any of those...

So, I'll just tell you about the time I found that lost thing.

2. Ext. Streetscape – Day

This is happened a few summers ago, one rather ordinary day by the beach. Not much was going on, I was, as usual, working tirelessly on my bottle top collection and stopped to look up for no particular reason. That's when I first saw the thing.

3. Ext. Beach Entrance – Day

I must have stared at it for a while. I mean it had a really weird look about it – a sad, lost sort of look.

Nobody seemed to notice it was there. Too busy doing beach stuff, I guess.

Naturally, I was intrigued. I decided to investigate.

The pre-storyboard script, clearly intended as a creative process document, runs for only six pages. The document was intended to be read with the picture book and so only included locations and narration. The film's key theme about belonging was captured in the following narration, towards the end of the film.

The Lost Thing Pre-Storyboard Script: Excerpt 2

9. Ext. Tram – Evening

Well, that's it. That's the story. Not especially profound I know, but I never said it was. And don't ask me what the moral is.

I mean, I can't say that the thing actually belonged in the place where it ended up. In fact, none of the things there really belonged. They all seemed happy enough though, so maybe that didn't matter. I don't know.

Third draft script of *The Lost Thing*

In 2004, the bare-bones structure of the pre-storyboard script was developed into a fully scripted screenplay. The third draft was written in conventional screenplay format, combining dramatic action with narration. It was written in Courier New font, designating it as the work of a professional screenwriter. The scene below follows a new opening.

EXT THE BEACH – DAY.SLOW PAN: Along a `footpath`, small bits of debris and junk

BOY (V.O.) So you want to hear a story? Well, I used to know a whole lot of pretty interesting ones.

Picks up bottle top.

BOY (V.O.) (CONT'D) Some of them so funny you'd laugh yourself unconscious, others so terrible that you'd never want to repeat them.

Discards bottle top

BOY (V.O.) (CONT'D) But I can't remember any of those

Picks up bottle top

BOY (V.O.) (CONT'D) So maybe I'll just tell you about the time I found that lost thing.

Shot of boy studying a bottle top

BOY (V.O.) (CONT'D) This all happened some years ago, one ordinary day by the beach. Not much was going on.

CUT TO

BOY (V.O.) (CONT'D) I was, as usual, working tirelessly on my bottle top collection.

He examines field guidebook and ticks off specimen and moves on.

BOY (V.O.) (CONT'D) It was a Tuesday.

Boy approaches pedestrian traffic lights. Camera pans up to top of light as he waits for what seem to be an exceptionally long time for lights to change (even though there is no traffic). Lights change he moves on and we pull out to see wide shot of a beach landscape. Industrial sounds in the distance. Boy descends a wide, long stairway and makes his way along the beach, passing numerous people doing numerous different activities.

BOY (V.O.) (CONT'D) I happened to stop and look up for no particular reason. That's when I first saw the thing.

Conventional script formatting

By comparison with the previous version, the more conventionally written third draft provides very little interpretative space for the reader. It has a fairly predictable rhythm as it interweaves dramatic action with The Boy's voiceover. It uses a number of technical terms, which do not make it an especially good read on the page. Its strengths, such as an attention to the qualities of light and sound, are largely hidden in a myriad of detail. *The Lost Thing*'s producer, Sophie Byrne, recalls that initially there was considerable uncertainty as to how long the film might be, and how it would be financed. The Third Draft of *The Lost Thing* was consequently written with an eye to securing production funding and presented in the format generally required by film funding agencies. The creative team decided to abandon this draft and adapt the film from Tan's storyboards instead, since the screenplay did not successfully evoke the distinctive visuals and atmosphere of the story.[43]

Scripting as improvisation

As is increasingly common, the boundaries between the formerly discrete stages of script development, production and postproduction were blurred. Shaun Tan was involved in nearly every stage of *The Lost Thing*'s production from writing and storyboarding to design. Tan previsualised most of the shots using pencil and colour pastel sketches. He took screen shots of work-in-progress, printed them out and drew over them in order to understand how they might be improved. In a similar approach to the soundtrack, Tan created scratch versions of the Foley track, for example, using household objects and digital recording tools. The film's production team – based in London and Melbourne – regularly exchanged digital files and discussed each other's work. *The Lost Thing*'s creative team took nine years to adapt the book to screen. I would suggest that their creative process drew on several styles of improvisation elaborated on by organisational psychologist, Karl Weick. Further, that the jazz metaphor for creative work groups is an increasingly important one in a digital era.

Different degrees of improvisation

Weick became interested in jazz because it defies the more traditional western distinction in music between composition and performance. Transposing this to organisational units, he suggested that the metaphor of jazz helps break down traditional distinctions between structure and process, plans and their implementation. He also proposed that there are four degrees of improvisation. They range from implementation of a plan through to embellishment, the introduction of unplanned elements and radical departure from a plan.[44]

If we consider Shaun Tan's writing process in the light of these 'degrees of improvisation', then the initial writing and composing of the illustrated book involved the greatest degree of improvisation. The world and story of *The Lost Thing* were generated from an initial doodle. The next stage of adapting the book *The Lost Thing* to the film medium via a series of draft screenplays involved *interpretation* and *embellishment*. During this phase, the creative team began working with a conventional prewritten script, only to find themselves losing sight of their creative goals. They subsequently decided to go back to working with a brief outline of the story and storyboard paintings. This placed more emphasis on the distinctive tone and visual world of the proposed film.

Weick and other writers on jazz as an organisational prototype propose that minimal structures bring projects alive. Minimal structures provide enough of a framework to give everyone a sense of a shared project. But structures should not be elaborated to the degree that individual's contributions are turned into a series of predetermined tasks. The two page synopsis and storyboards used to adapt *The Lost Thing* to film, served as an effective minimal structure on which to base the production. This collection of materials provided an alternative to the model of the script as a plan or blueprint to be implemented via production.

Relationships within improvising groups

One of the most significant aspects of organisational units that foster improvisation is that there are already close relationships amongst the individual members. Such relationships create the safety net required for risk-taking. Weick provides the example of four improvising musicians who had not previously played together. The musicians began working with highly structured songs, which provided minimal opportunities for improvising. They only began improvising when they were more comfortable working together.[45] In the case of the key creative team who adapted *The Lost Thing* to film, the writer/co-director, director and producer were all highly experienced in their respective fields of writing and illustration (Tan) and producing (Ruhemann and Byrne). Significantly, both Tan and Ruhemann proposed to work in new roles through co-directing the film. The three key collaborators had a very clear goal – to adapt *The Lost Thing* to film. How they should go about doing that was less clear.

I will recap on the translation of *The Lost Thing* from picture book to screen. The pre-storyboard script provided a loose structure. In an

effort to secure financing, the creative team moved towards a fully written industrial screenplay. Tan wrote the screenplay and Ruhemann and
Byrne provided feedback. The creative team abandoned this methodology at third draft because it did not convey as strong a sense of
the proposed film as Tan's book and paintings. Writing a screenplay,
though, played a significant role in building the relationships within
the group. The production script was essentially a set of storyboards and
a two-page story outline.

Collateral spaces

Collateral spaces are an important factor in enabling organisational
improvisation. Collateral spaces run side by side with principal spaces.
Activities carried out in collateral spaces are subject to less scrutiny than
those carried out in principal spaces. Participants in creative projects,
it has been suggested, need collateral spaces in which they can rehearse
improvising strategies that fall outside of their usual roles. Improvisation
is also more likely to be successful with fewer numbers of participants
since small groups can more easily self-organise. Plus, the more direct
communication enabled in small groups leads to less information distor-
tion than large groups.[46] In the case of *The Lost Thing*, Passion Pictures
provided a collateral space in which the small creative team could test
ideas and methodologies.

Beyond brainstorming

An aspect of *The Lost Thing* project development process worth noting
is that it alternated periods in which the key creatives worked individually with periods of working together. I asked Tan how he had made
the transition from shaping projects on his own to working in a collaborative medium like film. 'Although it's highly collaborative, each
person still works in relative solitude,' he said.[47] Despite the cliché of
writers gathered around tables brainstorming ideas, there is considerable
evidence that individuals are more successful at generating innovative
ideas while groups successfully evaluate and combine ideas.[48]

Retelling the story of writing *The Lost Thing*

The book and film of *The Lost Thing* were well received by critics, readers
and viewers around the globe. Consequently, Tan has had the opportunity to tell the story of his project numerous times. It is common

for the authors of books, or screenwriters and filmmakers to tell the chronology of their project in soundbites for the press. An agreed version of events is soon settled upon, often with the input of marketing specialists and publicists. The story is told and retold via book tours, press screenings, blogs and interviews. In the case of *The Lost Thing*, though, there are some additional factors at play. The book's publication in 2002 and the film's Academy Award win in 2010 provided two different contexts for the telling of how the screen idea was generated and elaborated. In 2002, Tan saw his story of a lost thing as being about the role of imagination in an increasingly uniform society. How to respond to refugees arriving by boat had become a hot button issue over that interval. In recent years, the issue has sharply divided Australians. Much of the political debate has focused on methods of processing refugees by the government departments that are responsible.

In a 2011 interview for the opening of an exhibition of artwork at the State Library of Victoria, Tan retold the story of the genesis of the project. After completing the first draft, he didn't give *The Lost Thing* much more thought. It was simply a story about a boy who finds a lost creature at the beach. 'It [the creature] is big and it's got tentacles and he takes it to a government department and it all becomes a bit sinister. That was my basic idea.'[49] *The Lost Thing* began as a semi-autobiographical story inspired by living on the coast of Western Australia and going beachcombing. It gradually evolved into a more universal story about belonging. Looking back, Tan realised that this was a major theme in his body of work, What does it mean for a person to belong to a place? What is an individual? What is a place? Is belonging a good thing? Can belonging be a negative thing? The emphasis in Tan's retelling shifted a number of times over the years. From being about imagination, to the experiences of refugees. From being a story about being lost, to one about belonging. In adaptations, each retelling emphasises a different theme.

In the future, says Tan, his preference would be to develop screenplays in the same way as he develops picture books. That is, via a combination of conventional scripts and concept drawings and storyboards:

> The problem of just using a script with the kind of work I do is that it does not by itself convey much sense of wonder...The bulk of work happens at a storyboarding level. The best scenes for me are usually somewhat inexplicable and even irrational, but through drawing you can still experience what they could feel like.[50]

I began this chapter by writing about adaptation and have ended with a discussion of improvisational strategies. Why? Improvisation by both individuals and groups is a significant strategy for rewriting and retelling stories. It helps generate the variations that give stories resonance in new situations. Indeed, as I have considered the case studies that make up one strand of this book, I have come to think that improvisation is the key practice that underlies screenwriting in a digital era – as a creative process and as a means of organising groups of collaborators. As Arthur Frank says, 'Stories echo other stories, with those echoes adding force to the present story. Stories are also told to be echoed in future stories.'[51]

6
Degrees of Improvisation

One of the defining characteristics of digital cinema has been a renewed interest in improvising with performers. Around the globe, from silent cinema onwards, there has been a long tradition of writers and filmmakers drawing on improvisation on set as a method of generating and refining screen ideas.[1] From silent film's Charlie Chaplin to British social realist Ken Loach and Iranian cinematic explorer Abbas Kiarostami. Filmmaker and screen theorist J.J. Murphy observes that improvisation, visual storytelling and psychodrama increasingly feature as one alternative to conventional scripts in the work of independent filmmakers in the United States.[2] These trends can also be seen in the cinema of Europe, the Middle East, Asia, Australia and the Pacific. Murphy suggests that the increasing prominence of improvisation can largely be attributed to digital technologies and a renewed interest in exploring the real on screen. Digital technologies have lowered production costs and radically transformed feature filmmaking.[3] Consequently, more and more writers and filmmakers are able to embark on low-budget features without the prewritten scripts typically required by financiers and studios.

One of the best-known contemporary filmmaking movements that draws on improvisation as a scriptwriting process is what has been dubbed 'mumblecore'. Like much digital low-fi cinema, mumblecore productions are characterised by handheld cinematography, natural lighting, real locations, an emphasis on close-ups of actors' faces and long takes. Stories play out in particular subcultures, and script processes are fluid. Not known for the quality of their sound recording, some mumblecore films are so dense with dialogue that some critics refer to them as 'The New Talkies'.[4] According to writer and director Andrew

Bujalski, who is closely associated with the movement, the genesis of mumblecore lay in his peer group's frustration with the failure of mainstream movies to address the circumstances of their lives. Bujalski's own films are 'microdramas, films that are tuned to frequencies not attended to by the mainstream'.[5] This suggests that mumblecore filmmakers have much in common with other writers and directors around the globe who wish to see more of the realities of life in their communities reflected on screen.

While improvisation has long been accepted as a legitimate practice in art forms such as music and theatre, the work of contemporary screenwriters and directors who use this creative methodology is frequently criticised as lacking story and dramatic shape. Why? Where do we draw the line between scripting and production? Is every aspect of improvising images and sound for the screen 'writing'? In order to address these questions, I would like to consider the writing and development processes of a number of films that draw heavily on improvisation with nonprofessional casts: Zavattini and de Sica's legendary *Shoeshine*[6] and *Bicycle Thieves*,[7] set in postwar Rome, *Putty Hill*[8] writer/director Matthew Porterfield's acclaimed micro-budget drama set in a Baltimore neighbourhood, and Ramin Bahrani's *Man Push Cart*[9] about a New York street vendor. All four films share an ethos of improvising with the camera in real situations. Ideas about an expanded notion of improvisation, drawn from different art forms, cultures and contexts, ripple through this book. In the previous chapter, I considered picturemaking as an act of improvisation and how the organisational structures of creative teams can make use of improvisation. In this chapter, I would like to consider improvisation in ideas generation, performance and production. So let's go back to the beginning. What do we mean by improvisation?

Beyond spontaneity

All creative processes take place within a continuum, with improvisation usually placed at one end and composition at the other.[10] While romantic notions of improvisation emphasise spontaneity, improvisation requires skill and expertise. The term's etymological roots lie in the word *improvisus* – or the unforeseen. One of the defining characteristics of improvisation is an emphasis on fluidity and creating in the present.[11] Music theorists stress that improvisation involves selecting a point of departure. 'The improviser always has something to work from – certain things are at the base of the performance, that he (or she) uses as the ground on which to build.'[12] That is, improvisation involves interacting with a given environment and other people. As a creative methodology, improvisation is process-orientated and privileges collaboration. Far from requiring no preparation, improvisation most often occurs within a loosely prepared structure.

Drawing on research into American jazz, organisational theorist Karl Weick proposed four degrees of improvisation, ranging from interpretation to *embellishment*, variation and fully fledged improvisation in which the performers radically depart from the plan.[13] Weick's conceptual model is particularly useful in that it focuses on how different kinds of creative processes shape the products that arise from them. It can be applied to a range of art forms and group processes.

Another valuable perspective on improvisation comes from Hamid Naficy, who traced the social history of Iranian cinema. Improvisation has a strong place in the creative arts of Iran and the Middle East and has been incorporated into its cinema. 'Improvisation is one of the key features of the Iranian literary and performing arts particularly of classic poetry, comic theatrical performances (*ruhozi* and *siabbazi*), oral epic storytelling (*naqqali*), classical art music, and now of cinema.'[14] In Iranian culture, loose narrative structures based around resonant themes and images are often more highly valued than tightly controlled and balanced narrative structures. Naficy identifies three key improvisational strategies in Iran. Firstly, *repetition*, in which motifs and sets of motifs are repeated to create complex patterns. Secondly, *ornamentation*, in which musical passages (and, I would add, the components of other art works) are enlivened and enriched. Thirdly, *centonization*, which is sometimes referred to as patchwork or montage. In the form of centonization common to the arts of Iran, recognisable motifs from various sources are quoted and pieced together to form a whole.[15] As discussed in Chapter 3, in the context of remix practices, within centonization the new contribution lies primarily in the way the elements are assembled. Ethnomusicologist, Bruno Nettl, recalled studying music in Iran in the 1980s. He began by learning to play the *radif*, around 300 short pieces, which provided a framework for improvisation.[16]

The new realism

Writer David Shields claimed that many contemporary artists shared a 'hunger for reality'. As Shields wrote in his influential manifesto *Reality Hunger*, 'a burgeoning group of interrelated (but unconnected) artists in a multitude of forms and media (lyric essay, prose poem, collage novel, visual art, film, television, radio, performance art, rap, stand-up comedy, graffiti)…are breaking larger and larger chunks of "reality" into their work'.[17] The complexity of contemporary life, Shields suggested, could not be explored in overly familiar narrative forms. Echoing Shield's insights, *New York Times* film critic A.O. Scott suggested that post 9/11, a new generation of American-based filmmakers asked themselves: what kind of films do we need now? Their response? Films that engage with the world.[18] In an insightful article, Scott pointed to recent American independent cinema he called *neo-neorealist*. Films such as those of Kelly Reichardt, Anna Boden, So Yong Kim and Ramin Bahrani. Typically, these low-budget digital films feature characters not often depicted on screen: a Senegalese cab driver in Winston-Salem; a baseball player transplanted from the Dominican Republic to Iowa; an African-American shopkeeper in the Mississippi Delta; or two young Korean girls abandoned by their mother.[19] Although many neo-neorealist films feature the stories of immigrants, for their writers and directors 'multiculturalism is not a theme but a fact'.[20]

Not everyone, however, agrees that contemporary, semi-improvised independent films are best characterised as following in the steps of neorealism. Richard Brody, for example, dismissed them as 'granola cinema' – contrived to seem good for you but hard to digest.[21] David Bordwell suggested that we simply call films that focused on the daily lives of working people, featured nonprofessional actors and were shot on location *verismo* – or working-class realism.[22] This may, however, be too restrictive; neorealism not only advocated particular themes and stories but ways of telling them. Ramin Bahrani, while acknowledging the influence of Italian neorealism and especially the work of Roberto Rossellini on his own, has rejected neorealism as a label. Perhaps not surprisingly, given that Persian culture and, more specifically, the writing and production practices of Iranian filmmakers, Abbas Kiarostami and Amir Naderi have also provided significant inspiration for his own films.[23]

Beyond the Archplot

Sociologist Arthur Frank observed that 'stories often shape, rather than simply reflect human conduct'.[24] Perhaps then, we need some new stories *about* stories? American screenwriting gurus such as Robert McKee insist that engaging screen stories have always followed a crisis–conflict–resolution pattern. McKee calls this the Archplot – a classical story design that is 'neither ancient nor modern, Western nor Eastern; it is human'.[25] He insists that material observed from real life should always be structured into this formula, which is 'the meat, potatoes, pasta, rice and couscous of world cinema'.[26] It is important to acknowledge, though, that not all screenwriters aspire to mass-market entertainment. The designation of a single storytelling model (no matter how worthwhile it might be as *one* model) as a universal, classical story design robs contemporary screenwriters of a history – and possibilities for the future. It denies audiences opportunities for engagement. Stories are not fixed. They live and breathe.

Neorealism and the screenplay

Neorealism proposed engaging with the present moment, wherever you might be. In the aftermath of the Second World War, Italian filmmakers invented neorealism. Director Vittorio De Sica, one of the filmmakers most strongly associated with the movement, recalled that after the Americans entered Rome in June 1944, there was initially chaos. Everyone lived for himself or herself. There were no studios or cameras or film stock to make films. Word spread that Rossellini had begun making films on the streets and De Sica and his colleagues began thinking about how they might follow suit.[27] As veteran screenwriter Suso Cecchi d'Amico observed, the neorealist filmmakers did not think of themselves as a movement at the time. They were simply 'a group of friends who wanted to make films and went out on the streets to do so'.[28] Their methods included 'the casting of nonprofessional actors, often portraying characters close to their real selves; the use of unadorned specific locations and an absorption in the ordinary details of work, school and domesticity'.[29] Neorealist filmmakers made their lack of resources a virtue. They favoured extensive research, location shooting, episodic narratives, and nonprofessional actors and improvised scenes. All of which sounds remarkably like the contemporary independent filmmaking environment.

Italian neorealism was more than a film style. It was, according to Robert Gordon, 'the prime response in the cultural sphere (in art, architecture, literature, theatre, cinema) to the transition from war to democracy'.[30] Writer Italo Calvino saw neorealism as linked to a spirit of renewal in postwar Italy. A community of writers and artists longed to share the stories they had witnessed in a time of great social, political and economic upheaval.[31] In his influential manifesto, 'Some ideas on the cinema', Cesare Zavattini, the novelist and screenwriter who worked closely with director Vittorio De Sica, declared that cinema had a 'hunger for reality'.[32] As already noted, David Shields recently made a similar observation about the arts in our era in his manifesto *Reality Hunger*.

The sense of urgency associated with neorealism is captured in a diary entry Zavattini made in 1944. He recorded an idea for a new way of making films. The project would not need much money. Zavattini and his collaborators would travel around Italy with a truck stocked with basic filmmaking supplies – cameras, lights and film. Encountering stories along the way, the filmmakers would record the country's liberation from war. In order to document the world in transition, the cinema 'must abandon its usual narrative methods and adapt its language to its content', claimed Zavattini.[33] Consequently, he and his collaborators would leave Rome with very few script pages actually written. Instead, Zavattini's basic film idea, which he could clearly see in his mind's eye, would constitute 'a political or moral rough draft'.[34]

News item storytelling

In 1946, Zavattini and Victor De Sica collaborated on *Shoeshine*[35] – one of the films that launched neorealism. It was an example of the *fatto di cronaca* (*news item*) or *film lampo* (flash film) storytelling that Zavattini advocated.[36] According to Vittorio De Sica, he first sketched out the idea for *Shoeshine* in a column for a short-lived magazine. He began a column entitled 'What Films Do You Want to Make?' 'Instead of shooting people, I argued, we should be shooting films...' De Sica envisaged a film about two homeless boys who tried to earn money for food by polishing the shoes of American soldiers.[37] His script outline was illustrated with a photograph from the streets. De Sica showed his article to Zavattini and the two collaborators were soon strolling the streets of Rome fleshing out the story idea. *Shoeshine's* central characters, Little Monkey and Big Hat, were based on two boys the filmmakers befriended.

La Bataille du Rail

In postwar France, the neorealist impulse was expressed differently. In the same year that *Shoeshine* was produced, French novelist and screenwriter, Colette Audry collaborated with director René Clément on *Railway Battle* (*La Bataille du Rail*) about the role of railway workers in the Resistance.[38] The film, based on Audry's extensive research, was initially commissioned as a short documentary. It was so well received that Clément decided to expand the film to feature length. The resulting

Railway Battle is made up of two parts: a documentary followed by a drama. It won Best Film at the Cannes Film Festival in 1946. Like many works associated with neorealism, *Railway Battle* did not feature a single protagonist or hero. Instead, it celebrated the collective efforts of railway workers in the Resistance.

Stories of lives

In Italy, much neorealist cinema focused on the plight of the urban poor. Inspired by a novella by Luigi Bartolini, *Bicycle Thieves* was Zavattini and De Sica's most celebrated collaboration. Zavattini bought the rights to adapt Bartolini's *Bicycle Thieves: A comic novel of the theft and recovery of a bicycle, three times over*.[39] He insisted, though, that the only link between the novella and his screenplay was the title.[40] Robert Gordon described the research and writing process for *Bicycle Thieves* as close to ethnographic fieldwork.[41] Zavattini quickly wrote a treatment to discuss with his collaborators. Although he took the lead writing role, ultimately eight writers worked on the completed film. Suso Cecchi D'Amico recalled that the writing team worked together closely for several months. Several writers usually accompanied Zavattini and De Sica as they walked around Rome searching for stories and locations. The group frequently stopped to stage improvisations with street characters they wanted to appear in the film.[42] As Zavattini wrote, he was 'interested in the drama of things we happen to encounter, not those we plan'.[43]

Bicycle Thieves' dramatic premise was simply this: a thief steals the bicycle of Antonio, who is unemployed. Along with his bicycle, Antonio loses the possibility of work. Trailed by his young son, he searches the city for the bicycle. This slender plot enabled the filmmakers to show audiences the complexity of daily life in postwar Rome. Ultimately, De Sica secured a relatively large budget for the film, which was shot on the streets of Rome over several months with a cast of largely nonprofessional actors. De Sica commented that 'Production costs and lack of money were a determining factor in making me – and certainly Rossellini in *Open City* – take such actual life as the subject matter so that reality could be elevated to the plane of poetry.'[44] He explained the deeply collaborative nature of his work with Zavattini; 'I weigh, experience, discuss and define with him [Zavattini], often for months at a time, each twist and turn of the scenario. In this way, by the time we start shooting, I already have the complete film in my mind.'[45] Zavattini, he added, often introduced poetic touches. For all their emphasis on encountering the real, Zavattini and De Sica's scripts frequently had a fable-like quality. Iranian cinema of the 1990s, such as *The White Balloon* (1995),[46] shared this sensibility.

Episodic stories

Critics praised *Bicycle Thieves* for its drifting narrative, in which nothing happened. According to Zavattini, *Bicycle Thieves'* evocation of the texture and feel of real life could not have been captured with a more traditional dramatic arc of crises and resolutions. Screen theorist Robert Gordon echoed many previous writers when he observed: 'Lived lives are not shaped like stories, but move in messy sequences, not going anywhere in particular.'[47] This aspect of neorealist storytelling has a strong contemporary resonance – and could almost come from the press kit of a digital 'long-take' film. I suspect, however, that Gordon overstates the degree to which neorealist screen narratives were messy. *Bicycle Thieves* could instead be described as an episodic narrative. This is not surprising given the degree to which it was informed by observations from life. Dismissing nineteenth-century German playwright Gustav Freytag's formulaic crisis–conflict–resolution plot (which McKee's Archplot closely resembles), Walter Ong noted 'the experience of real life is more like a *string of episodes* than it is like a Freytag pyramid'.[48] A drifting, episodic quality, ambiguity and a preference for open-ended stories over narrative closure are all central to art cinema.[49]

Some critics have suggested that *Bicycle Thieves* is a closer fit with classical narrative than may first appear. Frank Tomasulo, for example, analysed the published screenplay and broke it down into 11 sequences that he saw as corresponding with the classical plot development of Freytag's pyramid, Scribe's 'well-made play' and Aristotelian tragedy.[50] One of the difficulties with this kind of analysis of published screenplays – usually assembled in postproduction – is that they effectively project a favoured structure onto the work under discussion. Almost anything can be found to conform to the preferred structure. My emphasis here is on scripting practices rather than structure. In her nuanced analysis, Kristin Thompson wrote that *Bicycle Thieves* balanced the use of Hollywood conventions with novel departures motivated by notions of the real. In her view, the production's carefully constructed script only superficially resembled the classical screenplay. The film's editing and sound postproduction strategies, however, were more familiar to international audiences.[51] The scripting strategies adopted by Zavattini, De Sica and their collaborators were a significant factor in injecting *Bicycle Thieves* with a sense of aliveness.

From neorealism to Cinema Novo

The neorealist ethos has proved resilient, surfacing around the world at critical times. Variations on neorealism can be found, for example, in the cinema of 1950s India, 1960s Brazil and 1990s Iran.[52] Yet the impulse towards cinematic realism was expressed differently in each of these places; the literary and art forms specific to particular geographies and cultures playing a significant role in the adaptation. In 1960s Brazil, for example, Hollywood storytelling was rejected in favour of films informed by the 'aesthetics of hunger'. Like the Italian neorealists and contemporary micro-budget filmmakers, Cinema Novo practitioners made a virtue of necessity.[53] Due to Brazil's impoverished economy at the time, some filmmakers made a feature of recycling old film stock and embracing what they called a 'garbage' aesthetic. The Brazilian version of surviving by one's wits has long been known as *jeitinho* and some commentators identify this spirit in Cinema Novo's approach.[54] Brazilians were living under a military dictatorship, and a political dimension was part of the alternative film movement. The filmmakers of Cinema Novo rallied around the call to action: 'a camera in my hand and an idea in my head'.[55]

Writing from the streets

Historically, screenwriters were depicted at their typewriters. More recently, at their laptops. In studio offices, or even poolside, they gaze into the distance, fingers poised over keyboards. As if their storylines were conjured from little more than individual imaginations and Californian sunshine. By contrast, Cesare Zavattini was always captured in motion. Walking. Striding. Riding a bicycle. Trailed by kids. Gesturing. Shaking his head. Smoking. Arguing. Zavattini took to the streets, filling notebook after notebook with photographs, interviews, and observations.[56] He jotted observations on scraps of paper and stuffed them into his pockets as 'aides de memoire'. No matter where the camera found him, Zavattini's pockets overflowed with notes, and ideas tumbled from his pen. He advocated a new form of cinema: the *film inchiesta* or *inquiry*. Filmmakers were to be detectives, shadowing potential stories and characters.

In 2008, I travelled to Brazil researching a film project about local variations on Charlie Chaplin's Tramp character. I searched film archives and met with street performers who played Carlitos. (The latter was a character inspired by a combination of The Tramp and the Brazilian folk character, the *malandro* or 'a man without qualities'.) I soon learnt that Chaplin's *The Kid* had a special resonance in Brazil. It was not hard to understand why. Literally millions of children, their families unable to support them, live on the streets, vulnerable to violence and drug-related crime. I had not yet read Zavattini's manifesto but I soon witnessed a scene that could have inspired one of his screenplays.

Each day, I joined the throngs of local residents taking their constitutional at Rio's Copacabana Beach. One morning, I stopped to look at a pair of blue trainers in the window of a sports store. My own shoes were a bit the worse for wear. I noticed a kid, homeless from the look of him, carrying a wad of cash. The boy wore a T-shirt that was far too large. Somehow he had cobbled together enough money to buy shoes. The boy's eyes darted everywhere. The shop assistants treated him as their most important customer, bringing out box after box of shoes for his approval. After much deliberation, he rejected all the trainers with fancy colours and stripes in favour of a sturdy pair of leather boots. The shop assistants gathered to say farewell to him. Resplendent in his new shoes, the boy stepped out onto the pavement. He ducked out into the traffic and soon disappeared. Out of sight. That single incident could spark the kind of found story Zavattini advocated. Shadow any person in the city and you will find a story, he said.[57]

Some critics have attributed the success of neorealism to the fact that it minimised literature and scripts.[58] To my mind, this is far from the truth. At the heart of this movement were strong artistic partnerships between writers and directors. While some critics have romanticised the degree to which semi-improvised screenplays like these were the result of a purely spontaneous process, others have over-emphasised the degree to which they were preplanned. One thing that is clear is that screenwriters were central to many landmark neorealist films. Writers were not hired hands but valued collaborators throughout the scripting and production process. Many neorealist screenplays are best described as *variations* or *embellishments* on the original source material or plan – rather than radical departures. The initial spark could be a magazine story, a novella or an incident glimpsed on the streets. Films such as *Shoeshine* and *Bicycle Thieves* were based on fully drafted screenplays, with Zavattini leading a team of writers. Unlike industrial screenplays, though, these were fluid rather than fixed documents.

From improvisation to composition

Ethnomusicologist Paul Berliner, a classically trained trumpet player, read in a musical dictionary that improvisation was 'the art of performing music spontaneously, without the aid of manuscript, sketches or memory'.[59] Dissatisfied with this explanation, Berliner decided to spend some time hanging out with jazz musicians in New York. Over more than 15 years, he interviewed many musicians about how they learnt to improvise and even took lessons from some of them. Berliner noticed that, in addition to group and solo rehearsal, many jazz musicians indulged in imaginative compositional play when they did not have their instruments to hand. Jazz artists, Berliner observed, were 'especially attuned to the general soundscape of their environments and constantly assessing its features for musical value'.[60] Screenwriters do the same, constantly evaluating their everyday environments for their visual qualities. As Suso Cecchi d'Amico observed, screenwriters 'write with their eyes'.[61]

Many jazz players insisted, too, that improvising music was an intuitive process. But this ability was frequently the result of years of practice and learning about the history and techniques of their art form. Bruno Nettl made the same observation about improvised music in Iran. Berliner concluded that the idea of improvisation as 'performance without previous preparation' was 'fundamentally misleading'. The practice and knowledge of an individual's lifetime, the practice and knowledge of entire communities provided the setting for improvisation.[62] The Italian neorealist writers, I would suggest, provide an example of such communities of practice. Strolls through the streets of Rome and hanging out in cafes functioned as informal preparation for their collaborative work. As Berliner concluded, the practices of improvisation and composition are deeply intertwined in the authoring of new works.

My home town

Zavattini began his published diary with a 1940 entry 'A Film I'd Like to Make'. What was the unproduced story idea at the top of his list? A story simply labelled, 'My Home Town'. It would not begin with plot or action but would gather momentum through Zavattini's experiences living for a few months in Luzzara in northern Italy where he had grown up.[63] The neighbourhood he grew up in likewise inspired writer and director Matthew Porterfield's micro-budget feature *Putty Hill*. Porterfield recalls, 'I was raised in a Baltimore suburb wild with unkempt hedges, disheveled lawns and porches, yards full of car parts and swimming pools, and a church or a bar on every corner.'[64] Like Belgium's Dardenne Brothers and the United States' Kelly Reichardt and Ramin Bahrani, Porterfield is more interested in stories about *people* than *types*:

> The tradition of neorealism offers a more fluid development process because it's more connected to the world and open to what the world can offer… It draws more on life than narrative conventions. And subsequently the audience is allowed to encounter the characters more like we encounter the people we meet.[65]

Porterfield's work shares the new realists' interest in telling visual stories about particular places, working with minimal budgets, nonprofessional actors, improvisation and fluid scripts. Cities, neighbourhoods or streets provide the frame within which many micro-budget films are improvised and *Putty Hill* is no exception. For several years, Porterfield worked on an original screenplay, *Metal Gods*, a coming-of-age tale about a group of metal-heads skirting the fringes of Baltimore city. In a story that is only too common in independent cinema, he was about to go into production when the financing fell through. After his initial disappointment, Porterfield decided to develop another scenario, *Putty Hill*, using many of the actors he had already cast. 'The inspiration was definitely everything tangible that I'd found put into place developing *Metal Gods* – the cast, the people, the places, the precise locations, and some of the themes.'[66] While *Metal Gods* was fully scripted, *Putty Hill* was improvised from a five-page scenario based around 15 key locations. His nonprofessional cast improvised dialogue and narration. According to Porterfield, there were no lines that were memorised; it was all collaborative work that was done on location.

Integral to Porterfield's reconceptualisation of his film after the financing for *Metal Gods* collapsed was a pared-down story more suited to his low budget (raised online via crowd-sourced funding). *Putty Hill* revolved around a gathering of family and friends in a karaoke bar after 20-something Cory suddenly dies. Porterfield commented, 'The dead kid Cory functions a bit like one of Hitchcock's MacGuffins. It's a plot device to bring everyone together. But it's a device with a strong emotional centre that all the actors drew upon.'[67] Porterfield introduced a documentary element in the form of an off-screen interviewer who probed individual characters about their thoughts and feelings. His aim was to make the fiction and nonfiction elements seamless and therefore slightly unsettling. The initial idea for the fusing of these fiction and nonfiction elements came from a casting test Porterfield shot with two of the proposed principals for *Metal Gods*. One of the actors, Sky Ferreira, had written journal entries in the voice of her character. She incorporated them into the screen test. Porterfield decided to build on this by filming an interview with Ferreira in which she drew on her own life. This footage combined elements of both the 'written' character and the actor's own characteristics and gestures.

Floating narration

The floating narration of Kent Mackenzie's critically acclaimed 1961 micro-budget film *The Exiles*[68] was another influence for Porterfield. Mackenzie scripted his film in collaboration with the three central members of his nonprofessional cast. In Mackenzie's film, three residents of Los Angeles's Bunker Hill, a favoured destination for Native Americans who migrated from reservations to the city, played versions of themselves. Yvonne and Homer were a young Native American couple expecting a baby and establishing their new life in the city. Homer did little to contribute to the household. Tommy, a young Mexican friend fond of partying, shared their home in Bunker Hill.[69]

In this instance, the use of character monologues as narration came about through a combination of practical and aesthetic concerns. Mackenzie was adamant that he did not want to make a film that romanticised poverty; *Exiles* was to be collaboration between its filmmakers and the Bunker Hill residents. Produced for a very low budget, the film was initially shot with synchronised sound on a 35 mm Arriflex camera. The camera was covered with a blimp to reduce noise. The rental of the blimp, however, added so much to production costs that Mackenzie decided to shoot image and sound separately.[70] 'The cast was interviewed and these recordings were later used on the soundtrack to convey the characters' inner thoughts as monologue.'[71] Ultimately, this decision made a major contribution to the film's much-praised poetic style. Stream-of-consciousness narration was juxtaposed with striking imagery – often featuring the city at night. Yvonne wanders the Los Angeles retail district, gazing longingly in windows at mannequins sporting the season's new fashions. She recalls what motivated her to move. 'I always wanted to get away from my people and all that. Go someplace where someone will make me feel different and be happier. I'm glad I came up to Los Angeles.' Later, shopping for groceries, Yvonne voices her hopes for the future. 'I don't think I want to take a little baby back to San Carlos. I'd rather have him raised up here. I want him to speak English and try to go to college and become something. I would like the baby to have the things I didn't have in my life.'

Homer remembered some of what he had lost in the move to the city. 'My people roamed all over the place, two hundred years ago. Before the white man came, my people were all over the place from the Canyon back down again . . . they lived mostly off the land.' In the context of his cramped domestic environment, Homer's commentary is particularly poignant.

Mosaic

Porterfield's use of an off-screen interviewer to prompt interior monologues provided his *Putty Hill* characters with an ability to articulate their thoughts and feelings. In one of the film's opening scenes, a group of teenage boys are playing paintball in the woods. The youngest, whose brother Cory overdosed, drops out. The off-screen interviewer asks him a series of questions. His answers are mostly monosyllabic. 'Is this your first time playing paintball?' 'Did you like it?' 'Where's your brother?' Hearing that the boy's brother has died, the interviewer says that he's sorry. His questions continue. 'Have you been to a funeral before?' The questions quickly escalate from whether paintball is fun to what happens when we die. As Porterfield says, 'They have a hard time communicating with each other. The interview device is to get a little more out of them.'[72]

One of the points of departure for *Putty Hill's* improvisations was a series of photographs Porterfield assembled to demonstrate the intended visual style for *Metal Gods*. In a selling document for that film, he collaged black and white portraits from photographers such as Patrick O'Dell and Ed Templeton – as well as his own work. Handwritten excerpts accompanied the photographs from Porterfield's script. Many of them emphasised the relationship of people to everyday environments. Fourteen-year-old Shaun, for example, looks to the camera. He poses against a brick wall. The caption reads 'His closet door is overflowing . . . There's a mound of clothes on the floor.'[73] In another photograph, a boy faces his video console. This caption reads 'In the front room, the younger boys sit on the couch, playing video games.'[74] The work of many of the photographers Porterfield selected focuses on youth subcultures. Patrick O'Dell, for example, is well known as a documentary photographer and recorder of the American skateboard scene.

To use a computing metaphor, unlike plug-and-play software, neorealism is re-patched and updated for local environments. As Porterfield observed, 'I've always been into how people assert their identity through style, music, athletics, art, and leisure. In particular the youth, who have more time to seek out and adopt subcultural signs and signatures.'[75] The photographs of Ed Templeton were also key amongst Porterfield's visual inspirations for *Putty Hill*. Templeton began his career as a professional skateboarder before exhibiting drawings, graphics and photography. His projects have documented the suburbs, skateboarding, friends and family and he has been described as a photographer of the 'present-tense'. Significantly, Templeton's vantage point is always that of an insider in the various communities he depicts. Templeton and Porterfield's work shares an interest in chronicling aspects of suburban life and the artistic milieu to which they belong. As J.J. Murphy observed of *Putty Hill*, 'Because his story is not dialogue driven, Porterfield focuses instead on scenes that employ visual storytelling.'[76] The photographs Porterfield assembled functioned as a spur for the film's visual text. In contrast to fully written screenplays, he says, 'treatments are good for nailing transitions and conveying atmosphere'.[77]

Porterfield's film is infused by an aesthetic linked to still photography and the snapshot. Opening and closing montages present moving picture 'stills' from the interior of the empty house where Cory died. Throughout the film, its characters are presented portrait style, framed in their immediate surroundings – the woods on the edge of town, a tattoo parlour, a kitchen, a suburban lounge room or a backyard swimming pool. Characters are framed individually or in small groups; guys playing paintball, girls swimming, boys practising their moves in the skate park. There is a lyricism in the way light falls through the trees or bounces from a wall, a teenager flicks hair from his face or executes a great move on his skateboard. *Putty Hill* gradually assembles a composite portrait of a loosely connected group of friends and family. The film's characters long for a bigger life. They dream of leaving Putty Hill. But, at this stage of their lives, the only vehicles they have are the trail bikes and skateboards of teenagers. One of Porterfield's characters, a 20-something young woman who has come back to Putty Hill for her brother Cody's funeral is not exactly nostalgic for her former hometown. 'You think you miss the place you grew up in but as soon as you get back it's as if you never left.'[78] (Figure 6.1).

Days are Golden Afterparty

Postman-turned-philosopher Gaston Bachelard considered that the imagination of each individual has a season.[79] In the case of Matthew Porterfield, that season is summer. In his 'Writer's Statement' for the first planned version of his film, *Metal Gods*, Porterfield wrote this description

Figure 6.1   Putty Hill, 2010, Hamilton Film Group

of summer in his hometown. 'There's great beauty in Baltimore during the summer months: The long days, the sun, the speed of the
heat, the way it hangs humid above the trees and the pavement, the
sound of birds, insects, automobiles and lawnmowers; here, summer
is palpable.'[80] *Putty Hill* hums with that sensibility. Not surprisingly,
Porterfield's work has increasingly crossed cinema and photography –
his mosaic of camera phone shots, *Days Are Golden Afterparty*, for example, was selected for the 2012 Whitney Biennale where it won a major
award. The mosaic, made up of 72 photographs arranged as a large
rectangular grid, featured shots of friends, lovers, pets, places and everyday objects. *Days Are Golden Afterparty*, says Porterfield, celebrated the
everyday.[81] It was shot with a camera phone simply because this was the
only camera he owned. Yet this choice of format successfully echoed
Porterfield's subject matter. A second component of Porterfield's photographic installation contained many of the same camera phone shots
edited on video. Each image appeared briefly creating the effect of a
contemporary video 'flicker film'.

The space between words and pictures

Together with *Putty Hill*'s scenario, locations and cast, the photographs
Porterfield curated formed the architectural framework for his film. It is

in the spaces between words and images that films such as *Putty Hill* are improvised. Porterfield's films and photographic projects can be seen as part of a Northern American post 9/11 concern with chronicling the real in specific communities. An ethos shared not only by independent filmmakers but their counterparts across the visual and performing arts, writing and music. The narratives of many films associated with 'improvising the real' feature ensemble casts, multiple points of view and emphasise daily life in particular localities. 'I am interested in routines, in the daily life of my characters, so plot is often subordinate to the lesser, quotidian things.'[82] Porterfield's approach to narrative matches the threads of routine pattern that David Bordwell describes as a feature of much art cinema.[83]

Putty Hill is the only film that Porterfield has made from a brief treatment and collection of images. This was in part due to its micro-budget and, in part, due to the fact that atmosphere was so important and a treatment or scenario may more successfully convey this than a fully drafted script. His other features, *Hamilton* (2006)[84] and *I Used To Be Darker* (2013)[85] also featured ensembles of characters and multiple protagonists. The latter was fully scripted because it required a subtle balance between its four principal characters. One of the dangers of improvising from a brief document, Porterfield suspects, is that unless there is a specific formal device built into the treatment, you may veer into more familiar narrative territory. A more open and flexible scripting process has both advantages and disadvantages. 'A treatment is more open to the collective imagination – and where does that take us?'[86] (Figure 6.2).

Man Push Cart

Like *Putty Hill*, writer and director Ramin Bahrani's micro-budget feature *Man Push Cart* (2002) is structured around daily routines. In this case, those of Ahmad, a former Pakistani rock star who 'ekes out a living selling coffee and donuts to commuters from his pushcart in Midtown Manhattan'.[87] Bahrani spent two years researching with pushcart vendors on the streets of New York. He gradually got to know them, visiting the vendors at home and sharing meals with them and their families. Eventually, Bahrani asked coffee cart vendor Ahmad Razvi to play himself in the script he had written. The writer and director described *Man Push Cart* as inspired by two things: the image of Ahmad pushing his cart, day after day on the streets of New York and, secondly, literature. Specifically, Albert Camus's *The Myth of Sisyphus* and Persian poetry. The

Figure 6.2   Push Man Cart, 2005, Noruz Films

central image of Camus's book is a man whose fate is to push a stone up a hill, over and over again. Every time, just before he got to the top, the stone rolled back down and Sisyphus had to repeat the exercise. Peace came to Sisyphus when he accepted the fundamental nature of his task. For Bahrani, Amhad was condemned to a similar fate, pushing his coffee cart through the streets of New York. 'I'm interested in what we don't see in cinema', he says. 'For me the story must come from a sense of reality, a sense of location and character that is rooted in today's society.'[88] In an observation that echoes Matthew Porterfield's approach to scripting *Putty Hill*, Bahrani says, 'We were trying to avoid relying too heavily on story and dramatic clichés...I wanted to use Ahmad's character, his face, his actions, and the specifics of his daily routine to create the feeling of the film.'[89]

Many street vendors had worked in professional occupations as journalists, engineers and technicians in their former lives in Pakistani or Afghanistan. After migrating to the United States, they worked long hours for little pay in jobs that did not allow them to fully draw on their skills. Bahrani's own parents migrated from Iran to America before he was born. He grew up in Winston-Salem, where there were few other Persian families. In the late 1990s, he visited his family's homeland, intending to stay for a couple of months. But, fascinated by the complexity of Tehran, he stayed for three years. A city with almost twice the population of New York, Tehran threw many different people into close proximity. To such an extent that Bahrani described the city itself as a collage. He intended to make a film in Iran but in the wake of 9/11 his American financing fell through. Like Porterfield, Bahrani decided to make a virtue of necessity and produce a micro-budget film. Rather than film in Iran, he would shoot an Iranian-style film in New York.[90]

Bahrani writes for place. 'I usually have the locations before I start writing or while I've started writing. I write while I'm coming back and forth between locations. So the locations become truly integral to how the story is told... from the script stage.'[91] He does not show his script to his cast in order that some of the performers' own dialogue can be incorporated into the script throughout rehearsals and production.[92] Like many of his contemporaries, Bahrani rejects moral endings that do not seem true to life. 'If you look at Persian poetry, it has an acceptance of life as it is.'[93] That is particularly confronting to many American viewers, he notes. Like Rossellini and the Italian neorealists, Bahrani hopes his films will speak to their times. The improvisational practices of Iranian culture are also part of the mix. Bahrani drew, for example, on the device of *tazmin*, using lines from the Persian poet Rumi as a springboard for his script. 'We have something in Persian culture and poetry where one poet borrows a line or a verse from another poem and builds a whole new poem for it.'[94]

Bahrani has acknowledged the Italian neorealist Roberto Rossellini, British socialist realist Ken Loach and new wave Iranian filmmaker Abbas Kiarostami as inspirations for his own work. At the same time, he has expressed frustration with critics' desire to link him to Italian neorealism. Yet Rossellini's description of his central working methods could easily be applied to Bahrani and many other contemporary new realist filmmakers:

> In order to work I first need to gather an extraordinary amount of information, so as to know what I am going to be dealing with through and through, after which I allow myself total freedom of action. What one would call improvisation...[95]

The improvised script

Rossellini was opposed to scripts, to written forms of cinema, to a prewriting of cinema.[96] Over the course of his career, Rossellini increasingly came to believe that cinema was part of an oral tradition of storytelling rather than a literary one. Sometimes, of course, fully prepared scripts were necessary in order to reassure financiers and producers. He thought deeply before making a film. Rossellini considered that it would be crazy to improvise every aspect of a film on the spur of the moment. He and his collaborators (mostly) wrote scenarios but every aspect of the scenario was adjusted from day to day.[97] Sometimes, though, he went on set with the ideas fully formed only in his head. Like Zavattini, his pockets were full of notes. 'Neorealism came down to this' said Roberto Rossellini, 'the exceptional is arrived at through an investigation of reality'.[98] It rejected formulae, taking the world as its object, rather than the telling of a story.

One suspicion, in particular, seems to hover around the renewed interest in the improvised screenplay. Is improvisation simply 'writing' for non-writers? My own answer would be an emphatic 'no'. All writing involves elements of both composition and improvisation and where any individual project belongs on this axis is simply a matter of degree. Improvisation can lead to innovative and compelling storytelling. Or not. More traditional compositional techniques can lead to innovative and compelling storytelling. Or not.

One of the surprising things I learnt examining films that involved a high degree of improvisation with performers was that they featured fully written scripts as often as brief scenarios or storylines. The critical difference between an industrial screenplay model and one which values improvisation is not simply whether a script predates production. Rather, it is the degree to which the screenplay remains open to new material throughout production. Michelangelo Antonioni rejected the separation of the screenplay and the film. He called his whole process of filmmaking improvisation, regardless of whether he was working with a pre-written script or not. 'The script is a starting point...not a fixed highway.... In the script you describe imagined scenes but it's all suspended in mid-air.'[99]

Photographer and videographer Ed Templeton described an epiphany in which he understood that all places are connected:

> I sometimes marvel...walking from my front door and standing on the asphalt looking down at its grimy blackness, wishing I could rest my eye down on it and hear everything like the Indians in an old Western film. The pavements we stand on are connected to practically everywhere else. Ribbons of concrete tangled across North America.[100]

A footpath, a street or a shopping mall can be a microcosm of humanity. Filmmakers inspired by the *neo-neorealist* ethos, suggested A.O. Scott, 'expand the range of aesthetic possibilities and experiences available to

cinema by pressing to bring it into rough, thoughtful and lyrical contact with reality'.[101] At the heart of digital films exploring what might
be called the new realism is the notion of a search for community. The
Italian neorealists were a loosely connected group of artists who sought
to contribute to a sense of renewal in postwar Italy. The same could
be said for the contemporary micro-budget digital screenwriters and
filmmakers who find inspiration in their work. They research and screen
stories *with* and *about* marginalised communities. From *Bicycle Thieves* to
Putty Hill and *Man Push Cart*, place plays a major role in establishing the
framework for the improvised element of their stories.

7
Improvising Reality

Below are some of the opening scenes from *Ajami* (2009),[1] a semi-improvised crime drama set in a neighbourhood within the ancient port city of Jaffa in Israel. *Ajami* was nominated for an Academy Award in the 'Best Foreign Film' category in 2010.

EXT. THE KHALIFEH FAMILY HOME – DAY

Yihya is about to finish changing the tyre. Two unidentified men, riding a motor scooter (one sitting behind the other), suddenly appear from around the corner. They stop behind Yihya, fire two shots in his back and make a quick getaway. Stunned, Yihya gets up and walks towards the neighboring house.

INT. NEIGHBORING HOUSE – DAY

Yihya enters the house and collapses on the floor.

YIHYA

Grandma, I've been shot.

GRANDMA

Yihya!!! What happened?! Yihya!!![2]

The opening scenes of *Ajami* plunge us into the realities of daily life for the suburb of that name's residents. Violence is only too common. Produced for a budget of less than $1 million, *Ajami* is mostly in Arabic. It was co-written and co-directed by Yaron Shani, an Israeli filmmaker from Tel Aviv and Scandar Copti, a Palestinian filmmaker from Jaffa. The filmmakers improvised their film with a large cast of

Figure 7.1 *Ajami*, 2009, Inosan Productions

nonprofessional performers who participated without reading a script.[3] As we have seen, it is often erroneously assumed that screenplays, which have been arrived at (or partly arrived at) via a process of improvisation, are the result of a largely unstructured process. This, however, is clearly far from the truth. Over the seven years from initial idea to completed film, Shani and Copti drew on a method of working from a tightly written script while remaining open to the input of their large cast. In this case, the degree of formal preplanning was perhaps necessitated by the logistics of their ambitious project (Figure 7.1).

Framing place

Ajami shares a broad neo-neorealist ethos with many of the films discussed in the previous chapter. Screenwriters are usually urged to begin with story or character. But, looking at films in which improvisation plays a large part, it seems that beginning with a location might be a better idea. From *Bicycle Thieves*[4] to *The Exiles*,[5] *Kes*,[6] *Nashville*,[7] *Putty Hill*,[8] and *Man Push Cart*,[9] to *Ajami*, place plays a major role in improvised films. In the case of *Ajami*, its real world setting generated material later shaped into a compelling and highly energised crime narrative. The filmmakers' specific storytelling strategies can, however, be attributed to the particular aesthetic and social and political context in which their movie was made. In this chapter, I would like to explore the improvised ensemble film, and *Ajami* in particular, as an example of presenting the composite vision of a community. How does the responsibility to explore a particular social reality shape writing strategies? How have digital technologies and mindsets fostered such films?

The port city of Jaffa has been the site of successive waves of religious and political conflict since the area was first inhabited around 7500 B.C.E. Following partition in 1948, it was designated part of the Arab state. In recent years, Jaffa has attracted an influx of well-off Israeli residents. Luxurious villas are replacing the neighbourhood's rundown apartments, creating tensions within the community. Once famous for its citrus industry, the city is now best known for its thriving underworld and the conflicts caused by redevelopment and rapid gentrification. An Arab 'ghetto' inside the main Jewish centre of Israel, Jaffa had not previously been depicted in Israeli cinema.

Co-writers and directors, Shani and Copti, describe the Jaffa suburb of Ajami as 'a melting pot of cultures and conflicting views amongst Jews, Muslims and Christians'.[10] The neighbourhood and its history of tensions and crime fascinated them and they wanted to make a film to depict its vibrancy and complexity on screen. Financing their project was not without its struggles, since few investors were interested in backing what was essentially a cinematic experiment. Eventually, the German/French cultural broadcasters ZDF-Arte and film funds in Germany and Israel provided production funding. *Ajami* was shot in 23 days, a relatively brief shoot for a production with such a complex storyline and logistics. Local residents and businesses, including the restaurant where Copti worked as a waiter, provided the locations. Hundreds of other people in the neighbourhood contributed to the film by lending vehicles, helping with production or providing meals for cast and crew.

Devised stories

In recent years, an ever-expanding emphasis on a single story pattern – in the form of the crisis–conflict–resolution template – has infiltrated more and more areas of life, from online environments to workplaces. Stories are sticky, say marketing gurus Dan and Chip Heath.[11] They are devices to help us remember and communicate. We are wired for stories, says Jonathan Gottschall.[12] But what kind of stories? Contemporary storytelling advocates often describe their preferred crisis–conflict–resolution story pattern as universal. Surely, though, there is not only one model of storytelling applicable to all cultures and eras? Stories are, in part, ways of remembering the past and imagining a shared future. They help individuals and groups create a sense of meaning and continuity. As sociologist Arthur Frank writes, 'Stories are the ongoing work of turning mere existence into a life that is social, and moral, and affirms the existence of the teller.'[13] Frank draws attention to the fact that stories are negotiated and devised, not simply found.

The 'hardwired for story' advocates emphasise the ongoing aspect of narratives at the expense of fluidity and change. We live *by* stories, says Arthur Frank.[14] Stories are always a response to the particular context in which their tellers and audiences find themselves. Neorealist screenwriter Cesare Zavattini insisted that 'Life is not what is invented in "stories".'[15] Stories should help us understand our own times – an approach shared by Shani and Copti. Their film's storyline, dramatic action, gestures and dialogue were all devised in collaboration with the local residents depicted on screen. Shani and Copti then drew on their professional writing and filmmaking skills to shape the material. Their screenplay went through six drafts over some years, and continued to evolve throughout the production. A multi-stranded ensemble film, *Ajami* captured the contradictions and difficulties of living in a conflict-torn neighbourhood and resonated around the globe.

Ajami is told from a number of conflicting points of view. Its central characters: a young Israeli fighting a criminal vendetta against his family, a Palestinian refugee working illegally to finance lifesaving surgery, an Israeli detective seeking his missing brother and a wealthy Palestinian who dreams of a future with his Jewish girlfriend.[16] Screenwriter and film editor Yvette Biro describes parallel stories like this as using a polyphonic structure. Polyphonic (musical) compositions do not simply bring together many tones or voices. Rather, polyphony is 'a style of (musical) composition in which more independent but organically related voice parts sound against each other'. The individual strands of such stories have a cumulative effect and thus 'the physical and psychological relations of many characters carry more meaning than the sum of their parts'.[17]

Biro singles out Robert Altman and John Cassavetes as key examples of filmmakers who utilised parallel storytelling to create complexity. In this model, storylines eventually converge and previously isolated characters find common ground. It is not coincidence, I would suggest, that improvisation featured heavily in both Altman and Cassavetes's scripting and production methodologies. Improvisation and polyphonic compositions are a natural fit.

Screenplay analyst, Linda Aronson, suggests that one of the main features of ensemble films is that 'they have a large cast and a series of stories that run simultaneously and chronologically in the same time frame'.[18] It is one of the forms that writers around the globe use to explore individuals in social settings. One subcategory of the ensemble films, Aronson observes, is the 'tandem narrative'. She includes a diverse group of films in this category. *Traffic, Nashville, City of Hope, Lantana, Crimes and Misdemeanors* are just some of them. Typically, a similar sociopolitical issue affects all the characters within a tandem narrative and such films are usually, therefore, didactic in her view.[19]

Beginning in the middle of things

In the contemporary world, we hear more about the principles of Aristotelian drama rather than other forms of ancient drama. Careful set-ups and inciting incidents are advocated. Yet in many parts of the world, including the Middle East, oral storytelling often plunged its audience into the midst of events. Urgency about the story to be communicated took precedence over all else. In ancient Greek oral narrative, the epic was not plotted. Instead, the epic poet 'hastens into the action and precipitates the hearer into the middle of things'.[20] Like the epic poets of long ago, Copti and Shani chose to begin *Ajami* in the middle of things. As 20-something Yihya changes a tyre on his car, two men drive past and fire at him. The shooting is not covered in slow motion or from a number of angles. There are no lingering deathbed scenes. A sunny day with its domestic routines is suddenly fraught with grief and terror. 'Grandma, I've been shot,' says Yihya.[21] During the course of the film, the consequences of this event ricochet out into the community.

The filmmakers saw this kind of depiction of real-life events as lacking in much contemporary cinema. Take a car crash. In a documentary, a car might be depicted crashing into a wall. In a Hollywood film, one car crashing into a wall would cause a chain reaction. Ten cars might explode, burst into flames or fall from cliff tops. All this dramatic action would be covered from multiple angles. By contrast, when a real car crash occurs, the impact is felt in many people's lives. It was this *human* chain reaction that Shani and Copti wanted to explore in *Ajami*. 'There are many competing narratives in *Ajami*, not just those of Jews and Arabs but also of West Bank Palestinians under occupation versus Palestinians with Israeli citizenship, Christians versus Muslims and urban Arabs versus Bedouins.'[22] Their method of scripting *Ajami* aimed to infuse their screen narrative with some of this complexity.

Beyond the well-made script

Shani began to think about more fluid ways of writing and making films towards the end of a university course in Tel Aviv. He wrote a short script about two guys who sold drugs from a parking lot, which was the first version of *Ajami*'s story world. 'Filmmakers were taught a sequence of steps: imagining the script and its characters, writing down this material, casting, working with the actors to find their characters, rehearsing, designing camera movements and creating a rhythm for the film.'[23] The result was a short film that, by Shani's own assessment, featured reasonably sophisticated images and camera movement. But there was something missing. Reviewing his outtakes in the edit room, Shani frequently found himself more interested in how the actors behaved after he said 'cut' than during the actual take. 'I watched the interaction among the actors, and I realised that was what I wanted on film. That is, the genuineness of the way they were talking rather than the acting that had gone on in front of the camera.'[24] Initially, Shani was frustrated by this experience. In general, fiction films often seemed like 'filmed theatre'. 'Something was deeply lacking – something which I could find in documentaries and in real life'. In time, though, his dissatisfaction led to a new process. How could he get more of the qualities of the outtakes into a completed work? How could you inject a film with reality while maintaining the control that was necessary to create a fictional world?

Shani's graduation film, *Disphoria*, a 40-minute drama, explored another way of writing and making films. Although the scenes were improvised, they followed the path of Shani's prewritten script. The actors were thrown into real situations, without knowing anything about the script or its dramatic action. According to Shani, the actors improvised freely but months of preparation led their improvisations in a particular direction. The film's dramatic structure, too, was outlined in Shani's prewritten script. He regarded *Disphoria* as a career-changing experiment and wanted to utilise the same method in his first full-length feature film.

Seeking collaborators, he met Copti, an engineering graduate who had grown up in the Ajami neighbourhood. Copti recalled, 'I always had this passion for filmmaking but I wasn't brave enough to go to film school. I thought that films weren't for people like me, people from Jaffa or Ajami.'[25] He studied engineering but rejected it as a career in favour of working as a waiter. An opportunity came up to make a short film. Copti and a friend wrote and directed a well-received mockumentary *The Truth* (2003) that was set in Ajami.[26] Shani suggested they collaborate on a feature film script devised for the same setting. From the outset, it was their intention to structure the story so that events would be told from several points of view and out of chronological order. The audience would be placed in the middle of the story and gradually piece its elements together. It is this perspective that gives *Ajami* some of its dramatic power. Over a four-year period, the two collaborators regularly met to talk through their story ideas. By his own admission, Shani had little exposure to Arab culture until he consciously decided to explore it as a young adult. People from Jewish and Arab cultures in Israel live in close quarters, yet are disconnected from one another. He taught himself Arabic and immersed himself in the culture as part of the process of making the film.

An alarm goes off. A hand reaches out to stop it. It is still dark. We can just make out two forms at either side of a double bed. We hear two brothers squabbling in thick Yorkshire accents. In the small cramped cottage that is home, the pair shares a room. One brother sets off to work in the mines. His younger brother, Billy, will leave school and join him in three weeks – reluctantly. We cut to daylight. Billy runs through the streets of Barnsley on the way to start his early morning paper round. This is his last summer of freedom. We see his hometown from Billy's point of view. Industrial architecture, rows of terraced houses, kids playing hopscotch on pavements, cars slowly moving down the streets of the town, glimpses of rooftops and sky. In the distance, the chimneystack of the colliery dominates the countryside. In detective stories, we follow people through shadowy cities at night. In films that follow in the footsteps of neorealism, we shadow someone – often a child – on foot. Through the streets of the city, town or suburb they live in. The camera maps place.

* * *

The streets of a northern England mining town in the 1969 seem a long way from Jaffa in 2009. But for Yaron Shani, *Kes* was one of the films closest to his own vision. Looking for inspiration, he found that many of the films that interested him had a stronger affinity with theatre than cinema. On the other hand, Scandar Copti cites the non-linear Brazilian documentary *Bus 174* (2002), about the hijacking of a bus, as one of the many documentaries that influenced him.[27] Improvisation in film is connected to an ethos that values taking materials from contemporary life and, in particular, the immediate environment. Extensive research in the field and discussion with collaborators was an important aspect of *Ajami*'s scripting process. Shani and Copti described their mode of working as 'hanging out together, and gaining a strong friendship and trust':

It wasn't just centered around writing sessions. In the beginning it was more about telling each other stories we knew would eventually become the stories in *Ajami*...one of us would write something and we would discuss it together. Most of the stories were encountered in our everyday life in and outside Ajami. We had to adapt these stories to a very precise structure...[28]

Working towards the open edge

Ken Loach, the director of *Kes,* whose work is often described as part of 'the social conscience of cinema',[29] began his career in British television before moving into feature film. Loach believes that the stories of working-class communities often contain the seeds of compelling drama. 'Drama is most intense among people who have got little to lose...the stakes are very high if you don't have a lot of money to cushion your life.'[30] Shani's description of the epiphany that led him to abandon the established methodologies he had learnt and seek a new way of working sounds remarkably like Loach reflecting on his work of almost five decades earlier. In British television of the 1960s, it was standard practice to hold a read-through of the script with all the cast on the first day of rehearsals. Loach noticed that these were often the best performances. 'It was usually downhill from then on, because the director – which was me in that case – would come in would start asking daft questions, would give the moves, they'd rehearse it for two weeks, by the time they got to the end of the second week, they were bored to tears.'[31] He resolved to work in a different way, casting a mix of amateur and professional actors and adhering less rigidly to prewritten scripts.

Kes marked Loach's shift to a new creative process. Adapted from Barry Hines's novel *A Kestrel for a Knave,*[32] the film presents its dramatic world from the point of view of its central character, Billy. As an audience, we are only privy to the situations in which Billy finds himself. Shani and Copti took a similar approach to *Ajami*'s multiple storylines and protagonists so that we see the world from many competing perspectives. *Kes* was shot in and around the south Yorkshire locations in which its author had grown up. Some of Hines's former teachers appeared in the film. Over time, Loach developed a preference for working either with trained actors with some experience of the world being depicted in the film, or nonprofessional actors. In *Riff-Raff* (1991), for example, much of the action took place on a building site. The director stipulated that any actors auditioning for the film should have some experience working on a building site.[33] Even at the outset of his career, Loach explained: 'We try to get people who can draw on their own lives, on their experience...they're not emoting, [they're] not a blank sheet of paper on which you and they write the part.'[34] While he remains reasonably close to the script when shooting his films, ultimately he is not concerned when performers choose to depart from the scripted dialogue. The script is simply a point of departure from which to riff on reality.

Like Woody Allen and Mike Leigh, Ken Loach withholds much of the script from his cast in an attempt to elicit surprise and truthful performances. He prefers to film in sequence so that the story unfolds for the actors during production and each day's shoot becomes rehearsal for the next day. These were all methods Shani and Copti adapted for *Ajami*. Above all, improvising from reality embraces risk. Loach, for example, once likened his filmmaking process to house painting:

> You always have an open edge and the paint is always wet for your next brushstroke, and I think acting has to be like that. There has to be an openness about it, kind of an uncertainty, a sense of danger, because once it's sealed off and everybody knows what he is doing, when he is going to flick the ash off the cigarette, things die really.[35]

Loach's notion of *working towards the open edge* is just as relevant to writing as performing.

Improvisation as an investigation

It is almost impossible to talk about improvisation for film without discussing the work of another influential English director and writer, Mike Leigh. Known for a socially engaged body of work that focuses on the complexities of English working-class and middle-class life, Leigh has developed a much-emulated method for the improvised screenplay. When he initially trained at the Royal Academy of Dramatic Art in the 1960s, the approach to acting was mechanical. Actors learned their lines and where they should move but were not encouraged to discuss the play, let alone improvise. Leigh was determined to find a more collaborative method.

When Leigh begins working with his actors, he does not usually have even a one-page outline. He tells the actors that in a defined period of five months, or three months, or longer, they will go on location to make a film. Until then, they will assemble the raw materials for their investigation. He invites them to participate in an inquiry: the 'actors literally have to find their characters, through improvisation and research into the ways people in specific communities speak and behave'.[36] Leigh works closely with his cast to develop characters, scenarios and dialogue over months of individual meetings and group improvisations. 'It's a complicated process as we explore the situations that are going to be the actual scenes in the film, then gradually deconstruct relations and reconstruct them, experiment with them, pin then down, fix dialogue, change things around here and there, cut and paste until we arrive at something coherent and pithy that works.'[37] Leigh then takes responsibility for the final shape of the screenplay, which remains fluid throughout the production.

Many of the principles underlying *Ajami* were similar to those of British social realists, Mike Leigh and Ken Loach. That is, the story was shot chronologically and the first time that characters met in a scene was also the first time they met in real life. A major difference was the casting of nonprofessional – rather than trained – actors.

Living the situation

Ajami was developed with the intention of its performers not acting, but living the situations they depicted on screen. Shani described their scripting methodology as somewhere between fiction and reality:

> The writer drafts a script which the director uses as a working plan. This script is based on a deep understanding of the reality. The nature of the 'actors' is changing the script all the time. Up until the shooting, the actors become so identified with the characters that in one magic word – 'action' – they are in a parallel reality...The scene which was written beforehand becomes alive spontaneously in front of the camera.[38]

The co-writers and directors worked with their nonprofessional actors during a year of workshops. They were placed in dramatic situations and urged to react as they would in life. From hundreds of volunteers, the pair chose their cast and began the workshops. 'One of our tasks was to liberate them from the tendency to perform in front of a camera, so that they could become themselves,' Copti said.

The research, writing, casting and shooting of *Ajami* were all interlinked. The pair tackled scenes that involved the police, for example, by accompanying local cops on their shifts. Patrolling the neighbourhood, they gathered research. The next step was to cast people with experience as police officers in real life to play their fictional counterparts. A number of former policemen expressed interest. The nonprofessional actors participated in extensive improvisations, joining the performance workshops run by Shani and Copti. As Shani reflected, 'when I work with real cops…I do not teach them how to act. I simply devise an improvisation and observe how they behave.'[39] The workshops generated material that could be fed into the evolving script. Although Shani and Copti planned to improvise with nonprofessional actors, they also wanted a precise script to draw on during what was likely to be a complex and demanding shoot.

One of Shani and Copti's guiding principles was that they wanted to achieve a 'hyperrealism of emotion'. While key incidents were fully scripted, the screenplay was withheld from the performers so that they could react to events as they happened. The film's two cinematographers were the only members of the cast and crew with whom Shani and Copti shared their script. Since it was not clear how the nonprofessional cast would react to the story events unfolding in front of the cameras, the co-directors needed to plan alternative patterns of coverage. During the shoot, the film's directors essentially took *Ajami*'s improvisations out on the streets. Shani provided an example:

> In the film we see three cops on patrol in the Ajami neighbourhood. They get a command to go and arrest a drug dealer. They are all former policemen. But they all know each other as characters due to the workshops we have done together. During our workshops, they carried out police inquiries together. We filmed with the same cars and walkie-talkies that the local police used. We sent the nonprofessional actors playing the policemen on a shift. The police characters worked as a team, out on the streets as part of their preparation. While on patrol, the police characters ran into a junkie. They were not always sure what was expected of them.[40]

Shani described this method as placing the film's nonprofessional cast in a *reality state*. This approach to generating material continued into the production. During the shoot, for example, the police characters were given orders to go and arrest a drug dealer. They did so. The drug dealer character attacked them, though, and they became angry. How would they react? According to Shani, cinema is particularly good at capturing this state. He added that you needed to be careful with this method so that no one was hurt. As an audience, what we were seeing on camera was a real, spontaneous action rather a performance of anger.

Performing the world of the story

Israel has a strong tradition of community theatre and theatre for social change, with a particular emphasis on multicultural stories. It was within this context that *Ajami* was developed. Copti had participated in community theatre productions throughout his teens. Theatre actor and director Hisham Suleiman, who was employed as the film's acting coach, had directed nonprofessional actors such as construction workers on devised theatre projects. More than 300 neighbourhood residents participated in the initial *Ajami* performance workshops. They were divided into groups based on their age: children from 8 to 13, teenagers from 14 to 17, young men aged from 18 to 25, older men aged from 28 to 40 and from 40 to 70. Since there were very few women involved, a separate workshop was organised for women participants of all ages. A young male workshop participant recalled that the workshops began with typical exercises to loosen everyone up: 'In the workshop they gave us the beginnings of situations and we continued them the way we thought they should go.'[41] Thus the development of the performances and the script proceeded hand in hand.

One participant was amongst the group of former policemen that Shani had assembled after seeking recommendations from the area's Chief of Detectives. They met in community centres once or twice a week and were led through performance exercises aimed at helping them to relax in front of the camera. There was a good rapport between the participants who shared the worldview of ex-policemen. The strategy of running performance workshops organised into groups of like-minded characters to create shared histories and a sense of bonding extended to the key families depicted in *Ajami*. As the project moved towards production, the performers playing the roles of parents and siblings in a family were asked to meet regularly; visit each other's homes and share meals and everyday experiences. Throughout this phase of preparation, individual actors still participated in workshops with the young men or the women's group. In this way, the actors built up multiple allegiances within the ensemble, while allowing the writing and directing team to explore new material.

The boundaries between fiction and reality rapidly blurred. One of the ex-policemen described a scene that he found especially confronting. He and his fictional colleagues had been driving around the neighbourhood with the cinematographers in tow. As in documentary films, the social actors became so accustomed to the presence of the cameramen they began to forget the cameras were there. Over the radio, they received an instruction to apprehend a grey Honda Accord and arrest its driver, a suspected drug dealer. Local residents soon came to see what was going on and began pushing and shoving. The former policemen could see the hatred in people's eyes. The crowd believed they were real policemen. It was a sobering moment. One of the participants noted, 'There was no script...no one told us what to say. But, through our ongoing work, it was obvious what we should say'.

Another participant had more positive memories of the overlapping of reality and fiction. Although she was initially reluctant about getting involved in the project, she enjoyed the workshop exercises because they allowed her to release her inner feelings. After living amidst the conflict within *Ajami* for many years, she felt as if she was releasing a heavy burden. During the shoot, the writer/director team pulled her aside and asked her about her life. Their questions uncovered a personal sadness that she usually tried to hide. These feelings fed into the next scene. Her on-screen son, who had disappeared for some time, suddenly returned. She was angry and lost control, beating his arms and chest with her firsts as she sobbed. Scripting and rehearsal methodologies like this suggest the influence of psychodrama.

Psychodrama: From theatre to film

Jacob L. Moreno, the founder of psychodrama, first conceived of his therapeutic staged encounters in Vienna following the First World War. Much like the contemporary new realist filmmakers, Moreno aimed to inject more of the qualities of life into the theatre. Stints as a doctor in refugee camps, where large numbers of people with very different cultural and social backgrounds were forced to live together in close proximity, drew Moreno's attention to the social bonds we need to develop to live successfully in groups. Theatre should be more socially relevant, Moreno felt and, in his view, scripts were the problem. He began his Theatre of Spontaneity in a small hall in Vienna, devising performances that tackled urgent social issues, such as how Germany should be run following the war.[42] From theatre, Moreno turned his attention to film and developed a design for the Radio/Film, a device to record sound on discs. Moreno travelled to the United States in 1925 with the hope of commercialising his invention. Unsuccessfully, as it turned out.[43] It now seems ironic that the man whose influence is seen as contributing to an excess of dialogue in contemporary low-budget digital cinema should have migrated to America with a blueprint for a sound recording device in his pockets.

In the United States, Moreno was initially more successful at establishing psychodrama in hospitals than theatres. A purpose-built Therapeutic Theatre at Beacon, just north of New York, enabled him to stage psychodrama sessions with patients. He speculated on the possibilities of combining his interests in psychodrama and cinema. Psychodrama would not use prewritten scripts, but reenact scenes from life. Movements and gestures, believed Moreno, were as important as speech. Unlike psychodrama sessions run by psychologists to help patients, therapeutic films would use the techniques to achieve emotional catharsis for audiences.[44]

Watching Moreno's Therapeutic Theatre

A number of episodes of Moreno orchestrating psychodrama encounters survive on film. In 1948, he was filmed at the Therapeutic Theatre he had established. I watched the documentary online, courtesy of YouTube.[45] The camera is trained on a bare stage with a curtain as backdrop. An off-screen narrator announces Moreno's entrance. A larger-than-life character, Moreno appears rather like a TV host. 'How do you do?' he asks the audience, smiling. 'It's a great pleasure to meet you here.' Moreno appeals for someone to step up and allow him to demonstrate the technique of psychodrama. 'What about you', he asks, singling out an audience member. A young man in a suit and tie makes his way on to the stage. 'Anything on your mind?' asks Moreno. Appropriately for the founder of a technique that values movement as much as speech, Moreno is animated, waving his hands around as he speaks. This intensity of both speech and gesture is one of the hallmarks of the contemporary improvised films often described as psychodramas.

Psychodrama and independent cinema

For Adrian Martin, psychodrama is one of the dominant forms of contemporary low-budget cinema. Too many psychodramas are simply talkfests, he says, advising caution. 'At its crudest level, psychodrama leaves its ad-libbing actors flailing, as they hurl at each other prompt lines like: "Who are you, really?" "Why are you here, really?" and "What are you after, really?" '[46] Far from working in a 'let it happen in the moment' school of improvisation, filmmakers such as John Cassavetes in America and Maurice Pialat in France wrote, planned, staged, worked and reworked their material down to the last detail, Martin asserts. The filmmakers most frequently associated with improvisation were more rigorous in editing their material than some of their contemporary counterparts.

In his groundbreaking work on how independent and experimental filmmakers in the United States have successfully drawn on psychodrama as an alternative method of scripting, J.J. Murphy describes psychodrama on screen as 'those peak moments of dramatic intensity where the artifice of the performance or situation suddenly breaks down, and the performer as well as the audience experiences a heightened sense of reality'.[47] The films of John Cassavetes, Jonas Mekas and Andy Warhol contain many such moments. Indeed, many of the scripted, sound-synchronised films that Warhol made after he began collaborating with writer Ronald Tavel drew on psychodrama techniques to create 'a potentially combustible situation'.[48] According to J.J. Murphy, Warhol saw narrative as 'a series of situations in which his non-actor performers would engage in improvised role-playing in contrast to a carefully constructed plot'.[49] Their method was far from haphazard or unplanned. As Tavel explained, 'If you want to create spontaneity, improvisation, the accident, and so forth, you must set up a situation in which the spontaneous, the accidental, the improvised, the unexpected, will take place. That takes planning.'[50]

Psychodrama and social cinema

An interest in the social dimensions of life was a key aspect of Moreno's work across theatre, film and psychology. Historians of psychology credit him with developing therapeutic techniques for *groups* rather than solely *individuals*. This interest was on display in his presentations of 'Living Newspaper' productions in Vienna in the early 1920s and New York's Carnegie Hall in the 1940s. A cast of professional performers presented impromptu stories based on the newspaper stories of the day and suggestions from the audience. As a form, the Living Newspaper promotes social action and favours more experimental and expressive methods of theatre. In 1920s Russia, for example, some Living Newspaper productions simply involved actors reading newspapers from the stage.[51] Other forms, such as those developed by the U.S. Federal Theatre Project in the 1930s, involved teams of researchers and writers and complex productions.[52] Both psychodrama and the Living Newspaper used 'scenes from life' as a basis for improvisation.

Psychodrama, which has continued to evolve, has influenced the practice of both theatre and psychotherapy in Israel. Specifically, psychodrama with more emphasis on the individual in the community than might be the case in, for example, the United States. Nahman Ingber, a film critic and historian, says that in recent years the cinema, too, is beginning to more strongly reflect Israel's social problems. He attributes this to a new and more introspective generation of filmmakers. 'These are younger people making movies, and they ask the questions that you have to ask. "Is war always necessary? Do we deal with political situations properly?" '[53]

Reflective practitioner

The particular method of improvising on the streets used in *Ajami* was enabled by low-cost digital technologies. Specifically, lightweight digital video cameras allowed the team to shoot for hours on end and provided immediate feedback. Recalling his trajectory towards what he termed *Ajami*'s 'controlled spontaneity', Shani noted that his lecturers in film school were very supportive. Nevertheless, they discouraged him from pursuing a similar methodology during his film studies. It was considered too risky. During the production of *Ajami*, too, not all the crew was convinced that much would come of the experiment. 'Professionalism is our enemy. It makes people narrow-minded,' he said, observing that professionals in any given field are frequently less open to new methodologies than those at the beginning of their careers.[54]

After speaking with Shani, I was struck by the degree to which both *Ajami* and *Kes*'s writer/directors fitted Donald Schön's influential model of the *reflective practitioner*. Drawing on fieldwork with architects, town-planners, managers and other professionals, Schön developed an argument for reflection-in-action as an alternative to technical rationalism. Reflective practice is a dynamic process in which 'the unique and uncertain situation can be understood through the intent to change it, and changed through the attempt to understand it'.[55] Professionals approached problems of practice as unique cases, drawing on past experiences, while closely observing emergent situations. Separated by more than 50 years, *Kes* and *Ajami* – landmark films in the United Kingdom and Israel – came about as a break with the industrial working methods that Loach and Shani and Copti felt were not productive. Implicit in Schön's notion of reflecting-*in-practice*, reflecting-*on-practice* and reflecting-*as-practice* is the ability of professionals in a given field to draw on their tacit or implicit knowledge. That is, reflective practice is not simply a new competency to be taught in the seminar room. It arises from action and reflection.

Provocative competence

In the last chapter, I compared the practices of improvising musicians with those of screenwriters. I would like to do so again to explore the mindset of provocative competence. Frank Barrett combines a career as a professional trumpet player with that of organisational theorist. He suggests that improvising jazz musicians develop a mindset of *provocative competence*. Once players have built up the vast repertoire of musical phrases and patterns needed to play jazz, they are tempted to simply do what is feasible. That is, to play notes within their comfortable range rather than risk an incoherent piece. Responses quickly become routine. Jazz musicians thus make deliberate efforts to interrupt their patterns and habits. 'A transformation occurs in the player's development when he or she begins to export materials from different contexts and vantage points, combining, extending and varying the material.'[56] Veteran musicians learn to deliberately place themselves in unfamiliar and challenging situations. By contrast, screenwriters are usually encouraged to learn about the intricacies of the most dominant narrative structures, for example, rather than develop a repertoire of creative practices and story forms. The new methods developed by the writers and directors whose work I have discussed could all be seen as examples, too, of *provocative competence*.

When films cost sixpence

Cesare Zavattini asserted that much of what passed for collaboration in the industrial cinema was not really collaboration at all. Instead, financial backers imposed creative solutions on writers and filmmakers. 'It is obvious that when films cost sixpence and everybody can have a camera, the cinema would become a creative medium as flexible and free as any other,' he said.[57] Cameras still cost more than sixpence, but low-cost digital technologies were critical to the shaping of *Ajami's* complex shifting and multi-perspective narrative. In part, because tools such as film downloads and YouTube provided ready access for watching earlier models of social cinema such as the early films of Ken Loach. Low-cost and high-quality digital cameras and postproduction tools, too, enabled more open and collaborative scripting processes. *Ajami's* complex narrative, for example, was constructed from large volumes of recorded media. Matthew Porterfield's *Putty Hill* (discussed in the previous chapter) was improvised from a relatively simple storyline about a gathering of friends and family. Porterfield's 'mosaic of portraits' structure was thus more easily communicated in the five-page treatment and collection of photographs from which his film was improvised. The larger-scale and more complex logistics of *Ajami* required a more fully written script in order for Shani and Copti to keep track of their production and its multiple storylines. Albeit, a fluid script developed on the basis of extensive research and improvisation.

In an insight that is especially relevant to *Ajami*, Mike Leigh countered what he saw as popular myths about improvisation. According to Leigh, 'all art is based on improvisation *and* order'. Artists 'start something that grows all over the place and then figure out how to shape it into something that's coherent'.[58]

Composite vision

It is revealing that so many of the terms that best describe the practices for developing screen narratives that increasingly resonate in our digital era – such as polyphonic, mosaic, ensemble, improvised and remix – have migrated from music and performing and visual arts rather than literature. Ethnographic filmmaker and screen theorist David MacDougall observed that film and video, in particular, have some distinct advantages over text in recording social experience. 'The possibility of grasping a complex social event simultaneously through its various dimensions of gesture, facial expression, speech, body movement and physical surroundings is something that text can only approach with great difficulty.'[59] Movies evoke a flow of time. Film and photography offer a way of exploring social connections in the world often lost in writing.[60] They provide, says MacDougall, a *composite vision*.

Ajami provides just one example of a scripting and production process that used a complex and meticulously planned method of improvising on the streets to produce a composite vision of a community in transition. It is part of a robust tradition of social cinema, reinvented with digital tools and thinking.

8
Composing the Digital Screenplay

The term 'compose' is used widely across the visual, performing and literary arts – within the latter it is often applied to poetry. For musicians, composition, from the Latin verb *componere* meaning 'put together', implies the assembly and structuring of musical ideas. Composers invent and work with materials drawn from their own experience, and from the history of their art form.[1] In the arts, the term emphasises the way artists interact with their materials, arranging shapes, lines, colours and textures to create meaning and visual experience. In screen media, composition refers primarily to how the director and cinematographer frame events in front of the camera, often building on aesthetic strategies drawn from painting and photography. Yet, as pens, cameras and audio recorders merge, as writing becomes a process that involves creating and combining images, sound and words, the practice of composing becomes more and more relevant to screenwriting and filmmaking.

Writing with light

Learning to use a film-based SLR camera as a student in the mid-1970s, I pressed my eye to the viewfinder to check the balance of my composition. Held the camera still. Clicked. Now, I hold my smartphone away from my body and glance at the blocks of light and colour it registers. Click. Move. Click. The action is more casual, a scanning for impressions of the visual world. Photography is no longer still, but restless. It forms part of many modes of interaction and communication – we compose on the run.

After a long history of experimentation, photography arrived on the scene in the 1820s as a system of making images from light impressions.

John Herschel gave it the name photography in 1839, splicing together the Greek words for light and writing. In 1969, Apollo 11 made its trip to the moon, sending ghostly images of its surface back to a population huddled around TV sets. Yet the heavyweight 3.3 kg television camera on Apollo 11's packing list nearly didn't make it on to the flight, as space officials crossed off items to reduce onboard weight. It is fortunate that a place was found for the camera, since it was the technologies developed and tested on space missions that eventually found their way into the smartphones and mobile devices we now carry around in pockets and backpacks. Digital photography transforms *electrical* impulses into light pictures. Photography has shifted from a medium that is fixed to something that is transient, says Stephen Bull. Pictures can be made on the run. Individual pixels can be shifted and changed.[2] Photographs can be sent, transmitted, stored or erased – instantly.

Renowned documentary photographer Henri Cartier-Bresson defined 'the decisive moment' as when a scene is stopped and depicted at a point of high visual drama.[3] In his view, the shutter freezes a *geometric pattern* that gives the image life.[4] Not everyone was convinced. Some critics suggested the decisive moment was actually when the photographer decided which image to print from often dozens of shots of a particular scene.[5] Wherever we place it, in our digital era, that moment has stretched to become a series of decisive moments.

Cinema and photography followed mostly separate paths, while acting as muses to each other for over a century. The fluidity of mobile devices, digital cameras and hybrid cameras (capable of shooting both still and moving images) has called into question the traditional separation between the two media. Fred Ritchin, a former *New York Times* photography editor who has been at the forefront of analysing the impact of digital photography, says that everything in a digital world is constantly on the shuffle – being reordered and reassembled, from mp3 files on an iPhone to the pixels in a photograph.[6] Photographic images are no longer fixed but composed of millions of changeable pixels. Increasingly, photographers shoot both still images and moving stills.[7] According to Ritchin, rather than being a quote from appearances, photography in a digital environment serves as 'an initial recording, a preliminary script which may precede a quick and easy reshuffling'.[8] Writing with light has become electronic writing, a first impression of the world recorded not by pen, but by camera. The illiterates of the future will be ignorant of the use of camera and pen alike, wrote Hungarian photographer Moholy-Nagy in the 1920s.[9] It looks like he was right on the money.

Photo-film

Throughout the history of the medium, many art cinema practitioners have drawn on photographs as part of their scripting process: Jutta
Brückner, Chris Marker, Stanley Kubrick, Peter Greenaway and Wim
Wenders just some of them. As a student, I watched a black-and-
white feature film composed almost entirely of still photographs and
narration. It was one of the films that made me want to write and
direct my own. The film was Jutta Brückner's *Do Right and Fear No-one*
(1975),[10] about her mother, Gerda Siepenbrink and twentieth-century
Germany. Photographer August Sander's major project involved creating
portraits of a vast cross-section of ordinary Germans. This self-appointed
task began in 1910 and occupied him for around 30 years. Brückner's
film juxtaposed Sander's portraits of middle-class German citizens with
Siepenbrink's narration of her own life story. Brückner compiled photographs 'from photo agencies, from history books and scrapbooks' to
create what she called her photo-film.[11] Sander's photographic portraits
prompted her to make a film. The people who sat for his camera took
on a distinctive attitude as they composed themselves. How would her
mother present herself and her version of twentieth-century Germany to
the camera? Bruckner wanted to create a double-portrait of her mother
and of a social class.[12]

Instead of a conventional script, writer, photographer and filmmaker
Wim Wenders began filming *Wings of Desire* (1987)[13] with a collection
of photographs. He recalled:

> On my wall in my office I just had lots of pictures, photographs and
> Polaroids of all the places that had to appear in the film and of all
> sorts of people I wanted to discover via these angels, and lots of ideas
> for scenes... These angels could appear anywhere, and through their
> perception anything could be revealed. Not only were they invisible,
> they could also hear people's most secret thoughts.[14]

Later, Peter Handke, novelist, screenwriter and Wenders' regular collaborator, sent him poetic monologues to use in his film.[15] *Wings of
Desire* thus began with two texts: photographs and words. It was in the
gap between them that *Wings of Desire*'s distinctive poetic storytelling
emerged (Figure 8.1).

Cinécriture

The filmmaker most closely associated with 'writing with light' is Agnès
Varda. With an inventive and highly influential body of work spanning

Figure 8.1   *The Gleaners and I*, 2000, Cine Tamaris

photography, films and gallery installations, she has emerged as one of the key innovators of digital cinema – and writing for the screen. Varda studied art history and philosophy before working as a photographer and then filmmaker. She is often credited with launching the French New Wave with her first film *La Pointe Courte* (1955).[16] Her innovative low-budget film used location shooting, a mix of professional and nonprofessional actors and editing that emphasised discontinuity rather than continuity. The film introduced her distinctive method of splicing together two narratives: one personal and one social. *La Pointe Courte* combined a nonfiction story about people in a fishing village with the fictional story of a couple deciding whether to stay together. Or not.

While Varda insists they did not see themselves as a formal grouping at the time, she is strongly associated with the Left Bank filmmakers within the New Wave of the late 1950s and 1960s.[17] The group included her husband Jacques Demy, Chris Marker and Alain Resnais. By comparison to their New Wave counterparts, the Left Bank had a stronger interest in aesthetic innovation, nonfiction filmmaking, politics and the arts beyond cinema.[18] In recent years, the success of Varda's digital essay films – *The Gleaners and I* (2000),[19] *The Gleaners and I: Two Years Later*

(2002),[20] and *The Beaches of Agnès* (2008)[21] – has created renewed interest in her back catalogue and working methodologies.

Varda favours an approach she terms *cinécriture*, or film-writing. 'The cutting, the movement, the points-of-view, the rhythm of filming and editing have been felt and considered in the way a writer chooses the depth of meaning and sentences, the type of words, number of adverbs, paragraphs, asides, chapters which advance the story or break its flow, etc.'[22] While Varda has long worked across drama and documentary, the practice of *cinécriture* arose from her nonfiction work. The blurring between once separate creative roles and production phases that digital technologies foster has resulted in a climate even more conducive to her preferred methodology. Varda has been at pains to explain that film-writing is a different concept from that of the screenplay. Writing a film does not begin and end with a written document, but continues through every phase of the production.

> The encounters I have and the shots I take, alone or together with a team, the editing style...the wording of the voiceover commentary, the choice of music, all this isn't simply writing a script, or directing a film or wording a commentary...all this is the film writing that I often talk about.[23]

Cinécriture even extends to approving publicity materials. Like weaving, Varda sees filmmaking as an activity carried out by artisans in an *atelier* or workshop.

Atelier

Genetic studies in literature and music typically examine a body of avant-textes or pre-texts, such as sketches and drafts, in order to shed light on the evolution of a composition. Screen theorists have tended to focus on genetic approaches repurposed from literature but the work of musicologists is highly relevant to screenplay composition, since music and film are both time-based media. The French musicologist Nicolas Donin has borrowed the term *atelier* to refer to a thinking space rather than a physical space. According to Donin, who studied the work of contemporary composers of art music, compositions develop as both a piece and an *atelier*, with the two interacting throughout the process. He defined the *atelier* as all the materials and actions available during the compositional process. The *atelier*, which acts as a wellspring for the work-to-be, can include the composer's library and all the sketches generated during the composition of a work.[24] Assembling the reference materials and sketching the preliminary ideas that form the *atelier* is essential to creating works of imagination and resonance.

Gleaning images

In the case of *The Gleaners and I*,[25] Varda's *atelier* extended to the French countryside. In order to produce *her* film, Varda travelled to rural areas with a handheld digital video camera and a small crew in search of people who scavenge in potato fields, apple orchards and vineyards, as well as in rubbish dumps. Her resulting film is both a personal diary and an essay about the history of scavenging in French culture. Varda recalls that very little was planned in advance; she did not research a list of gleaners she would like to work with but sought them out during the shooting phase. 'I wanted to glean images as one jots down travel notes.'[26]

The Gleaners and I takes its title, and some of its inspiration, from an 1857 painting by Jean-François Millet. As writer and critic John Berger observed, *The Gleaners* is one of the best-known oil paintings in the world, endlessly reproduced on cards, engravings, ornaments and even plates.[27] The painting shows three women in a cornfield, stooping to pick up sheaves and kernels left behind after the harvest. Each of the three women adopts a different pose: one is doubled over searching the ground, one picks up an ear of corn and another straightens herself up. The three figures are all clothed in blue, standing out against fields of yellow. Although the gleaners are poor, in the background there are images of plenty: a man on a horse surveying the fields, haystacks and a cart filled with harvesters. The fields bathed in the golden light of midday; legally, gleaners were required to carry out their work during the day so that they did not take any full sheaves.

En plein writing

Millet spent several decades researching the lives of peasants in rural France. Just as lightweight digital cameras have liberated filmmakers, in the 1850s, the invention of the collapsible zinc paint tube made oil painting in the open possible. Droves of artists left their Paris studios for the countryside to paint *en plein*, or open air. Millet, who grew up in a family of peasant farmers, was part of a group of realist painters who travelled regularly to the village of Barbizon to work.[28] Many of his paintings depicted seasonal work such as scything, sheering, splitting wood, potato lifting, digging, shepherding and pruning. Millet was known for his nuanced use of tone, mixing endless tints and shades from a palette of only five colours. The artist made dozens of preliminary drawings, a small painting and even an engraving before settling on his final composition for 'The Gleaners' in his studio.[29]

Varda described her rhythm of working on *The Gleaners and I* (2000):

> I can start shooting for two weeks and then immediately proceed to edit. Meanwhile we keep finding new locations. Then we start shooting again and editing more... then the commentary text begins to take shape, words give rise to new ideas and call for new images. New information comes up, new contacts. We then go back on the road again.[30]

Like Millet's method of painting, Varda wrote by gathering materials on location and taking them back to her edit room, repeating this trajectory over and over again. Varda compared her process of assembling the film to that of jazz musicians.

> They take a theme, a famous theme. They play it all together as a chorus. And then the trumpet starts with a theme and does a number. And then, at the end of his solo, the theme comes back, and they go back to the chorus. And then the piano takes the theme again.[31]

Varda riffed on images throughout her film, moving back and forth from fantasy to history to reality. The central theme that underscored *The Gleaners and I* was this: many of us sustain ourselves on what others throw away. It was having this clear central theme that allowed Varda the freedom to riff and digress.

Mise-en-cycle

The Gleaners and I was enormously well received and its sequels *The Gleaners and I: Two Years Later* (2002) and *The Beaches of Agnès* followed a similarly fluid process of composition. The notion of a compositional *mise-en-cycle* provides a useful prism through which to consider Agnès Varda's trilogy of autobiographical essay films, since each work builds on the next. Examining sketches and drafts, Nicolas Donin studied how composers develop cycles of compositions.[32] He discovered cycles often resulted when a number of compositional ideas and strategies from a first piece invited further elaboration. As the composer worked on her new piece, the earlier compositions become integrated into the composers' *atelier*. Donin termed this compositional technique the *mise-en-cycle*.[33] According to Varda, the third film in her trilogy, *The Beaches of Agnès* drew on her personal memories, and so a greater proportion of the material was scripted and planned. 'I like to play off words, which becomes a play of images.'[34]

Weaving Nashville

As a film student in the 1970s, I was entranced by Robert Altman's critically acclaimed *Nashville* (1975) which interwove the stories of a number of characters to create a microcosm of America. *Nashville* was the first published screenplay that I owned and I scanned its pages eagerly seeking insights into writing characters and dramatic action. I was in awe of writer Joan Tewkesbury's skill in introducing and marshalling the film's 24 character ensemble while tackling some big resonant themes about America. Like Varda, Tewkesbury drew on the concept of weaving to describe how she structured her idea. Although Robert Altman was known as a director who liked to improvise, Joan Tewkesbury's screenplay provided the point of departure for *Nashville*. Moreover, when we look at them now, her sketches and draft materials point to some new possibilities for the screenplay.

In an in-depth interview with Chuck Sack in 1978, Tewkesbury described the genesis of both her film career and the film's script.[35] After beginning work in theatre and dance, Altman agreed to back her first feature film. When they had difficulty raising the finance, Altman asked Tewkesbury to take on the job of continuity on *McCabe and Mrs. Mill*er (1971). A western, adapted from Edmund Naughton's novel, the film was shot in location in West Vancouver. Although Altman and McKay had co-written a selling script for *McCabe and Mrs. Miller*, the film was widely acknowledged to have been shot without a traditional screenplay. Altman recreated the 1890s setting of Naughton's novel by building an entire frontier town. He began shooting before the sets were finished and, as the town took shape, the production company migrated to the new sets. One of the key insights Tewkesbury took from this experience was the significance of locations to screenplays: Leon Erickson's set provided Altman with the spine of his movie.

The script as photo-essay

When Altman asked Tewkesbury to work with him on his new film about country music, she agreed to be involved if she could start from scratch rather than rework anyone else's material. Tewkesbury began by making a three-day research trip to Nashville. At Altman's suggestion, she kept a diary. Tewkesbury, however, failed to find inspiration in the country and western museums her music industry minders arranged for her to visit. Several months later, Tewkesbury made a second research trip, arriving at Nashville Airport to a scene of chaos, with everyone jockeying to catch sight of an unidentified celebrity. On this trip, she managed to shake off her music industry minders and spent a week watching musicians play and interact, scrawling notes as she sat in on rehearsals and recording sessions. Evenings, she hung out at the Exit Inn, listening to country and western music performers. Tewkesbury was struck by the intimacy of the relationship between the singers and their audience. 'I'd take my notebook and write; I'd write a lot of dialogue as I hear it ... By the end of five days I was inundated with material.'[36] After her last evening at the Exit Inn, Tewkesbury went back to her hotel and wrote 17 pages capturing her initial thoughts.

An essay in Joan Didion's *The White Album* begins: '1969: I had better tell you where I am and why. I am sitting in a high-ceilinged room in the Royal Hawaiian Hotel in Honolulu watching the long translucent curtains billow in the trade wind and trying to put my life back together.'[37] Sitting in her hotel room, banging out her script on a typewriter, Tewkesbury compared herself to the more established Didion, whom she much admired. Like Didion, she was also putting her life back together. Unlike Didion, however, she was not staying in the palatial Royal Hawaiian Hotel but in a modest hotel in Music City with a name that sounded like a Wim Wenders movie: Kings of the Road. Alone. Like the characters in the film she was writing, Tewkesbury desperately wanted something – to make it in the movie business.

Tewkesbury's first attempt to capture her ideas for *Nashville* was in the form of an essay and a collection of photographs. The film's overall structure was inspired by the city with its circular roads and revolving doors and sense of everyone constantly running into each other. She set her story over five days, observing: 'It's like weaving a rug to get all the colours. I used Friday, Saturday, Sunday, Monday and Tuesday: yellow, red, blue, green, orange. Then each character becomes a different colour and you line them up the other way: Tom, Linnea, Albuquerque.' The film would involve overlapping of the characters, which Tewkesbury described as a thematic structure.[38] After discussing her photo-essay with Altman, she produced a sprawling first draft. Unaccustomed to screenplays featuring dozens of lead characters, the studio backing the film was not convinced that what Tewkesbury had produced was actually a script. It declined to proceed with the project. Another backer stepped in, however, due to the film's extensive use of music.

Their reasoning: if the film failed at the box office, a soundtrack album might make up the revenue shortfall.

From improvisation to composition

While all creative processes draw on both composition and improvisation, ethnomusicologist Bruno Nettl suggests that western music has created a hierarchy in which composition is much more highly valued. Improvisation, linked to jazz musicians and outsiders, has long been regarded as requiring less skill. Nettl proposes that, instead of considering improvisation and preplanned composition as opposites, we view them as part of a continuum.[39] He suggests that we simply distinguish between *slow* and *fast* modes of composition.[40] While *Nashville* is sometimes described as an improvised film, Tewkesbury's fast composition provided its structure, characterisation and themes.

Kiarostami and poetry

Composition is also a term associated with poetry – which brings us to the work of Abbas Kiarostami. Kiarostami works across photography, video and film, which he sees as part of the same spectrum. 'Even when I am in a taxi looking out the window, I put everything in a frame. This the way I see painting, photography and film – all interrelated and connected because they capture reality in frames.'[41] Like Agnès Varda, Kiarostami has embraced the more fluid working methods enabled by digital technologies.

Kiarostami, who has frequently compared his films to poetry, began his career in film after starting out as a graphic artist. He described his rather unconventional introduction to screenwriting. 'They [Tabli Films] asked me to write a sketch about an isothermal water-heater. I spent the night writing a poem about water-heaters. Three evenings later, to my great astonishment, I saw a commercial on TV with my poem in it.'[42] His work in commercials eventually led to designing credit sequences and making films. Iran has a long and rich tradition of poetry, architecture, music and storytelling, which its filmmakers have increasingly drawn on. Kiarostami is associated with the Iranian New Wave, which began in the 1960s. Its techniques include the use of poetic narratives and allegory, which became even more pronounced after the country's 1979 revolution. As Iranian director Amir Naderi observed, the constraints of repressive regimes foster innovation in cinema. Kiarostami prefers to describe this homeland as restrictive rather than repressive.[43]

To see with borrowed eyes

Kiarostami favours the use of 'pared-down scripts', asserting that his scripts and films are necessarily half-made, so that the viewer completes them in his or her mind.[44] Every audience member will experience a slightly different film: seeing is an interpretative act. He draws on a Persian expression to explain this concept – to see with 'borrowed eyes'.[45] Like poetry, his films provide the interpretative space for audience members to draw more fully on their own imagination. As viewers, we complete his 'pared-down stories' and make them our own. He has referred to a quatrain by the thirteenth-century Persian poet Rumi to explain his method.

> You are like the ball to my polo stick.
> I set you in motion
> But once you're off and running,
> I am the one in pursuit.
> You're making me run, too![46]

Digital cameras

Kiarostami first learned photography during the 1979 revolution when it was impossible to make films. Escaping to the countryside, he began taking pictures. Kiarostami initially began working with digital technologies as a form of note taking, taking video cameras on location trips to store impressions and ideas. On *ABC Africa* (2001),[47] he shot research footage on location, with the intention of returning to make his film. Kiarostami soon realised that the digital camera was more suited to the intimacy he wanted to capture in his films and edited his film from the research footage. *ABC Africa* marked his transition to a more impromptu and intimate method of scripting and production. The films he has made in this more impromptu spirit are amongst his strongest, Kiarostami has observed. 'A good movie is made by an initial burst of energy that contributes to the quality of the work...with projects that are meticulously planned, you look at the end result and it is full of emptiness.'[48]

In the last 15 years, Kiarostami has produced a number of minimalist films and gallery installations exploring, in part, the narrative possibilities of film and photography. They include *Five* (2003);[49] five long takes featuring aspects of the natural world, such as waves breaking on the shoreline and the moon shining on a lake, and *Ten* (2002) which consists of ten conversations conducted by women as they drive. While many filmmakers and screen theorists have compared lightweight digital cameras to Alexandre Astruc's *camera-stylo* or camera-pen, Kiarostami has taken this idea one step further by referring to the digital camera as his 'drafting pen'.[50]

Hidden patterns

Five (2003) lies at the crossroads of poetry, photography and film. Originally designed as a gallery installation, it consists of five long shots filmed by the Caspian Sea. In his documentary *About Five* (2005), standing at the edge of the sea and tossing a piece of wood into the water, Kiarostami muses on life and the cinema. He credits the *digital* camera with the ability to reveal the hidden patterns of the visible world. Much cinema relies too much on storytelling, he complains. People don't listen to music expecting a story, complained Kiarostami. Looking at an abstract painting, viewers do not only think about narrative. They are more likely to arrive at a sense of meaning through a series of associated images, for example.[51]

Mobility

Cars feature heavily in Kiarostami's cinematic output. Perhaps not surprisingly, since he has suggested that mobility is one of the central attributes of the new digital cinema. In his documentary *10 on Ten* (2004), Kiarostami provided the background to his film's production. A camera fixed to the car window, Kiarostami drives through Tehran voicing his thoughts. One sequence is devoted to the script. He explains that he begins by outlining the initial idea. 'I don't usually write my scripts as accurately as screenplays are normally written. My first ideas are no more than half a page. I then develop this into three pages by which time I know the film can be made.'[52] In the next phase, he begins making notes about people he has known in real life that may be useful for the character. Typically, this process takes around six months and production begins on the basis of his outline.

Although he wrote full screenplays earlier in his career, Kiarostami found that he usually lost interest in them by the time they were finished and handed them over to colleagues to produce. As his career progressed, he no longer needed to present scripts for his producers and the Ministry of Culture to approve. Everyone understood that it was unlikely his films would actually resemble his prewritten scripts.

Kiarostami adds that while he finds it almost impossible to remain faithful to screenplays, he always remains faithful to the original idea of a film. 'It is in the process of shooting and production that daily changes shape the film. The screenplay finds its final form as the film is being made.'[53]

Ten (2002) began when Kiarostami heard the story of a woman psychoanalyst who began consulting in her car after her office was closed by the government. After some initial research, Kiarostami ran into an obstacle translating this idea to cinema: psychoanalysts listen far more than they speak. He set the project aside and did some more research, this time focusing on potential characters. The car would become a mobile space into which he could bring characters from very different backgrounds. All of his films bring together people from varied cultural and social backgrounds. A typical cast list might include 'an intellectual, a child, an office worker, a high-ranking government employee, a taxi driver'.[54] Each of those characters has their own culture, language and words that they use to express feelings. When Kiarostami began working with nonprofessional actors, he wrote dialogue for them but was dissatisfied with the results. He now prefers his cast of actor-characters to extemporise instead of memorising prewritten lines. 'Rather than pulling them towards myself, I travel closer to them; they are very much closer to real people than anything I could create.'[55]

Open texts

In the world of western classical music, 'open form' compositions flourished in the postwar period with composers such as John Cage and Henri Pousseur and others creating more fluid, open works that gave more freedom to performers. Umberto Eco distinguishes between *open texts* and *open forms*. Open texts could be interpreted in many ways while closed texts could not. By contrast, *open forms* combined some elements that were fixed with others that were malleable.[56] Over the last several decades, there has also been a move within theatre and performance, to 'open texts'. In this context, the term is often used to describe productions in which visual, aural and movement-based texts are given more weight alongside the written text with the aim of opening up the composition process.[57]

Structure as repetition

Filmmaker and screen theorist Alex Munt described *Ten* as a serial narrative, linking Kiarostami's structuring devices in this and other minimalist films to the work of Godard.[58] Both the serial narrative and modular scripts (such as *Five* and *Ten*) have considerable resonance in our digital era with its 'cut and paste' aesthetic and ability to endlessly copy and modify images and sounds. Taking a longer-term view, an even more significant influence in Kiarostami's work is the rich legacy of Iranian culture. The process of creating a composition in classical Persian music can involve combining a number of short pieces to create a larger work. As discussed in Chapter 6, a basic framework is extended through repetition, ornamentation and centonization.[59] The latter, derived from the Latin word for patchwork, is the joining together of recognisable musical motifs. An important part of Kiarostami's compositional practices is the use of the rhymes, refrains and repeated patterns associated with both poetry and music in Iran. 'Repetition is a characteristic of all Iranian oral, musical, visual and performing arts, from art music to pop music, from poetry to carpets, from calligraphy to Islamic architecture, and from miniature paintings to film.'[60]

Moving stills

Long before the advent of hybrid digital cameras, Kiarostami insisted that cinema and still photography were part of the same creative enterprise. He elaborated on this theme while discussing his photography exhibition *Rain*, a series of images taken from his car:

> There is a connection between my photography and my cinema. If there was no movement in what I photographed then I would have felt no need to take those pictures. Yet even though you can hear the sound and see the path of the wiper, my photography is capturing one specific moment. The same applies in my cinema: even though it's a moving image, I'm still capturing a specific moment.[61]

According to Kiarostami, the same desire to capture a moment in time as an image underlies his poems. He offered the following as an example:

> A white foal
> emerges through the fog
> and disappears
> in the fog.[62]

Kiarostami's films, photographs installations and writings celebrate the poetry of the everyday – roads, rain, trees, light and the patterns and cycles of time. We only notice the everyday when we place a frame around it, says Kiarostami. He began using the car window as his frame, driving around the countryside with one hand on the wheel, the other holding his camera. 'I had spent years looking through my car windscreen, admiring the rural landscape, admiring the raindrops and the effect of light on them. I tried taking photographs through the windscreen, but at that time I was using film, and I could hardly ever get the right light effect to make the pictures work.'[63] It was the advent of lightweight digital cameras that made it possible for Kiarostami to explore his idea. Similarly, a photographic exhibition, *Trees in Snow* grew out of his long walks into the countryside to find film locations. Covering hundreds of miles on foot, Kiarostami began photographing the world around him. *Trees in Snow* depicts the patterning of trees against drifts of snow, the outlines of the trees forming a repeated motif in a field of white. Photography curators have described Kiarostami's landscape images as pictures of 'emotional states'.[64]

Digital and the incomplete

In Kiarostami's view, digital images are always incomplete. Films and photographs are never finished but are constantly in a state of coming into being. All photographs are ephemeral since they inscribe a single moment. If you take a photograph and glance back at the subject of your composition, invariably everything has changed. Due to his preference for minimal scripts and structures prior to production, his digital films are often thought of as primarily improvised. I prefer to think of them as compositions by an artist deeply versed in the history and practices of the visual and performing arts, cinema and poetry. Kiarostami says his ideas begin as images. 'It's said that in the beginning was the word, but for me the beginning is always an image. When I think about a conversation, it always starts with images.'[65] Increasingly, while based in Tehran, Kiarostami shoots his films abroad due to political restrictions in Iran. 'The world is my workshop,' he says.[66] While Agnès Varda has termed herself a *cinécriture* or film-writer, I cannot think of a better credit for Kiarostami than *composer* – or someone who structures and assembles screen ideas.

Journey to the End of *Coal*

> White letters appear on a black background.
> The sounds of a station announcement in Chinese.
> Voices.

Snatches of music.
'As a freelance journalist, you have decided to investigate the shadow of China's economic miracle.'

I click the mouse. Take the train to Shanxi. Visit homes, mines, factories, talk to people. Navigate my way through the story. The choices repeat themselves: Move on. Ask a question. Get more information. Show map. I am watching photojournalist Samuel Bollendorff's acclaimed web documentary, *Journey to the End of Coal*, on my laptop.[67] I select: Get more information.

Bollendorff's body of work presents a social vision of institutions, focusing on hospitals, schools, law enforcement and prisons. He has used photography and documentary film as tools to interrogate life in the housing projects of outer Paris, the shadowy side of China's economic growth and other subjects. His photographs could be described as social thought. Bollendorff's work combines considerable skill, balancing visual rhythm and colour – with the rigour of an investigative journalist. It is not surprising that he has chosen to take advantage of the expanded possibilities for visual storytelling offered by online environments.

I spoke with Samuel Bollendorff via Skype. No one went anywhere. I was in Sydney, he was in Paris. For Samuel, it was Friday morning at the office, while for me, it was Friday evening and the end of the week – but I quickly became engrossed in our conversation. How did he script *Journey to the End of Coal* which combines stills, video footage, text and elements of the computer game? On a trip to China, he photographed stories of people he saw as the victims of China's economic miracle. Bollendorff wanted to meet the people he regarded as left behind in China's booming economy, putting faces and hands to what were otherwise mere statistics. Government officials trailed him everywhere, blocking access to subjects and he was forced to work undercover with a local journalist to try and find out more about the terrible conditions in the coal mining industry.

During this research trip, Bollendorff took thousands of photographs – many of them portraits. He also recorded brief audio interviews. Over the next several years, he made a number of trips to China in order to gather the images and evidence needed for his project. The work was first exhibited in a gallery with around 50 images culled from several thousand photographs. Laying out the photographs for an essay is like constructing a sentence with 40 or 50 images, he told me. Rhythm is important. You must not repeat yourself. 'Cut and cut, and cut some more. The pictures will lead people to the texts.' He assembled his photographs and wrote a brief text for each – four or five lines. Here are some examples:

(Figure 8.2)

Figure 8.2   Journey to the End of Coal, 2008, Samuel Bollendorff

[A middle-aged woman poses with the soft toys she produces.] Mrs Pao has been a factory worker for fifteen years. Once a factory worker reaches a certain age, without qualifications, it is impossible to find another job. She has chosen to stay in this factory where she is paid 1 euro a day.

(Figure 8.3)

[An isolated town in the snow.] 'We work from sunset until the middle of the night so as to avoid the inspectors.' Mr. Chang. Although officially closed down, the private mine in Shiqianfeng is still operating.

(Figure 8.4)

[An older woman shovels waste from the road. Like Agnès Varda's gleaners, she is looking for cooking fuel.] Linfen, in the heart of the steel-making and coal-processing industrial areas, is one of the ten most polluted cities in the world. Mrs Qi, 60, is unemployed. She

Figure 8.3   Journey to the End of Coal, 2008, Samuel Bollendorff

Figure 8.4   Journey to the End of Coal, 2008, Samuel Bollendorff

collects scraps of coal, hydrocarbon waste and other toxic products left behind by trucks at the entrance to the steel plant, and then uses it as fuel for cooking. She says 'No, there's no pollution here'.[68]

These photographs and captions formed pre-texts for Bollendorff's documentary *Journey to the End of Coal* (2008) produced with Honky Tonk Films. He migrated to online documentaries because pictures alone could not convey the stories he wanted to tell. For Bollendorff, working with images and words has always been central to his role as a photographer. As a founder of the photographic agency Œil, he insisted that images could only be displayed online with the captions he provided. 'I didn't want our images to be disassociated from their context.'[69] Once they were sold, however, he could not prevent his pictures and texts being separated and so he decided to produce projects that integrated his written story with the images.

You are a foreigner

Journey to the End of Coal is influenced by video games but Bollendorff believed it was important not to make the suffering of the Chinese coal miners a game. Instead, he based the narrative on his own investigation, inviting viewers to put themselves in the place of a journalist in China researching and telling this story. What choices would you make? *Journey to the End of Coal* uses the branching narrative method favoured by many games; in this case, 'choose your own adventure' is mixed with reality. The structure evolved from one of the themes in Bollendorff's exhibition and book. In one photograph, for example, he turns his camera back on the officials following him. They were trying to ensure he did not depart from the authorised story.

(Figure 8.5)

[A man has stepped out of his car to make a call. His companion, a young woman, waits inside the warmth of the car.] 'You are a foreigner, you don't know where the good things are, that is why the Government is here to show you the good places. If we were to hide anything, it would mean that we weren't showing you reality.' Hu Xiaodong, Deputy Director of Information in Xinjiang.

The path less travelled

Your journey begins in Datong which is located just a couple hours away West from Beijing. You travel from there all around the region and visit

Figure 8.5 *Journey to the End of Coal*, 2008, Samuel Bollendorff

its major coal mines, from the 'best' state-owned complex to the worst private coal plants. In and around the coal mines, you get the story first hand from the mingong, the rural migrants traveling their country looking for work.[70]

Many of the choices offered to *Journey to the End of Coal's* viewers come down to this: take the approved itinerary, or branch off to investigate. Visit a village with the official delegation, or find a way to talk to a miner about his working and living conditions; conduct the interview on the streets, or accept an invitation to visit his home. Unlike a traditional 'choose your own adventure story', text features strongly in the mix of elements and, at almost every turn, there are opportunities to read background information.

Bollendorff and his collaborator Abel Segretin prepared a plan for their project's branching narrative. 'The script is the reconstruction of your investigation in a particular subject matter. You need to know whom you are going to talk to and what you will include. You also need to think about how you will integrate your captions into your images and online.'[71] At its simplest level, their outline resembled a mind-map, with a series of alternative scenes, each encapsulated in an image and a brief description, hanging from a branch. One of the first issues they faced was to find a relatively simple way for viewers to navigate the programme. Bollendorff came up with the idea of using 'a video-game interface with a series of familiar buttons at the bottom of the computer screen. It means that when you see it for the first time, you know how it works. You recognise the interface.'[72]

Words and pictures

After authoring a number of web-based projects, Bollendorff says that *Journey to the End of Coal* made him think more deeply about creating online works. Such environments offer the possibility of working with images, sound and words, adding new information to older information as needed. He wished to move beyond simply placing photographs online and create more dynamic texts. In 2012, he produced an online documentary about the housing crisis in France titled *Nowhere Safe*.[73] It combined 16 four-minute portraits, each made up of still and moving images, ambient sound, text and data on screen. Like *Journey to the End of Coal*, the programme combined big picture analysis with personal stories.

Nowhere Safe's first portrait introduces a young girl who rides around and around on her bicycle in an empty room. The image freezes and we travel outside. A series of stills introduces her parents and siblings, who are living in a caravan. We hear excerpts from an audio interview expressing her mother's sense of frustration living with a young family in such cramped conditions. How can one imagine a future here, the programme asks? *Nowhere Safe* presents us with relatively few navigational choices as viewers. We can learn more, skip a story or proceed to the next. Words are an even more important element in this programme than *Journey to the End of Coal* and, throughout the documentary there are opportunities to learn more by reading pages of text.

I don't want to click

Bollendorff added a button – 'I don't want to click' – for viewers who preferred to watch *Nowhere Safe* straight through. This move, I would suggest, is indicative of shifts in how we think about interactivity in a digital environment. While user-controlled navigation was once emphasised as the key to interactivity and viewer engagement, we now take a broader view. Media theorist Gunther Kress has suggested that increasingly the most significant aspect of interactivity concerns the interplay between words, images and sounds.[74] *Journey to the End of Coal* and *Nowhere Safe* are inspiring examples of online multimodal texts that present two markedly different approaches to composing web documentaries. In the shift from pages to screens as writing and viewing displays, images have not replaced words. According to Bollendorff, in his own work, words now play a more significant role due to the need to contextualise his pictures in a veritable torrent of images.

From draft to composition

Writing about musical composition, Alex Stewart observed that 'fixing compositions in their final form, particularly in notation or in recorded medium, allows for reflection, revision and refinement'.[75] Composers of popular music rarely use notation, more commonly arriving at their pieces through improvising in the recording studio. Their compositions are written down after the fact, with preliminary recordings and 'demos' providing the means of reflecting, revising and refining their works.

In screen media, the prewritten screenplay has occupied a privileged position as the authorised form for fixing the idea for a screen work at various stages in its composition. Yet there are many alternatives – as evidenced by the works of Agnès Varda, Abbas Kiarostami and Samuel Bollendorff. Like players in a branching narrative, they have all taken the road less travelled, often working with smaller budgets to retain creative freedom while exploring some of the big issues of our time. Films made with small budgets are small in name only. The size of their budgets does not necessarily correspond with their significance or breadth of vision.[76]

In front of a computer screen, headphones on, we dip into research notes, retrieve images from a digital camera roll and begin writing; words, images and sounds at our fingertips. As we move to multimodal texts combining text, images and sound, music, poetry and photography provide a wealth of alternative ways of thinking about composing screen works – perhaps none more so than photography. After all, in our digital world, photography is becoming more like writing. According to Fred Ritchin, 'the ephemeral and easily malleable online photograph can be increasingly be considered the expression of a particular point of view, a commentary more akin to writing than a definitive recording'.[77] The converse is also true: writing is becoming more like photography. More and more, the digital screenwriter is a cine-composer.

9
Collaboration: Writing the Possible

Like the fresco paintings of medieval Europe, which employed the skills of large numbers of people under the supervision of a master painter, cinema is often described as an intensely collaborative activity. Does collaboration simply mean the contribution of a large number of people and their skills towards a given project? Social psychologist, Karl Weick, suggests that organisations come into being when individual (or, sometimes, individuals) realises that the task they want to complete is beyond their abilities. They can choose to abandon the task or collaborate with others. When the group comes together it has already identified a purpose and task and, over time, the interests of the individuals gradually become enmeshed.[1] Sans Façon, the long-term collaboration between architect Charles Blanc and artist Tristan Surtees, notes that collaboration is often used to describe a number of people with a specific skill, each working on part of a project. In Blanc and Surtees' view, however, 'collaboration should ideally take the project somewhere else – a place where you didn't expect it to end up, as the input of all the collaborators reshapes the project into something altogether new'.[2]

Film production is often compared with going to war. 'Making a movie is like going to war.' 'I wear a uniform because to me a movie is war.'[3] In my 20s, I did a short intensive course to qualify as a camera assistant in order to subsidise work on my own scripts. The camera assistant's certificate course might better have been described as camera assistant's boot camp. South Australia was at the forefront of the renaissance in Australian cinema in the 1970s and a former munitions factory was quickly repurposed as a film factory. Once we had mastered the technical details of light meters and loading film magazines, we were required to do tripod sprints. The course leader, a former soldier, timed our efforts with a stopwatch. Each morning, we sprinted 100 metres, heavy tripods designed to hold 35 mm cameras slung over one shoulder, set it up, adjusted the spirit levels, folded it down and ran for our lives. We repeated the exercise *ad nauseum*. Never a fan of military organisation, I soon went AWOL, stopping off for an espresso and a quick scan of the morning papers on the way. Perhaps, I mused, I was more suited to the guerrilla-style, small, agile crews associated with independent cinema and documentary.

Collaboration in early cinema

Early American film production was intensely collaborative until around 1908, according to screen historian, Charles Musser. Typically, two partners with complementary skills produced short films together in an informal and non-hierarchical manner. 'The originator(s) of a story would often direct the actors, appear in the films, operate the camera, develop the exposed raw stock, cut the negative and – if required – run the projector.'[4] Filmmakers had an in-depth knowledge of all aspects of their craft. Around 1907–1908, this collaborative system gave way to the hierarchical central producer system. According to Janet Staiger, who dates the emergence of this system several years earlier, it contained many of the elements that dominate industrial filmmaking today. As the length of films grew from an average of 18 minutes to features of 75 minutes or more, studios developed techniques of mass production.[5] The producer used a detailed shooting script known as the continuity script, to plan and budget the film before crew was hired, sets built and shooting began. The 'scientific management' principles of Frederick Taylor, enthusiastically embraced by the manufacturing industries, found their way into film production, resulting in a separation between the work of developing ideas and executing them.

Taylor, who came from a wealthy Philadelphia family, dropped out of his studies at Harvard to join a manufacturing company as an apprentice machinist. After a spectacular rise from the factory floor to the position of chief engineer within six years, Taylor began his time-motion experiments aimed at maximising efficiency in factories. In one of his first studies, he assigned two workers to shovel iron ore and two more to monitor them. The plan was to break the action into its components in order to teach workers the most efficient method. 'A manager must plan and control all decisions and steps in the work process so that waste could be eliminated.'[6] Henry Ford combined the principles of scientific management with the methods of slaughterhouses to invent the assembly line. In his factories, each worker carried out a specialised task – such as attaching the handle on the left-side door of the car as it moved down the assembly line.[7] Like Charlie Chaplin's famous factory floor scene in *Modern Times* (1932), the assembly line could stop for no one. Workers performed increasingly specialised tasks faster and faster.

Scriptwriting in early Hollywood

The emerging Hollywood style and the development of feature-length films contributed to a scriptwriting process in which 'technical experts...specialised in translating a story into a continuity script'.[8] Four or five experts discussed the script in detail and attempted to eliminate every flaw in structure before passing it on to the director. Such a system did not restrict itself to maximising efficiencies in production but also attempted to standardise products in the name of quality. Before long, scripts might just as well have been Model T Fords, rolling off the assembly line after a series of technical experts had each made their contribution. Planning departments determined the costs of each project in advance, calculating materials and each worker's role. Records, paperwork and memos were the order of the day and the script soon became part of this paperwork. 'It [the continuity script] could function as a paper record to coordinate the assembly of the product shot out of order, prepared by a large number of people spread at various places throughout the world...and still achieve a clear, verisimilar and continuous representation of causal logic, time and place.'[9]

Maintaining the continuous time and space that was a growing feature of Hollywood screen narratives involved coordinating and tracking vast amounts of information.[10] Paper plans were more reliable than the memories of individuals who would otherwise need to track this data. It was cheaper and more efficient to employ staff to solve continuity problems prior to production than deal with them on set. A flood of 'how to' books helped standardise the continuity script format – just as screenplay manuals helped standardise Hollywood's preferred three-act structure from the mid-1970s onwards. 'Scientific management also intensified production-planning work so that the director's tasks subdivided: the producer planned and coordinated the work while the director specialised in managing the shooting activities.'[11] Writers were split into two categories – those who created stories and those who rewrote them.

Paper explosion

Over the last 50 years, many commentators have predicted a move to the paperless office as a result of new technologies. In the late 1960s, animator Jim Henson was commissioned to make a five-minute film for IBM, promoting the virtues of the then-new Dictaphone machines. His witty montage, *Paper Explosion* (1967), presented a succession of harried-looking men and women in their offices. 'There is not enough time for paperwork', 'In the past, there were always enough time and people', 'There is no time for paperwork', they chorus. Management, secretaries, engineers, accountants alike, no one has time for the ever-expanding paperwork associated with the modern workplace. Enter the Dictaphone. Rockets launch into space. They blow stacks of papers sky-high. 'Machines should work, people should think', 'Machines work, people think' intone the relieved office-workers. Despite the advent of mass computing, nearly five decades later, the brave new world of the paperless office is still a distant dream. Clearing my desk of piles of funding applications, reports and memos, I wonder whether digital tools have not instead spawned more paperwork.

In recent years, a number of books tracing the intellectual history of paperwork have appeared including, notably, Ben Kafka's *The Demons of Writing: The Powers and Failures of Paperwork.*[12] The evolution of bureaucratic paperwork is often described as a move towards rationality and order but Kafka (like his famous namesake) tends to think otherwise. In one of his stories, the novelist invented a sea god, Poseidon, who was so overwhelmed with the demands of bureaucratic paperwork that he never actually got to swim.[13] According to Ben Kafka, paper records are actually associated with crisis and disruption just as often as order. Yet much film production still relies heavily on a mountain of paperwork in the form of scripts, revisions, schedules, memos, lists and call sheets. Such paperwork is often associated with professionalism and the possession of insider knowledge.

Challenges to the industrial script

Cinema has a long history of writers, actors and filmmakers forming collectives and collaborative groups in order to realise their projects. They range from Charlie Chaplin, Douglas Fairbanks and Mary Pickford, who banded together in 1919 to form United Artists, to Godard's Dziga Vertov Group, assembled in 1968. David Bordwell noted that most challenges to Hollywood and classical film have evolved from individual filmmakers or filmmaking groups, with the status of the script being nearly always a major site of difference.[14] Many of the films discussed in this book – the works of Agnès Varda, Guy Maddin, Matthew Porterfield, Yaron Shani, Abbas Kiarostami, Lucien Castaing-Taylor and others – were produced without traditional scripts. Some filmmakers write scripts they do not use, others work from notes instead of scripts or some combination thereof. Wim Wenders wrote his road movie *Kings of the Road* each night before shooting in order to take advantage of local conditions. The six cameramen who filmed the feature documentary *The Battle of Chile* (1975–1977) participated in extensive theoretical discussions in order to prepare for the shoot. The filmmakers shot for two weeks without a script and then met to decide production roles and the film's final argument.[15] They did not eschew planning, it simply took a different form. Gus Van Sant's feature *Elephant* (2003) was produced without a traditional script, relying instead on a treatment and map.[16]

Dogme and collaboration

In 1995, Danish filmmakers Lars von Trier and Thomas Vinterberg announced their ten rules for low-budget filmmaking: the Dogme Manifesto. The rules primarily involved making films that drew on the resources of particular localities and rejecting any unnecessary technologies. They were intended as a spur to creativity and built on the notion of 'creativity under constraints' proposed by Norwegian philosopher Jon Elster.[17] Surveying the history of art, Elster suggested that artists commonly worked with three kinds of constraints: imposed, chosen or incidental, any of which could hinder or foster artists' creativity. Screen theorist Mette Hjort observed that the shift towards a viable low-budget model of filmmaking promoted collaboration within production teams. While directors often wrote Dogme films, a collaborative ethos surrounded their production. Rune Palving from the National Film School explained that in Danish low-budget filmmaking 'The production structure is very flat. You have your area of responsibility but there is a lot of interaction. The films are small – as are the budgets – and this means there has to be a lot more consultation.'[18] Building on this model, Dogme countered the 'institutional complexities and hierarchies of costly feature-length film with rules for feature films devised from intensely collaborative, low-budget production'.[19]

Rune Palving recalled Lone Scherfig's approach to finding locations on the Dogme-certified *Italian for Beginners* (2000). 'I was sitting in this house ... I looked out the window and that was my film. I take the easiest concept I can think of exploring instead of adopting some really complicated concept that then has to be scaled down.'[20] Ake Sandgren took the opposite approach on *Truly Human* (2001). His starting point was instead: 'What if I took this fantasy character and special effects movie and turned it into something that could be a Dogme movie?'[21] Many movements and initiatives devoted to low-budget filmmaking have emerged since – from mumblecore in the United States to microwave in the United Kingdom. One of their defining characteristics is a shift away from the long cycles of script development that characterise the Hollywood studio system in favour of embracing constraints, and writing for local contexts.

Ephemeral organisations

Natural disasters such as earthquakes and hurricanes provide one of the key settings for sociologists to study the organisations that emerge when the usual social structures break down. After an earthquake in Italy in 1953, sociologist Lanzara observed the impromptu organisations that emerged to meet the immediate needs of communities.[22] He identified a number of differences between formal organisations and those he termed *ephemeral*. The latter form quickly and spontaneously in response to a crisis. Commitment of group members is more likely to be based on intrinsic rewards than external rewards, such as money and status. Ephemeral organisations make use of a loose division of labour, with tasks and positions defined broadly. Roles are self-proscribed rather than mapped by authorities, work units tend to be small and activities are likely to be *ad hoc* and informal. Ephemeral organisations are emergent and collaborative and so better at innovating than established organisations. Self-directed and self-managed teams are agile, flexible, efficient and adaptive.[23] According to Lanzara, 'they do not assume their own survival or permanence as a requirement for identity and effectiveness of performance'.[24] By contrast to their formal counterparts, ephemeral organisations measure their performance by their achievements rather than economic efficiencies. There are some clear parallels with the screen production ecologies of both early cinema – and digital cinema.

Court 13

It is appropriate that the critically acclaimed independent feature *Beasts of the Southern Wild* (2012), co-written by Benh Zeitlin and Lucy Alibar, should be the focus of a discussion of methods of collaboration, since its story is set in Florida in the aftermath of Hurricane Katrina. Where better to trial a new way of organising a film production? Many of the members of the film's large production unit belonged to a collective called Court 13, with whom writer, director and composer Benh Zeitlin had long worked. Court 13 describe themselves as a grassroots, community-based filmmaking collective, a mix of 'artists, animators, constructionists, editors, musicians, and storytellers'. Sometimes they even call themselves an independent filmmaking army. Court 13 initially formed to support a member's college thesis film, an eight-minute retelling of *Moby Dick*. They regularly met on a basketball court, hence their name, and subsequently participated in the production of a number of short films. The collective made a boat out of junk and sailed it on Lake Pontchartrain for their short film *Glory at Sea*. The success of this film, written and directed by Zeitlin, led to the opportunity for the group to take on a larger project (Figure 9.1).

Significantly, much of the production financing for *Beasts of the Southern Wild* came from a not-for-profit organisation, Cinereach. The collective began, said Zeiltin, because he wanted to 'give a lot of agency to the individual artist to breath their own creativity into whatever element of the film they're in charge of'.[25] A methodology and ethos that could be applied to larger projects emerged as they worked together in New Orleans. Many of the people who worked in the art department on *Beasts of the Southern Wild*, for example, spent most of their time producing their own sculpture, painting or music. Unlike most feature film crew members, they were not itinerant freelancers moving from production to production. Instead, group members worked on individual projects and came together quickly for larger productions. They were

Figure 9.1   Beasts of the Southern Wild, 2012, Court 13 Pictures

self-described 'animators of junk who seek to tell huge stories out of small parts'.[26]

Temporary organisations

Court 13 shares some of the attributes of the temporary professional organisation. Not all such organisations are ephemeral: temporary *professional* organisations are associated with the knowledge industries and product development in areas such as software, film, theatre and sports.[27] Sociologist Zygmunt Bauman describes our current era as a liquid society. As more and more aspects of our life are in flux, temporary professional organisations play a significant role in more people's lives. Itinerant professionals, usually in creative or administrative roles, are contracted to work on specific projects for defined periods. Such organisations are more informal and less hierarchical than their ongoing counterparts. The Court 13 filmmakers and artists constructed a hybrid organisation, combining aspects of the temporary professional organisation with the grassroots collective. Its structure also owes something to the recent resurgence in artist-run initiatives, cooperatives and studios in other art forms. Contemporary musicians, for example, have long embraced an ethos of artist-led initiatives, often belonging to a number of different ensembles formed to realise different projects.

Fluid script

The story of *Beasts of the Southern Wild* began like this. Benh Zeitlin was homeless in Prague after Hurricane Katrina devastated his hometown. Two separate ideas began to mesh. After attending an informal reading of the short play *Juicy and Delicious*,[28] written by his friend Lucy Alibar, he raised the possibility of adapting it to film. Later, having completed the short film, *Glory at Sea*, Zeitlin began considering a new story to be set in Louisiana. In response to Hurricane Katrina, the new film would focus on a group of people who refused to leave their homes at the height of the crisis. The two ideas converged when Zeitlin decided to combine his story of a community losing its place with Alibar's storyline about a small girl losing her father. The latter had the potential to provide the emotional storyline the film required to connect with audiences. The core narrative that Zeitlin eventually took from *Juicy and Delicious* was 'what responsibility do you have to be there for someone or something as it slips away in front of your eyes?'[29]

On location

The script, expanded from *Juicy and Delicious*, was guided by extensive on site research and improvisations throughout rehearsals and production. The filmmakers travelled to Louisiana and established their production base in an abandoned convenience store. The pair worked on their script, holed up in a marina 'where the road ends and the Gulf begins'.[30] Research amongst the local communities included conversations with fishermen, oilmen and other local residents. It was always intended that *Beasts of the Southern Wild* mesh not only two storylines but two tonal registers: the real and the fantastic. Thus, one of the major tasks of the development period was to find a means of creating the heightened world of the narrative with a very low budget. Zeitlin and Alibar had known each other since their early teens and were close friends so were comfortable in taking risks. Zeitlin commented on their decision to write the character Hushpuppy as a six year old – rather than as an 11 year old – and the casting challenges that created: 'we sort of go into abysses and impossible challenges like that fairly regularly so it wasn't totally out of the blue'.[31] Sundance Laboratory became involved and attached the writers to experienced mentors. As they developed their screenplay, Zeitlin and Alibar gradually heightened the fantasy element.

The director described the strategies he used to prepare the nonprofessional actors for a large and relatively complex production. The local baker, Dwight Henry, was cast in a similar role in the film (to that of his real life) and so the filmmakers recorded a version of the entire script that he could listen to while baking. Zeitlin and Henry also interviewed each other, relating particular scenes in the film to the baker's own life. Some of the material generated was then incorporated into the script. A different kind of reading was staged for the six-year-old actor. Zeitlin told her the story 'I would sit down with her and I would tell her the story like it was a folk tale'[32]. He began the story with 'Once there was a Hushpuppy', a line which found its way into the film and opens the narration.

Amidst the swamps and mosquitoes and heat of Louisiana, Court 13 went 'off the grid', embracing whatever technology was available. The collective even went so far as hand-raising the animals that feature in the film so that they would be comfortable around people. This provided an alternative to expensive digital effects. Court 13's volunteer casting army made it possible to canvas a given town, working with local school superintendents to pass out flyers in public schools, and holding auditions in churches and libraries. In some areas, they went door to door, inquiring about people who might be interested in being cast. Looking for locations followed the same process. The ability to mobilise a large pool of committed professionals who were willing to take on tasks outside their specialisations gave Court 13 the ability to embark on a much more ambitious scale of production than would usually have been possible with their modest budget.

Workshop draft

The co-writers drafted one draft of the screenplay fast and then collaborated on three or four more versions. 'The characters and tone and basic shape of the story came from the play, more than a page-to-page adaptation.'[33] At that stage, they completed casting the film and began incorporating their community cast's input. Zeitlin said, 'the final draft was a sort of collaborative process of rehearsing scenes, interviewing actors and bringing in elements of their lives to the characters'. The last draft was a workshop script, primarily aimed at translating the dialogue and action into the speech and rhythms of the nonprofessional actors. Zeitlin has elaborated on Court 13's approach to writing: 'We do not finish a script and then have a document that is executed line-by-line. The script is written while we're casting and finding places. It's a very fluid thing. If we find a person, a place or an object that reflects the essence of the story, we're able to incorporate that.'[34] This methodology gradually evolved as Court 13 made *Beasts of the Southern Wild*.

Choose-your-own-adventure game

Despite its hardships, Court 13 director and Special Effects Coordinator Ray Tinder compared making *Beasts of the Southern Wild* to an adventure. Court 13 aimed to treat their film's production as a series of challenges that would test their limits, an ethos that has strong overtones of online gaming worlds like Second Life and 'choose-your-own-adventure' video games. Zeitlin and his collaborators' accounts suggest a deeply immersive experience played out over an extended period. The lack of funds to realise their complex production helped build an ethos in which those challenges would be faced as obstacles to be overcome in order to move to the next level.

Adhocism

According to architect Charles Jencks, *adhocism* is a mongrel term first used in architecture in the late 1960s. Deriving from *ad hoc* which means 'for this particular purpose', it involves using an available system in a new way to solve a problem quickly. 'Adhocism denotes a principle of action having *speed* or economy and *purpose*, and it prospers like most hybrids on the edge of respectability.'[35] As a movement, adhocism favours multiple solutions rather than any single solution. It favours mass *customisation* over mass production. Creativity, asserts Jencks, depends on the coming together of disparate material. In their 2013 manifesto for adhocism, Jencks and Nathan Silver explicitly link the revival of adhocism to the aftermath of events such as Hurricane Katrina and the earthquake in Haiti. In such situations, people make do with whatever is at hand. On *Beasts of the Southern Wild*, adhocism was both a production methodology and a way of life. 'Our life was the process of building something out of nothing and trying to create art out of whatever was around.'[36]

Milkyway and improvisation

Hong Kong-based director Johnnie To founded Milkyway Image with his longtime business partner Wai Ka-Fai in the mid-1990s. The company has since established an unusually collaborative means of scripting and producing films. One of the key characteristics of their slate is alternating films that mix elements of the action genre with art-house films and more populist comedies. For David Bordwell, Milkyway's major achievement has been to reenact the crime film. 'Their characters are not die-cast, the plots are labyrinthine, the images are at once lustrous, ominous, and deceptive.'[37] In 2007, Milkyway produced the critically acclaimed *Mad Detective*. Co-written by Wai Ka-Fai and Au Kin-Yee, it is story of a burnt-out detective who solves cases by reenacting crimes and intuiting crooks' inner personalities. *Mad Detective* unfolds through the perspectives of different characters and their interior personae, combining elements of action, philosophical musings and even black comedy (Figure 9.2).

Whilst Wai Ka-Fai and Au Kin-Yee are credited as writers on *Mad Detective* and Johnnie To as director, the creative roles on Milkyway productions are unusually porous. To prefers not to have a concrete script before beginning production so that he can continue to introduce new ideas throughout the film shoot. Too much planning, he says, limits creativity. This is how To describes Milkyway's usual scripting process: 'The scriptwriter and I would discuss the script together; many other people could also contribute their ideas during the shoot. The scriptwriter combines them in the final script.'[38] It is not unusual for the term 'creative

Figure 9.2 Mad Detective, 2009, Milky Way Image Company

team' to appear in the credits of Milkyway productions because many people contribute.

Milkyway's creative process

I spoke with writer and member of the Milkyway Creative Team, Au Kin-Yee on her trajectory into writing for film. Collaboration is one of the hallmarks of the Milkyway process and our interview was in the same vein. As we Skyped, Kin-Yee's colleague interpreted from English to Cantonese and back again. At our respective computers in Sydney and Hong Kong, we Googled for more information on the Milkyway Image back-catalogue and Kin-Yee's earlier work. She took up a position in dramatic writing at the Hong Kong broadcaster TVB after graduating from high school and learnt on the job. TVB produces series across many genres with a particular focus on police procedurals and comedies. Typically, a supervising writer leads a team of three or four writers on a series, which runs for 50 or more episodes. The writing team develops storylines and scene breakdowns together. Individual writers then split off from the group to complete full episodes. Kin-Yee gained a great deal of experience writing for television within a relatively short time as part of a team whose work was constantly in production.

Kin-Yee regards her best work at TVB as her contribution to the series *At the Threshold of an Era* (1999–2000). An epic story of more than 100 episodes, the series was commissioned to mark the turn of the millennium. Its narrative took place over a 20-year period and, in a bold storytelling decision, the entire series was narrated as a continuing flashback. On completion of the work on the series and after ten years of working within TVB's drama department, Kin-Yee was invited to join

Milkyway Image. While her experience working with genre, interweaving story lines and writing for large casts stood her in good stead in her new role, Milkyway Image has a radically different working process. Writing teams for feature films are usually smaller with a scriptwriter collaborating with one or two others. The expanded role of the screenwriter at Milky Way involves not only discussing and scripting ideas but going on location to work with the actors and director during the shoot, working with the editor on an initial cut of the film, and working with the actors on ADR (Additional Dialogue Recording).[39]

Mad Detective

The genesis of the critically acclaimed *Mad Detective* was the desire of Milkyway's founders to commemorate the company's ten-year anniversary through a new approach to storytelling. One starting point was to consider how to reinvigorate the police stories that were some of the company's most successful productions. The writers began by considering the main character Bunt and the possibilities of using the concept of karma that had featured in their previous films like *Running Out of Time* (1999) to justify presenting his inner visions on screen. Doing the reading and research that typically launches a Milkyway project, the writers noticed that American films often used mental illness as a device to justify seeing visions. By contrast, the topic of mental illness would rarely be explored in Chinese cinema. Ka-Fai and Kin-Yee discussed an unusual range of sources, from Buddhist notions of karma to popular American novels on the phenomenon of multiple personalities and biographies of Vincent van Gogh. Kin-Yee observed 'In some ways, the idea of multiple personalities is ridiculous. But it is also a very useful idea cinematically because it provides a rationale for seeing different versions and identities within a single character.'[40]

Four-part structure

Unlike the contemporary American model of three acts, Chinese filmmakers break down their stories into four parts: set-up, deployment, twist and resolution. In the case of *Mad Detective*, *qi cheng zhuan he* was simply one of the ideas in the mix. Tracing this four-part story pattern, I find that it dates back to classical Chinese rhetoric, poetry and drama and named after its four parts of (*qi* (opening), *cheng* (continuing), *zhuan* (turning) and *he* (synthesis)). According to Kin-Yee, 'the story simply needs to fulfil this dramatic structure. It is not a mechanical process with recommended page counts and so on.'[41] Dating back to the Tang dynasty, four-part structure is thought to have migrated from China to Japan and Korea, and from poetry to prose to music-theatre and drama. Most recently, *qi cheng zhuan he* has turned up in Japan as *kishōtenketsu* where it is used to structure some graphic novels and 'four cell' mangas. Kitano Takeshi has said his films, which begin from images and not stories, are structured in four parts – like four-panel mangas – and follow the principles of *kishōtenketsu*.[42]

Rather than being a fixed structure, *qi cheng zhuan he* has continued to change and morph across cultures and art forms. As a story pattern, it places less emphasis on plot and a rising narrative line than the three-act structure popularised by Syd Field and favoured by many American script gurus. Instead, its emphasis on frequent twists and recurring images and scenes helps convey the sense that we are continually seeing scenes afresh from different perspectives – one of the features of Milkyway's most successful projects.

Story fragments

In the Milkyway script development process, the writers prepare a summary document, which they forward to the film's director. Once he or she has approved it, they begin filling in the detail. The summary document resembles a jigsaw puzzle with many of the pieces missing. Two key images, for example, kick-started the scripting of *Mad Detective*. Firstly, the opening scene in which the main character, Bunt, cuts off his ear in the police squad room. Secondly, the scene in which a woman urinates standing up – like a man. The summary document contains a series of clues to the story; clues about themes, characters and imagery or key scenes. In a departure from the more conventional model of an outline which summarises the script's entire plot, 'the task of the writers is to find the story from these fragments'.[43]

The writers proceed with a scene breakdown and, once the film begins shooting, the director becomes a third collaborator. The films of Milkyway Image often go into production without a fully drafted script since shooting starts before all the locations have been found. The collaborators might decide on particular locations which suggest new ways to tell the story and the writers revise or adapt scenes to be shot there. The writers regularly visit locations to give actors their scenes and make script revisions as a result of the actors' and directors' feedback. When a writer takes script pages out to location it will often be the first time that anyone has seen the fully scripted scene. Milkyway Image generally follows the Hong Kong practice of adding sound in postproduction. Since Hong Kong action films are not dialogue heavy, the director has more space to create a mood on location, says Johnnie To. More emphasis is placed on the rhythms of visual storytelling than static dialogue scenes with actors. It is not uncommon for scenes to be shot in the company's building or on their roof as well as the streets of Hong Kong. As David Bordwell suggests, this not only enables filmmakers to shoot more quickly, and hence with low budgets, but gives Hong Kong films the fluency of silent cinema.[44]

One practical consideration that plays a role in Milkyway Image's production methodology is that films are made with a particular cinema release date already set. The time from initial idea to cinema release has varied from as little as a month to as much as three years. While *Mad Detective* completed shooting within 30 days, it took longer to edit than usual because of its complex storyline. Johnnie To described *Mad Detective* as 'a film that follows no rules.... Every day on the set felt like an experiment.'[45]

Milkyway's creative team

Milkyway's writing and production process is an organic one in which everyone helps each other out, even when they are all working on several different scripts. Rather than deciding on precise roles at the beginning of a project, decisions about who takes on the roles of writing, producing and directing are sometimes made in the process of making a given film. Consequently, it is common for scripts to be credited to the Milkyway Creative Team.

The Milkyway creative methodology shares many of the features of the new collaborative mindset emerging in the screen sector. While writers have extensive experience in their field, they contribute in multiple roles and across the whole of the production process. Skilled teams work on the run, improvising as they go. Scripts are flexible and fluid, and constantly revised throughout production and editing. They function primarily as a record of creative ideas rather than as part of the production paperwork. Nothing could be further from the industrial method of production with its highly specialised division of labour and separation of ideas and their execution.

Collaboration with other art forms

George Lucas compared digital cinema to oil painting due to its malleability. By contrast, pre-digital cinema was like fresco painting, which required large numbers of assistants to apply plaster and paint to largely preplanned compositions. Writer and director Robert Rodriguez enthused, 'It's the speed and power of being almost a paintbrush in your hand.'[46] Perhaps most importantly, digital cinema has led to an outpouring of collaboration with other media and art forms.[47]

Bricolage

Karl Weick defines *bricolage* as 'using whatever resources and repertoire one has to perform whatever task one faces'.[48] Michael Chanan, tracing the prehistory of cinema, observed that *bricolage* is the polar opposite of the mass production methods of industrial societies. Even cinematography itself is a kind of *bricolage*, 'the invention of cinematography created a sort of intellectual *bricolage* which knocked together bits of theory and practical know-how to bring the photograph to life'.[49] Weick suggests that those who make skilled use of *bricolage* combine a detailed knowledge of the available resources with careful observation, listening and a trust in intuitive insights. They exhibit a confidence that any enacted structure can be self-correcting if one's ego is not too heavily invested in it.[50] Too much preplanning, Weick suggests, can stifle creativity because it does not leave room for experimentation, improvisation and surprise. Traditional organisations concern themselves with planning, policy, procedures and controls, with the aim of maximising efficiency. In times of change, crisis and complexity, Weick suggests, these strategies are ineffective. Conflict, ambiguity and uncertainty are necessary aspects of the looser organisational structures that foster innovation.

A collaborative partnership

The Belgian-based brothers Jean-Pierre and Luc Dardenne, who share writing and directing credits, have developed their own collaborative scripting methodology over a suite of political documentaries and low budget features. Their films *Rosetta* (1999) and *L'Enfant* (2005) were awarded the Palme d'Or at Cannes, while *La Promesse* (1996), *Le Fils* (2002), *Le Silence de Lorna* (2008) and *Le Gamin au velo* (2011) have attracted numerous awards and a strong critical response. Their work, often associated with the new realism, features working-class characters dealing with shifts in their living conditions and crises of conscience of various kinds. Luc Dardenne has described the camera as 'a blowtorch...to heat bodies and objects'.[51] The camera, he says, creates an intensity, which burns and reveals the incandescent in the everyday.

Each project takes around three years to write and realise and their shooting periods are considerably longer than is usual on relatively low-budget films. Like the collaborative partnerships of early cinema, the Dardennes carry out many of the tasks of preparing their production themselves: writing, producing, finding locations and casting. During the shoot, however, they are joined by their team of regular collaborators.

Jean-Pierre and Luc Dardenne begin by discussing the script. 'We talk, we talk, we talk,' they say. The initial spark may be something the brothers have seen, heard or read about.[52] According to Luc Dardenne, literature and music act as spurs to his own writing. Before beginning to write, he reads widely and listens to music, especially Beethoven's piano sonatas and concertos.[53] After all, like music, each film has a particular rhythm. 'A numbered outline emerges, with some 50 points, listing action, spaces, situations and dialogue.'[54] The written document is a record of their thinking and so continues to shift and evolve. Ultimately, Luc Dardenne writes up to six or seven drafts of a screenplay.

Writing the possible

The Dardenne brothers' now well-established methodology might be seen as another example of provocative competence, emerging after an unsatisfactory experience making the feature film *Je pense à vous* (*Thinking of You*) in 1992. Their intensely collaborative method stems from their work in theatre and the desire to recreate the film production unit as a theatre troupe. Luc and Jean-Pierre Dardenne began their respective careers in the arts in the 1970s, working with poet, filmmaker and theatre director Armand Gatti. Gatti had been a member of the French Resistance and was loosely associated with France's Left Bank filmmakers. His work has been described as part of an attempt to 'leave classic production behind in favour of a participative approach of research, encounter and dialogue with people'.[55] A charismatic theatre director, Gatti led his company in the creation of group-devised works. His performances ranged from theatrical happenings to survey plays. In the latter, actors visited the homes of schoolchildren, agricultural workers and others and asked them to write on specific topics. A philosophy of *wandering* or *drifting theatre* underlay much of his work. Gatti called his work *l'écriture du possible* or 'writing the possible'.[56]

After a stint working with Gatti, where they learnt to make videos, the Dardenne brothers established a political video collective and made a number of broadcast documentaries about the working-class suburb of Seraing within their hometown, Liège. Their video collective was supported through state arts funding. The Dardennes explained their motivation: 'a lot of these workers' have no communal space, and so there's no place for people to talk to each other, so we decided that we would go and film these people and tell their stories, perhaps of moments in their lives where they come up against some injustice. So we would film them during the week and then on the weekend show the films in a café or a local church. And that was a way for people to see and listen to other people in the same estate.'[57] As their work gradually attracted more attention, the pair took the opportunity to move into feature filmmaking. They wanted to tell their own stories and imagined that fiction would enable a collaborative process like they had experienced working in the theatre. 'We lived as a community and every evening ate together', they recalled. They hoped to develop a method of collaborating with actors to 'tell stories from the inside of history'.[58]

By the time it was produced in 1992, the Dardennes' first full-length feature *Je pense à vous* (*Thinking of You*) had been in development for seven years. It explored subject matter the Dardennes knew well: the impact of unemployment on a steel-working family. Renowned screenwriter Jean Gruault, who had worked extensively with Truffaut and Godard, advised them, helping to 'extract characters from the clay of documentary'.[59] In a departure from their work until then, however, the screenplay that resulted from working with Gruault was highly plot driven with extensive dialogue. Once the budget was raised and the film went into production, the apparatus of professional filmmaking kicked in. The Dardennes considered that the film was made 'not against us but without us'.[60] The director of photography, assistant director, actors and many crew were chosen without their input. On set, the conventions of professional filmmaking prevailed. Whenever they hesitated, the smooth-running machinery of a professional film unit took over. They believed they had been frozen out of their own production. Years later, reflecting on the experience, the Dardennes believed that designing individual shots had been privileged over all else. 'Do that and you end up losing the fluidity, the energy, the tension.' In an in interview about their next film, *La Promesse* (1996), the Dardenne Brothers compared their unsatisfactory experience on *Thinking of You* to being the shop floor managers in a factory. Their role had simply been to create employment for others and ensure that the job was done rather than lead a collaborative effort.

A period of soul-searching began. Should they give up filmmaking? Luc Dardenne began keeping an artistic diary, 'Behind Our Images', detailing encounters, thoughts on news events and film ideas, reflections on literature. Its underlying theme was how the two could continue to collaborate since they rejected many of the devices of mainstream cinema as merely putting 'into images and music an increasingly trivial, flatly obvious, dramatic mechanism'.[61] In interviews, they articulated a new way of working. 'We would not work with well-known actors; we would work in locations chosen only by ourselves; the crew around us would be friends and people chosen by us; and we would organise every aspect of the shoot ourselves. And, most of all, we would have the least possible amount of technology, of technical mediation.'[62] They would no longer work with people who blocked them with their professionalism or people whose instincts were always 'to steer them towards the familiar'.[63] On set, behaviour would be characterised by the satisfactions of everyone working towards the realisation of a shared project. The ethos of the cooperative would replace the industrial film production unit.

Since embracing their new methodology, the Dardenne brothers have drastically increased the amount of time spent on scripting and location finding. They take along digital cameras to act out scenes themselves in potential spaces. After all, the relationship between the spaces and the bodies of their actors is vital to the aesthetic of their films. The pair adopt multiple roles, finding locations, advertising for nonprofessional actors in local newspapers, choosing wardrobe items for their actors and spending weeks discussing characters with them prior to the shoot. Locations, cast and crew are all available for the whole shoot so that scenes can easily be reshot if required. In one of the biggest shifts from the industrial model, the Dardennes' films are shot in sequence. Rather than being broken down into individual scenes and shots and scheduled in the most efficient way possible. Their scripts can function as a fluid record of an evolving creative idea, rather than as a continuity script.

Films of the middle

Some of the difficulties Jean-Pierre and Luc Dardenne faced in retaining creative control over their script and production process were connected to the problems of 'films of the middle'.[64] In France, there was a long tradition of quality films produced with medium budgets of between three and eight million euros. In 2008, a French group of screen professionals known as Club 13 produced a report that was highly critical of the quality of such films. The situation was serious, asserted Club 13, titling their report *The Middle Is No Longer a Bridge but a Fault Line*. Both the number and quality of such films were in decline, the report claimed, linking this to the multiple financing partners now needed to finance mid-budget films. According to Joseph Mai, 'this means multiple voices, often with contradictory interests, beginning with the screenplay, which sometimes undergoes many last-minute rewritings'.[65] This, in turn, led to overworked screenplays, half-hearted directing efforts and too much control by well-known actors. The screenplay had become a site of control. (A problem increasingly shared by documentaries requiring higher budgets and needing contributions from a number of international partners.) These problems are not confined to France, of course, but shared by screenwriters and filmmakers around the globe, who prefer to work outside the industrial screen production model.

Screenwriters as bricoleurs

Stories always echo other stories and, in that sense, all screen stories are collaborative. Storytelling is the work that communities undertake in order to assemble fragments of experience into whole narratives that can be retold and reassembled. 'Cinema is about showing things that are changing,' insists Luc Dardenne.[66] As the methodologies of Court 13, Jean-Pierre and Luc Dardenne and Milkyway Image demonstrate, the role of screenwriters has expanded in our digital environment. Fundamental to the flexible, collaborative screen production is the ability to tailor stories to specific environments and resources. Screenwriters, too, must be *bricoleurs*.

Conclusion: Sustainable Screenwriting

This collection of essays is an account of my attempt to understand more about shifts in writing for the screen during a time of rapid change, the fluxes and flows that sociologist Zygmunt Bauman calls *liquid modernity*.[1] An era in which many of us seek a sense of belonging, coherence and community, fearful of finding ourselves disposable in a consumer-driven, globalised world. The story, however, is not all bleak. We look for groups to which we can belong in a world in which all is shifting and nothing is certain. Yet many people resist *liquid modernity*, they attempt 'to arrest the constant flows and fragmentation of contemporary life'.[2] According to sociologist Richard Sennett, who has traced the return of the craftsman, we create narratives about our working lives to generate a sense of coherence, agency and meaning in a social world that often works against this.[3]

Not all of this is new. Early American film production was intensely collaborative until around 1908, according to screen historian, Charles Musser. Typically, two partners with complementary skills produced short films together in an informal and nonhierarchical manner. Against our current backdrop of social anxiety and fragmentation, various forms of collaborative writing and creative arts production are reemerging. This trend is not confined to screen media but is evident across the media arts, theatre, design, architecture and the visual arts.

Screenwriting as an art

Just as stories are made afresh in each retelling, screenwriting is a living art, constantly in transition. Cinema can be seen as a continuation and transformation of screen practices including the magic lantern, photography and the slide show. Likewise, screenwriting is a transformation of earlier modes of writing for screens, visual media, poetry and performance. Far from beginning in America, it is a form of writing with images that can be linked back to the picture storytellers of India in the sixth century B.C., the picture reciters of China's Tang Dynasty (618–907), the shadow playwrights of twelfth-century Egypt and the magic lantern shows of Europe. All of these storytellers used images to breathe life into their stories. Poet and shadow playwright, Ibn Daniyal, who was forced to flee from his homeland to Cairo in the thirteenth century, perhaps deserves to be recognised as one of the founders of writing for the screen. Like many innovators in the arts and screen media since, he devised a manifesto aimed at reinvigorating an art form – in his case, the shadow play. He advised embracing local conditions and working with small, mobile troupes. Could Daniyal be the patron saint of sustainable screenwriting?

Beyond the speculative screenplay

In our era, studios increasingly purchase not scripts, but intellectual property in the form of television series, comics, books, games, blogs, graphic novels and toys. They buy up these for exploitation across a variety of platforms. In this environment, a single high-profile author is seen as a guarantee of quality across the various elements of a transmedia project.[4] Budgets climb to dizzying heights. In the summer of 2013, Hollywood studios released 13 films with individual budgets of over $100 million aimed at the international blockbuster market. In an attempt to attract the highest possible global audiences, committees will pore over the scripts, often demanding wildly conflicting story elements.[5] Their focus is entirely on financial outcomes – art has been edited out of the picture. Will this play in the cinemas of North America, China (the two largest markets) and the rest of the world? While a few of these blockbusters will succeed at the box office, most will fail.

In the next level down, script development processes shape screenplays into preexisting templates primarily designed to meet the needs of industrial film production. Along the way, a plethora of well-meaning consultants and advisors assist in eroding the distinctive qualities of works, reader's report by reader's report, draft-by-draft. Increasingly, data reports on previous similar screenplays that have performed well at the box office play a part. Reports generated by entities such as the Worldwide Motion Picture Group reduce scripts to data. Although vast numbers of feature-length 'speculative screenplays' are developed around the globe, studios purchase only around 100 of them each year. An ancillary industry of infotainment seminars, consultancies and how-to-write-a-screenplay manuals is arguably where more viable, long-term careers are actually forged. Far more people earn a living advising the writers of speculatively written screenplays than do the writers themselves. The industrial models are focused on maximising profits for their backers. In this extraordinarily wasteful system, countless hours of human labour and creativity and vast amounts of resources are simply not factored into the equation. This is one problem that simply paying a carbon tax offset on the flights of celebrity actors and executives will not solve. This method of writing and producing scripts is unsustainable.

Write for production

Fortunately, there are alternatives emerging. Alternatives that place writing for the screen within a smaller-scale, collaborative arts ecology. As digital technologies and processes allow more writers and filmmakers to produce work with high production values more inexpensively, there has been a dramatic increase in the number of low-budget features, nonfiction and hybrid works produced outside traditional funding structures. The new screen storytelling is transnational. Writers and filmmakers who have long been at the forefront of innovation in screen media – such as Agnès Varda, Abbas Kiarostami and Guy Maddin – have emerged as some of the spokespersons for this new digital cinema. More and more, screen storytellers are working across cinema, television and gallery contexts. Across art forms and in multiple roles. A plethora of script formats is emerging that combine images, sound and text, or in which other works act as *avant* texts or *ghost* texts. Increasingly, screenwriting (and theatre) are becoming more genuinely collaborative as people write for *specific* contexts and production parameters. Howard Shalwitz, Artistic Director of independent theatre company Woolly Mammoth, described this as a shift from *script* development to *production* development.[6]

Multimodal writing

Increasingly, we write with images, sound and text. There is a shift to multimodal texts that combine a complex interplay of written text, images and graphic elements. While user-controlled navigation was once emphasised as the key to interactivity, we now take a broader view. In this new environment, one aspect of interactivity is the arrangement of words, images and sounds within a given text. Screens have not replaced pages: both are being transformed. We increasingly communicate via images and photography in a digital environment that serves as 'an initial recording, a preliminary script'.[7] Photography can be seen as a new form of writing.

I began with a long list of screenwriting practices. It included prototyping, designing, adapting, remixing, reenacting, photographing (or writing with light), collaborating, composing and improvising. I added some more along the way. Ultimately, though, I discovered that there are two key practices: improvising and composing. And most projects involve both.

Writing as accretion

The term accretion, often applied to writing, can be usefully applied to screenwriting. Accretion is 'a process of gathering, evaluating and piecing together elements, materials, emotions and desires, as a way of giving expression to the world of the story'.[8] Novelist Nelson Algren compared writing to making pictures. Over many drafts and revisions, he built up the surface of his stories like a painter until he had found the right emotional register.[9] On other occasions, he compared his process of producing endless drafts to 'the slow geological layering that shapes mountains and continents over millennia'.[10] In an especially resonant insight, essayist and nature writer Richard Mabey says that the densest, richest, most ancient landscapes are the opposite of a palimpsest in which each layer of writing is obliterated by the next. Just as earlier formations are visible in landscapes, the traces of earlier writing shine through and influence what comes later.[11]

Spatial stories

Spatial stories enact our struggles to possess, transverse or access spaces. They cross and organise spaces, select and link them together. Spatial stories can be loosely structured since they do not depend on narrative progression or character development to engage us. They explore *worlds*.[12] Perhaps most importantly, stories go ahead of social practice to open up new fields.

Co-lateral spaces

Agnès Varda, Guy Maddin, Lucy Alibar and Benh Zeitlin, Jean-Pierre and Luc Dardenne, Shaun Tan, Matthew Porterfield, Rahmin Bahrani and Milkyway Image are just some of the contemporary screen storytellers who write to their own briefs. Seeking to understand their scripting and production processes, I found myself returning again and again to the work of sociologists and social psychologists who study groups, and the insights of those who write about the theory and practice of jazz music and photography. Minimal structures bring projects alive. Improvisation is not simply a means of generating script material or working with nonprofessional actors, but is a method of organising and making sense of experience. Whatever you care to call it – organisational improvisation, *adhocism* or *bricolage* – sustainable screenwriting embraces the ethos of 'making do' and repurposing whatever is at hand with a vengeance. As art forms, jazz and photography challenge the traditional distinction between structures and process, ideas and their execution.

Sustainable screenwriters work in co-lateral spaces. The co-lateral spaces that foster improvisation exist side-by-side with principal spaces and provide a way of rehearsing new strategies that fall outside the participants' usual roles. Co-lateral spaces tend to be occupied by smaller groups since they promote direct communication and hence collaboration. In the new screen media ecology, ensembles, collectives, cooperatives and collaboratives are all flourishing. They are part of what I would term *sustainable screenwriting*. Improvisation is a key creative practice in sustainable screenwriting just as organisational improvisation is the preferred means of organising.

Collaborating with the past

A key aspect of our digital era is that we can access the past more easily via digitised archives, databases and online sites. In Guy Maddin's evocative term, we collaborate with the past. Writing increasingly involves 'writing back' to the stories of other cultures and eras and the digital screenwriter is deeply versed in the practices of a number of art forms. We never start with a clean slate. 'The site on which we build is always cluttered: the past layers are visible in the present in which the future tries to take root.'[13]

Workshops, ateliers and cooperation

The idea of the workshop or laboratory as spaces for fostering the development of ideas, skills and cooperation resonates throughout the work of the writers and filmmakers whose work I have discussed in *Screenwriting in a Digital Era*. Agnès Varda's process is that of an artisan working in her *atelier* while Errol Morris's discovery-driven method of testing ideas and technologies has the rigour of a research scientist in his laboratory. Shaun Tan and Passion Pictures' script and production development process for *The Lost Thing* brought together a small team who collaborated from their respective sites in London and Melbourne via digital transfers and uploads. Court 13, a collective of artists and designers who collaborated with Benh Zeitlin and Lucy Alibar on *Beasts of the Southern Wild*, could be described as what Zygmunt Bauman called a *neo-tribe*. Rather than simply clinging together in search of community and coherence, though, Court 13 realised a complex script and production with limited resources, forging a new collective methodology that resulted in an Academy Award-winning feature.

Scandar Copti and Yaron Shani's workshop was the streets of the Jaffa suburb where they wrote and shaped their crime drama *Ajami* in a seven-year long collaboration with local residents. Small films are not in any way small in their artistic or intellectual ambition.

I found Richard Sennett's study of the resurgence of the craftsman in the new economy particularly illuminating. In the Middle Ages, the craftsman's workshop was a small, face-to-face place of work containing, at most, a dozen people. Much like contemporary small screen and arts companies, workshops struggled to stay afloat. In the medieval era, apprentices undertook seven years' regular bench-work in a workshop; just as it is recommended today that anyone learning a professional skill-set dedicate 10,000 hours to deliberate practice. A workshop or *atelier* was a place of absorbed concentration. In an analogue version of contemporary networks, collections of workshops in a given field were organised as guilds. They facilitated introductions and fostered a sense of community for workers on the move. 'Workshops present and past have glued people together through work rituals; whether these be through a shared cup of tea or the urban parade, through mentoring... through face-to-face sharing of information.'[14] The workshop was a space where people work together cooperatively.

We do not simply learn from our mistakes, asserts Richard Sennett, challenging what he considers an oversimplification of creative process. Any work process has to 'dwell temporarily in mess – wrong moves, false starts, dead ends... in technology, as in art, the probing craftsman does more than encounter mess; he or she creates it as a means of understanding working procedures'.[15] As he or she produces work, the craftsperson (or writer or filmmaker) engages in a dialectical process. He or she tries to head in a particular direction, steers off course and corrects their route. Over and over again – until this method is written in the body. 'The confidence to recover from error is a learned skill.'[16] As Shaun Tan, writer and director of *The Lost Thing*, says, making art is guided by questions rather than answers, as we 'amass a series of often accidental and mysterious ideas'.[17] Jazz theorist Ted Gioia's term 'provocative competence' suggests something similar for experienced artists. Improvising jazz musicians deliberately set out to move beyond ingrained patterns and habits.[18]

A manifesto for sustainable screenwriting

In that spirit, if I had to sum up the insights gleaned from these writers and filmmakers into a manifesto, it would go something like this:

1. Reject script development in favour of production development. Research. Produce. Release. Find the collaborators with whom you wish to work and begin working towards production from the very beginning.
2. Think small. Resist unnecessary resources and funds that will co-opt your project and steer it towards overly familiar ways of doing things.
3. Think big. Embrace big ideas and creative and intellectual ambition.
4. Write for place. Decide on a setting for your script and write for it. It can be a room, an abandoned building, a street – or a wilderness.
5. Use what you have. Grab any low-hanging fruit.
6. Embrace constraints – imposed, incidental or accidental.
7. Collaborate. Screenwriters are collaborators involved in every aspect of designing and executing the screen idea. Accept nothing less.
8. Embrace provocative competence. Challenge yourself to work outside the zone where you feel comfortable.
9. Work both on and off 'the grid'. Use social networks to mobilise people and resources. But work 'off the grid' to foster deep reflection.
10. Develop prototypes. Work quick and dirty. Your script can be a map, sketches, photo-texts, a wiki, a list, scenes that form part of a jigsaw, a graphic novel, a video trailer, a short film – whatever works.
11. Recycle everything – ideas and resources. Adopt adhocism, bricolage, and improvisation.
12. Cast your net wider. Have more projects on the go at any one time. An evolving network of enterprises maximises the chances of accidental discoveries. Write and collaborate for other art forms.

13. A film should never be able to be summed up in a topic sentence.
14. Remember: life is infinitely richer than most of the stories told by the cinema.

As though it were a river

I am going to give writer, critic and visual artist John Berger the last word – I cannot find a better definition of sustainable screenwriting than to borrow his definition of drawing. Drawing and writing are provisional; they are processes of discovery.

> A line, an area of tone, is not really important because it records what you have seen, but because of what it will lead you on to see ... Each mark you make on the paper [or screen, I would add] is a stepping stone from which you proceed to the next, until you have crossed your subject as though it were a river, have put it behind you.[19]

Notes

Introduction

1. *Parklands*, directed by Kathryn Millard (1996; Sydney: Magnolia Pacific, 2003), DVD.
2. *Travelling Light*, directed by Kathryn Millard (2003; Sydney: Magna Pacific, 2003), DVD.
3. Brooks Barnes, 'Solving Equation of a Hit Film Script, With Data', *The New York Times* (5 May 2013), http://www.nytimes.com/2013/05/06/business/media/solving-equation-of-a-hit-film-script-with-data.html?page wanted=all&_r=0.
4. Andrew Boone, 'Modern Movie Magic', *Popular Science* (May 1936), pp. 29–32.
5. *Follow the Fleet*, directed by Mark Sandrich (1936; Los Angeles: Universal Pictures, 2005), DVD.
6. *Top Hat*, directed by Mark Sandrich (1935; Los Angeles: Universal Pictures, 2005), DVD.
7. Tino Balio, *Grand Design: Hollywood as a Modern Business Enterprise 1930–1939* (Berkeley: University of California Press, 1995), p. 222.
8. *The Boot Cake*, directed by Kathryn Millard (2008; Sydney: Ronin Films, 2009), DVD.
9. *Random 8*, directed by Kathryn Millard (2012; Sydney: Ronin Films, 2013), DVD.
10. Charles Musser, *The Emergence of Cinema: The American Screen to 1907*, vol. 1 (Berkeley: University of California Press, 1994), p. 16.
11. Ken Dancyger and Jeff Rush, *Alternative Scriptwriting: Successfully Breaking the Rules* (Burlington: Focal Press, 2007), pp. 17–18.
12. Austin E. Quigley, *The Modern Stage and Other Worlds* (London: Methuen, 1985), p. 70.
13. Musser, *The Emergence of Cinema*, p. 1.
14. Ibid.
15. See Erkki Huhtamo, 'Natural Magic: A Short Cultural History of Moving Images' in *The Routledge Companion to Film History*, ed. William Guynn (Abingdon: Routledge, 2011), pp. 3–9.
16. Musser, *The Emergence of Cinema*, pp. 17–19.
17. Ibid., pp. 42–3.
18. See Erkki Huhtamo, 'Screen Tests: Why Do We Need an Archeology of the Screen?', *Cinema Journal* 51, no. 2 (2012): pp. 144–8.
19. Jean-Claude Carrière, *The Secret Language of Film* (New York: Pantheon, 1994).
20. Jean-Pierre Geuens, *Film Production Theory* (Albany: State University of New York Press, 2000).

21. J. J. Murphy, *Me and You and Memento and Fargo: How Independent Screenplays Work* (New York: Continuum, 2007); J. J. Murphy, *The Black Hole of the Camera: The Films of Andy Warhol* (Berkeley: University of California Press, 2012).
22. Paul Wells, *Basics Animation 01: Scriptwriting* (Lausanne: AVA Publishing, 2007).
23. Adam Ganz, ' "Leaping Broken Narration": Ballads, Oral Storytelling and the Cinema' in *Storytelling in World Cinemas*, vol. 1: Forms, vol. 1, ed. Lina Khatib (New York: Chicago University Press, 2012), pp. 71–89.
24. See Adrian Martin, 'Making a Bad Script Worse: The Curse of the Scriptwriting Manual', *Australian Book Review* (April 1999): pp. 23–6; Adrian Martin, 'There's a Million Stories, and a Million Ways to Get There from Here', *Metro Magazine* (October 2004): pp. 82–90.
25. Adrian Martin, 'Where Do Cinematic Ideas Come From?', *Journal Of Screenwriting* , Vol. 5, Number 1, 1 March 2014, pp. 9–26(18).
26. Theodor Adorno, 'The Essay as Form' in *Notes to Literature*, vol. 1, ed. Rolf Tiedemann, trans. Shierry Weber Nicholsen (New York: Columbia University Press, 1991), pp. 3–23.
27. John Berger, *And Our Faces, My Heart, Brief as Photos* (London: Bloomsbury, 2005), p. 8.
28. Pamela Cohn, 'Rotating Constellations', *Bomblog* (blog) (9 October 2012), http://bombsite.com/issues/1000/articles/6855.

1   The Picture Storytellers: From Pad to iPad

1. See Siegfried Zielinski, *Deep Time of the Media: Toward an Archaeology of Hearing and Seeing by Technical Means*, trans. Gloria Custance (Cambridge: MIT Press, 2008).
2. Philip Pullman, 'The Challenge of Retelling Grimms' Fairy Tales', *The Guardian* (22 September 2012), http://www.guardian.co.uk/books/2012/sep/21/grimms-fairy-tales-philip-pullman.
3. *The Boot Cake,* directed by Kathryn Millard (2008; Sydney: Ronin Films, 2009), DVD.
4. *Sanjog,* directed by Abdul Rashid Kardar (1942; Concord: Samrat International, 2000), DVD.
5. *The First National Collection,* directed by Charles Chaplin (1923; Los Angeles: Image, 2000), DVD.
6. Monahar Varapande, *History of Indian Theatre: Classical Theatre* (New Delhi: Abhinav Publications, 2005), p. 115.
7. Govind Nihalani, Gulzar and Saibal Chatterjee, eds., *Encyclopaedia of Hindi Cinema* (New Delhi: Encyclopaedia Britannica (India), 2003), pp. 313–4.
8. Priyanka Jain, 'Syd Field: How to Make Your Own Movie', *Rediff News* (11 January 2007), http://www.rediff.com/getahead/2007/jan/11syd.htm.
9. *The Great Dictator,* directed by Charles Chaplin (1940; New York: Criterion, 2011), DVD.
10. Quoted in Victor Shklovsky, *Literature and Cinematography*, trans. Irina Masinovsky (Champaign: Dalkey Archive Press, 2008), p. 64.

11. *The Gold Rush*, directed by Charles Chaplin (1926; New York: Criterion, 2012), DVD.
12. Adam Ganz, 'Time, Space and Movement: Screenplay as Oral Narrative', *Journal of Screenwriting* 1, no. 2 (2010): pp. 225–36.
13. Richard Rorty, ed., *The Linguistic Turn: Essays in Philosophical Method* (Chicago: University of Chicago Press, 1992), p. 49.
14. Arthur W. Frank, *Letting Stories Breathe: A Socio-Narratology* (Chicago: University of Chicago Press, 2010), p. 2.
15. Virginia Woolf, 'A Sketch of the Past' (1939) in *Moments of Being: Unpublished Autobiographical Writings*, ed. Jeanne Schulkind (London: Chatto and Windus for Sussex University Press, 1976), p. 98.
16. Victor H. Mair, *Painting and Performance: Chinese Picture Recitation and Its Indian Genesis* (Honolulu: University of Hawaii Press, 1988), p. 98.
17. *Beasts of the Southern Wild*, directed by Ben Zetlin (2012; Los Angeles: Fox Searchlight, 2012), DVD.
18. See Mair, *Painting and Performance*, pp. 123–7.
19. Ibid., pp. 111–32.
20. Ibid., p. 11.
21. Ashoka Da Ranade, *Hindi Film Song: Music Beyond Boundaries* (New Delhi: Promilla & Co., 2006), p. 75.
22. Bhagwan Das Garga, *So Many Cinemas: The Motion Picture in India* (Mumbai: Eminence Designs, 1996), pp. 10–11.
23. Ibid.
24. Ashish Rajadhyaksha and Paul Willemen, *Encyclopedia of Indian Cinema* (New Delhi: BFI and Oxford University Press, 1994), p. 17.
25. Garga, *So Many Cinemas*, pp. 12–13.
26. Kirin Narayan, *Storytellers, Saints and Scoundrels: Folk Narrative in Hindu Religious Teaching* (Philadelphia: University of Pennsylvania Press, 1989), p. 257.
27. Amitabh Sengupta, *Scroll Paintings of Bengal: Art in the Village* (Bloomington: AuthorHouse, 2012), p. 9.
28. Manohar Laxman Varadpande, *History of the Indian Theatre: Classical Theatre*, vol. 3 (New Delhi: Abhinav, 2005), p. 49.
29. Ikumi Kaminishi, *Explaining Pictures* (Honolulu: University of Hawaii Press, 2006), p. 156.
30. Om Prakash Joshi, *Painted Folklore and Folklore Painters of India: A Study with Reference to Rajasthan* (New Delhi: Concept Publishers, 1976), pp. 29–32.
31. Manohar Varadpande, *History of the Indian Theatre: Panorama of Folk Theatre*, vol. 2 (New Delhi: Abhinav, 1992), p. 116.
32. Sengupta, *Scroll Paintings of Bengal*, p. 33.
33. William Mason and Sandra Martin, *The Art of Omar Khayyam* (London: I.B. Tauris, 2007).
34. Richard Abel, *Encyclopedia of Early Cinema* (New York: Routledge, 2005), p. 587.
35. Muhammed Badawi, *A Critical Introduction to Modern Arabic Poetry* (Cambridge: Cambridge University Press, 1975), p. 329.
36. Bruce Elder, *Harmony and Dissent: Film and Avant-Garde Art Movements in the Early Twentieth Century*, vol. 3 (Waterloo: Wilfred Laurier University Press, 2008), p. 97.

37. Li Guo, *The Performing Arts in Medieval Islam: Shadow Play and Popular Poetry in Ibn Daniyal's Mamluk Cairo*, vol. 93 (Leiden: Brill, 2011), p. 95.
38. Ibid., p. 93.
39. Ibid., p. 95.
40. Elder, *Harmony and Dissent*, pp. 96–7.
41. Lotte Reiniger, *Shadow Theatre and Shadow Plays* (London: Batsford, 1970), p. 16.
42. John Gassner and Edward Quinn, eds., *The Reader's Encyclopedia of World Drama* (Mineola: Dover, 2002), p. 393.
43. Reiniger, *Shadow Theatre*, p. 29.
44. Gonul Donmez-Colin, ed., *The Cinema of North Africa and the Middle East* (London: Wallflower, 2007), pp. 7–8.
45. Terri Ginsberg and Chris Lippard, *Historical Dictionary of Middle-Eastern Cinema* (Lanham: Scarecrow Press, 2010), p. 405.
46. Quoted in Jubin Hu, *Projecting A Nation: Chinese National Cinema Before 1949* (Hong Kong: HKU Press, 2003), p. 31.
47. Yingjin Zhang, *Chinese National Cinema* (New York: Routledge, 2004), pp. 50–1.
48. Zhang Zhen, *An Amorous History of the Silver Screen: Shanghai Cinema 1896–1937* (Chicago: University of Chicago Press, 2005), pp. 132–4.
49. George Stephen Semsel, Hong Xia and Jianping Hou, eds., *Chinese Film Theory: A Guide to the New Era* (New York: Praeger, 1990), p. 195.
50. Zhen, *An Amorous History*, pp. 161–4.
51. Ibid., p. 98.
52. Mair, *Painting and Performance*, pp. 114–15.
53. See Eric Nash, *Manga Kamishibai: The Art of Japanese Paper Theatre* (New York: Abrams, 2009).
54. Tze-Yue G. Hu, *Frames of Anime: Culture and Image-Building* (Hong Kong: HKU Press, 2010), p. 100.
55. See Robert S. Peterson, *Comics, Manga and Graphic Novels: A History of Graphic Narratives* (Santa Barbara: ABC-CLIO, 2011).
56. Hu, *Frames of Anime*, pp. 42–5.
57. Mair, *Painting and Performance*, p. 14.
58. A wide range of forms of storytelling in Japan were known as etoki or 'explanation by picture'. They are thought to date back to the Heian period (749–1185). See Mair, *Painting and Performance*, p. 111.
59. Mair, *Painting and Performance*, p. 114.
60. Barbara A. Biesecker and John Louis Lucaites, eds., *Rhetoric, Materiality, and Politics*, vol. 13 (New York: Peter Lang, 2009), p. 140.
61. Stanley Hochman, *McGraw-Hill Encyclopedia of World Drama*, vol. 1 (New York: McGraw Hill, 1984), p. 50.
62. See Anne-Marie Christin, *A History of Writing*, 2nd ed. (Paris: Flammarion, 2002).

2 Post Courier 12

1. *Travelling Light*, directed by Kathryn Millard (2003; Sydney: Magna Pacific, 2003), DVD.

2. For a discussion of protagonists in classic Hollywood scripts versus those of independent film, see Ken Dancyger and Jeff Rush, *Alternative Scriptwriting: Successfully Breaking the Rules* (Burlington: Focal Press, 2007).
3. Abraham Maslow, *Religion, Values, and Peak-Experiences* (New York: Viking, 1970), p. 92.
4. Ron Burnett, 'Atom Egoyan: An Interview', *Film Views* 16 (Spring 1988) (Text accessible online at http://www2.cruzio.com/~akreyche/aeai1.html).
5. Kathryn Millard, 'Writing for the Screen: Beyond the Gospel of Story', *Scan: Journal of Media Arts Culture* 3, no. 2 (2006).
6. J. J. Murphy, *Me and You and Memento and Fargo: How Independent Screenplays Work* (New York: Continuum, 2007), p. 266.
7. Noelle Janaczewska, 'That Development Sceptic Again', *outlier-nj* (blog) (27 July 2008), http://outlier-nj.blogspot.co.uk/2008_07_01_archive.html.
8. Ian Macdonald, 'Disentangling the Screen Idea', *Journal of Media Practice* 5, no. 2 (2004): pp. 89–100.
9. Lewis Hyde, *The Gift: Creativity and the Artist in the Modern World* (London: Vintage, 2007), p. 187.
10. Mike Ware, 'John Herschel's Cyanotype: Invention or Discovery?', *History of Photography* 22, no. 4 (1998): pp. 371–9.
11. Macdonald, 'Disentangling the Screen', p. 91.
12. Ibid.
13. Walter Murch, 'A Digital Cinema of the Mind? Could Be', *The New York Times* (2 May 1999), http://www.nytimes.com/library/film/050299future-film.html.
14. Macdonald, 'Disentangling the Screen', p. 91.
15. The Academy of Motion Picture Arts and Science, 'Screenwriting Resources – Formatting Tips', http://www.oscars.org/awards/nicholl/resources.html, accessed 1 July 2013.
16. Tom Vanderbilt, 'Courier Dispatched', *Slate* (20 February 2004), http://www.slate.com/id/2095809/.
17. Jesse Lasky quoted in Marc Norman, *What Happens Next: A History of American Screenwriting* (London: Aurum, 2008), p. 193.
18. Vanderbilt, 'Courier Dispatched'.
19. For a discussion of the relationship between the self help industry and the screenwriting template see Millard, 'Writing for the Screen'.
20. Vera John-Steiner, *Notebooks of the Mind: Explorations of Thinking*, 2nd ed. (Oxford: Oxford University Press, 1997), pp. 128–9.
21. Jean-Pierre Geuens, 'The Space of Production', *Quarterly Review of Film and Video* 24, no. 5 (2007): p. 413.
22. For discussion of the systems theory of creativity see Howard Gruber, 'The Evolving Systems Approach to Creative Work' in *Creative People at Work: Twelve Cognitive Case Studies*, ed. Howard Gruber and Doris Wallace (Oxford: Oxford University Press, 1989), pp. 3–24.
23. Edward Douglas, 'EXCL: Guy Maddin's Brand Upon the Brain!', *ComingSoon.net* (9 May 2007), http://www.comingsoon.net/news/movienews.php?id=20244.
24. Ibid.
25. Keith Sawyer, *Group Genius: The Creative Power of Collaboration* (New York: Basic Books, 2007), p. 170.

26. Ibid., p. 169.

27. Andrea Ketchner, 'Screenwriter Jim Taylor Talks Comics', *The Student Life* (3 March 2006), http://www.tsl.pomona.edu/index.php?article=1371, accessed 3 August 2009.

28. Ibid.

29. Paul Wells, *Basics Animation 01: Scriptwriting* (Lausanne: Ava Publishing, 2007).

30. Rocco Versaci, *This Book Contains Graphic Language: Comics as Literature* (New York: Continuum, 2007), p. 11.

31. Ibid., p. 13.

32. Ibid., p. 14.

33. Jon J. Muth, *M: A Graphic Novel Based on the Film by Fritz Lang* (New York: Harry N. Abrams, 2008).

34. John-Steiner, *Notebooks of the Mind*, p. 109.

35. Kevin Alexander Boon, *Script Culture and the American Screenplay* (Detroit: Wayne State University Press, 2008).

36. Andrew Gay, 'Notes UFVA Presentation', *Screenplayology: An Online Center for Screenplay Studies* (blog) (20 August 2008), http://www.screenplayology.com/2011/08/20/notes-on-ufva-presentation/.

37. Adam Ganz, 'Play from Slide Show: PowerPoint, Screenwriting, and Writing on Screen'. Presented at Screenwriting in a Global and Digital World, 6th Screenwriting Research Network International Conference in Madison, 2013.

38. For more discussion of *District 9* and alternatives to the industrial screenplay, see Kathryn Millard, 'The Screenplay as Prototype' in *Analysing the Screenplay*, ed. Jill Nelmes (Abingdon: Routledge, 2011), pp. 142–56.

39. Jay Fernandez, 'Evolution of a Screenwriter', *Hollywood Reporter* (24 July 2008), http://www.hollywoodreporter.com/news/evolution-a-screenwriter-116289.

40. Ibid.

41. Quoted in Will Straw, 'Reinhabiting Lost Languages: Guy Maddin's *Careful*' in *Canada's Best Features: Critical Essays on 15 Canadian Films*, ed. Eugene P. Walz (Amsterdam: Rodopi, 2002), p. 313.

42. Henry Jenkins and David Thorburn, eds., *Rethinking Media Change: The Aesthetics of Transition* (Cambridge: MIT Press, 2003), p. x.

43. Richard Koman, 'Remixing Culture: An Interview with Lawrence Lessig', *O'Reilly* (24 February 2005), http://www.oreillynet.com/pub/a/policy/2005/02/24/lessig.html.

44. Jean-Pierre Geuens, *Film Production Theory* (Albany: State University of New York Press, 2000), pp. 82–3.

3 The New Three Rs of Digital Writing: Record, Reenact and Remix

1. Quoted in David Trend, *The End of Reading: From Gutenberg to Grand Theft Auto* (New York: Peter Lang, 2010), p. 137.

2. Mary Carruthers, *The Book of Memory: A Study of Memory in Medieval Culture* (Cambridge: Cambridge University Press, 1990), p. 12.

3. Roland Barthes, *Image, Music, Text* (London: Fontana Press, 1977), p. 146.
4. See Jay David Bolter, *Writing Space: Computers, Hypertext, and the Remediation of Print* (Hillsdale: Lawrence Erlbaum, 1991).
5. Gunther Kress and Theo van Leeuwen, *Reading Images: The Grammar of Visual Design* (Abingdon: Routledge, 2006), p. 17 (emphasis added by author).
6. Gunther Kress, *Literacy in the New Media Age* (London: Routledge, 2003), p. 5.
7. See Gunther Kress, *Learning to Write*, 2nd ed. (London: Routledge, 1994).
8. Patrice Pavis, *Dictionary of the Theatre: Terms, Concepts and Analysis* (Toronto: University of Toronto Press, 1998), pp. 60–1.
9. Ibid.
10. *Sweetgrass*, directed by Lucien Castaing-Taylor and Ilisa Barbash (2009; New York: Cinema Guild, 2010), DVD.
11. Lucien Castaing-Taylor, 'Director Lucien Castaing-Taylor on the making of Sweetgrass', *The Arts Desk* (23 April 2011), http://www.theartsdesk.com/film/director-lucien-castaing-taylor-making-sweetgrass.
12. Ibid.
13. Patricia Aufderheide, *Documentary Film: A Very Short Introduction* (Oxford: Oxford University Press, 2007), pp. 44–9.
14. Ibid.
15. Quoted in Yael Zarhy-Levo, *The Making of Theatrical Reputations* (Iowa City: University of Iowa Press, 2008), p. 45.
16. Joram ten Brink, *Building Bridges: The Cinema of Jean Rouch* (London: Wallflower, 2007).
17. Jean Rouch, *Ciné-Ethnography*, vol. 13 (Minneapolis: University of Minnesota Press, 2003), p. 267.
18. Paul Henley, *The Adventure of the Real: Jean Rouch and the Craft of Ethnographic Filmmaking* (Chicago: University of Chicago Press, 2009), p. 268.
19. Errol Morris, 'Truth Not Guaranteed: An Interview with Errol Morris', *Cineaste* 17, no. 1 (1989): pp. 16–17.
20. Anna Grimshaw and Amanda Ravetz, *Observational Cinema: Anthropology, Film, and the Exploration of Social Life* (Bloomington: University of Indiana Press, 2009), p. 65.
21. Ibid., p. 82.
22. Lucien Castaing-Taylor, '*Sweetgrass*: On Shooting an American Elegy', *Arts Desk* (14 April 2011), http://www.theartsdesk.com/film/sweetgrass-shooting-american-elegy.
23. Mark Feeney, 'A Very Different Kind of Western: Following the Final Sheep Drive in Montana', *The Boston Globe* (28 March 2010), http://www.boston.com/yourtown/newton/articles/2010/03/28/sweetgrass_filmmakers_talk_about_documentaries_the_intersection_of_journalism_and_anthropology_and_some_of_their_new_films_subjects_sheep/.
24. Ibid.
25. Jay Kuehner, 'Keeper of Sheep Lucien Castaing-Taylor on Sweetgrass', *Cinema Scope* (Winter 2010), http://cinema-scope.com/cinema-scope-magazine/1107/.
26. Robert Koehler, 'Agrarian Utopias/Dystopias: The New Nonfiction', *Cinema Scope* (Fall 2009), http://cinema-scope.com/features/features-agrarian-utopiasdystopias-the-new-nonfiction/.

27. Charles Mahoney, ed., *A Companion to Romantic Poetry*, vol. 73 (Chichester: Wiley Blackwell, 2011), p. 167.
28. *Leviathan*, directed by Lucian Castaing-Taylor and Verena Paravel (2012; New York: Cinema Guild, 2013), DVD.
29. Hilary Weston, 'A Conversation with "Leviathan" Directors Lucien Castaing-Taylor & Vérena Paravel', *BlackBook* (27 February 2013), http://www.blackbookmag.com/movies/a-conversation-with-leviathan-directors-lucien-castaing-taylor-v'‰C3‰A9rena-paravel-1.59202.
30. Koehler, 'Agrarian Utopias/Dystopias'.
31. Ibid.
32. Timothy Corrigan, *The Essay Film: From Montaigne, After Marker* (Oxford: Oxford University Press, 2011), p. 197.
33. *Nanook of the North*, directed by Robert J. Flaherty (1922; New York: Criterion, 1999), DVD.
34. *Stories from the North*, directed by Uruphong Raksasad (2006; Bangkok: Extra Virgin, 2010), DVD.
35. Kong Rithdee, 'Uruphong Raksasad: Self Sufficiency Filmmaking', *Bangkok Post* (27 October 2006), http://www.criticine.com/feature_article.php?id=34.
36. Ibid.
37. Endel Tulving, *Elements of Episodic Memory* (Oxford: Oxford University Press, 1985).
38. Rouch, *Ciné-Ethnography*, p. 267.
39. Laura Tunbridge, *The Song Cycle* (Cambridge: Cambridge University Press, 2010), p. 3.
40. *Sunrise: A Song of Two Humans* Photoplay, directed by F. W. Murnau (1927; Los Angeles: Fox Films, 2009), DVD.
41. Jean-Pierre Geuens, *Film Production Theory* (Albany: State University of New York Press, 2000), p. 90.
42. *Agrarian Utopia*, directed by Uruphong Raksasad (2009; Bangkok: Extra Virgin, 2011), DVD.
43. R. Emmet Sweeney, 'Robert Flaherty Seminar 2010, Part 1: Unseen Labor', *Notebook* (21 July 2010), http://mubi.com/notebook/posts/robert-flaherty-seminar-2010-part-1-unseen-labor.
44. Uruphong Raksasad, *Agrarian Utopia Director's Statement*, http://www.filmfestival.be/pressfiles/Agrarian‰20Utopia.pdf, accessed 22 July 2013.
45. *Patience (After Sebald)*, directed by Grant Gee (2012; New York: Cinema Guild, 2012), DVD.
46. W. G. Sebald, *The Rings of Saturn* (London: Random House, 1998).
47. Pamela Cohn, 'Rotating Constellations', *Bomblog* (blog) (9 October 2012), http://bombsite.com/issues/1000/articles/6855.
48. Damon Smith, 'Grant Gee – Patience (After Sebald)', *Filmmaker* (9 May 2012), http://filmmakermagazine.com/45517-grant-gee-patience-after-sebald/.
49. *Patience (After Sebald)*, directed by Grant Gee (2012; New York: Cinema Guild, 2012), DVD.
50. Phillip Lopate, 'In Search of the Centaur: The Essay-Film' in *Beyond Document: Essays on Non-Fiction Film*, ed. Charles Warren (Middletown: Wesleyan University Press, 1996), p. 245.
51. Cohn, *Bomblog*.

52. Lise Pratt and Christel Dillbohner, eds., *Searching for Sebald: Photography After W.G. Sebald* (Los Angeles: Institute of Cultural Inquiry, 2007), p. 104.
53. Ibid., p. 23.
54. Cohn, 'Rotating Constellations'.
55. Lawrence Lessig, *Remix: Making Art and Commerce Thrive in the Hybrid Economy* (New York: Penguin, 2008), p. 69.
56. *My Winnipeg*, directed Guy Maddin (2007; Montreal: Seville Pictures, 2008), DVD.
57. Personal correspondence with Guy Maddin, June 2012.
58. *Walking from Munich to Berlin*, directed by Oskar Fischinger (1927; Los Angeles: CVM, 2006), DVD.
59. Oskar Fischinger, 'CVM's Fischinger Pages', *Center for Visual Music*, http://www.centerforvisualmusic.org/Fischinger/OFFilmnotes.htm, accessed 5 August 2013.
60. 'How Guy Maddin Found His Winnipeg', *The Globe and Mail* (11 May 2009), http://www.theglobeandmail.com/arts/how-guy-maddin-found-his-winnipeg/article4273398/?page=all.
61. Guy Maddin, *My Winnipeg* (Toronto: Coach House Books, 2009), p. 6.
62. Ibid.
63. *Keyhole*, directed by Guy Maddin (2011; Thousand Oaks: Monterey Media, 2012), DVD.
64. Guy Maddin, 'Guy Maddin', *Dream the End* (2008), http://www.dreamtheend.com/#/?cat=171.
65. Personal communication (2012).
66. Gaston Bachelard, *The Poetics of Space*, trans. M. Jolas (Boston: Beacon Press, 1994).
67. Personal communication (2012).
68. William Beard, *Into the Past: The Cinema of Guy Maddin* (Toronto: University of Toronto Press, 2010), p. 284.
69. Ibid.
70. Personal communication (2012).
71. Michael Temple and James Williams, eds., *The Cinema Alone: Essays on the Work of Jean-Luc Godard 1985–2000* (Amsterdam: University of Amsterdam Press, 2010), p. 34.
72. Dziga Vertov, *Kino-Eye: The Writings of Dziga Vertov*, trans. Kevin O'Brien (Berkeley: University of California Press, 1984), p. 199.
73. *Three Songs of Lenin*, directed by Dziga Vertov (1934; Los Angeles: Image Entertainment, 2000), DVD.
74. Vertov, *Kino-Eye*, p. 199.
75. Ibid., p. 120.

4 14 Lessons on Screenwriting from Errol Morris

1. Lawrence Weschler, 'Errol Morris, Forensic Epistemologist', *Public Books* (18 June 2012), http://www.publicbooks.org/interviews/errol-morris-forensic-epistemologist.
2. Errol Morris, 'The Making of *The* Thin Blue Line 1/2', *YouTube*, http://www.youtube.com/watch?v=2xa2CiiPJt8, accessed 12 July 2013.

3. *The Thin Blue Line*, directed by Errol Morris (1988; Los Angeles: MGM, 2005), DVD.

4. *The Fog of War: Eleven Lessons from the Life of Robert S. McNamara*, directed by Errol Morris (2003; Los Angeles: Sony Pictures, 2004), DVD.

5. *Standard Operating Procedure*, directed by Errol Morris (2008; Los Angeles: Sony Pictures, 2008), DVD.

6. Richard Koman, 'Remixing Culture: An Interview with Lawrence Lessig', *O'Reilly Network* (2005), http://www.oreillynet.com/policy/2005/02/24/lessig.html.

7. Howard Gruber, 'The Evolving Systems Approach to Creative Work' in *Creative People at Work: Twelve Cognitive Case Studies*, ed. Howard Gruber and Doris Wallace (Oxford: Oxford University Press, 1989), pp. 3–24.

8. Howard Gruber, 'Network of Enterprise in Creative Scientific Work' in *Creativity, Psychology and the History of Science*, ed. Howard E. Gruber and Katja Bödeker (Dordrecht: Springer, 2005), p. 103.

9. *Man with a Movie Camera*, directed by Dziga Vertov (1929; London: BFI, 2000), DVD.

10. *Land Without Bread*, directed by Luis Bunuel (1928; New York: Kino, 2000), DVD.

11. *Psycho*, directed by Alfred Hitchcock (1960; Los Angeles: Universal Pictures, 2003), DVD.

12. Mark Singer, 'Errol Morris Profile', *The New Yorker* (6 February 1989), http://www.errolmorris.com/content/profile/singer_predilections.html.

13. *Gates of Heaven*, directed by Errol Morris (1978; Los Angeles: MGM, 2005), DVD.

14. *Vernon, Florida*, directed by Errol Morris (1981; Los Angeles: MGM, 2005), DVD.

15. Errol Morris, 'Harvard Book Store', errolmorris.com/content/lecture/brattle.html, accessed 20 July 2013.

16. Singer, 'Errol Morris Profile'.

17. Simon Ings, *The Eye: A Natural History* (London: Bloomsbury, 2008), p. 134.

18. Gruber, 'Network of Enterprise', p. 254.

19. Vera John Steiner, *Notebooks of the Mind: Explorations of Thinking* (Oxford: Oxford University Press, 1997), p. 112.

20. *The Thin Blue Line*, directed by Errol Morris (1988; Los Angeles: MGM, 2005), DVD.

21. Errol Morris, 'Thin Blue Line: Synopsis', http://www.errolmorris.com/film/tbl.html, accessed 20 July 2013.

22. Eric Kohn, 'Errol Morris: "The Thin Blue Line" Would Not Have Saved Randall Adams Today', *Indiewire* (15 July 2011), http://www.indiewire.com/article/interview_errol_morris_the_thin_blue_line_would_not_have_saved_randall_adam.

23. Errol Morris, 'Play it Again, Sam: Re-enactments Part 1', *New York Times* (3 April 2008), http://opinionator.blogs.nytimes.com/2008/04/03/play-it-again-sam-re-enactments-part-one/.

24. Rebecca Pahle, 'My Golden Rules: Errol Morris', *Moviemaker* (15 September 2011), http://www.moviemaker.com/?s=Errol+Morris%2C+My+Golden+Rule.

25. David Bordwell, 'Errol Morris: Boy Detective', *David Bordwell's Website on Cinema* (4 November 2010), http://www.davidbordwell.net/blog/2010/11/04/errol-morris-boy-detective/.

26. Carlo Ginzburg, 'Clues: Roots of an Evidential Paradigm' in *Clues, Myths, and the Historical Method*, trans. John Tedeschi and Anne C. Tedeschi (Baltimore: Johns Hopkins University Press, 1989), p. 102.

27. Errol Morris, 'Werner Herzog in Conversation with Errol Morris', *The Believer* (March/April 2008), http://www.believermag.com/issues/200803/?read=interview_herzog.

28. Taylor Segrest, 'Career Achievement Award: The Cinematic Investigations of Errol Morris', *Documentary.org* (Winter 2010), http://www.documentary.org/content/career-achievement-award-cinematic-investigations-errol-morris.

29. Morris, 'Werner Herzog'.

30. Nicolas Rapold, 'Errol Morris Interview Uncut', *Film Comment* (27 June 2011), http://www.filmcomment.com/article/errol-morris-interview.

31. Roy Grundmann and Cynthia Rockwell, 'Truth Is Not Subjective: An Interview with Errol Morris', *Cineaste* 25, no. 3 (Summer 2000), p. 4.

32. Brad Schreiber, 'Errol Morris: Writing the Documentary in Your Head', *Absolute Write*, http://www.absolutewrite.com/screenwriting/errol_morris.htm, accessed 5 July 2013.

33. Keith Phipps, 'Errol Morris', *The Onion* (9 December 1997), http://www.avclub.com/articles/errol-morris,13493/.

34. 'The Morris Microscope', *Creativeplanetnetwork.com*, http://www.creativeplanetnetwork.com/dcp/reviews/morris-microscope/15220, accessed 5 July 2013.

35. Emanuel Levy, 'Standard Operating Procedure: Conversation with Errol Morris', *Cinema* 24/7, http://www.emanuellevy.com/interview/standard-operating-procedure-conversation-with-errol-morris-9/, accessed 6 August 2013.

36. Mongrel, 'Standard Operating Procedure: Press Kit', http://www.mongrelmedia.com/press_info/?id=1458, accessed 6 August 2013.

37. Geoffrey Macnab, 'Return to Abu Ghraib', *The Guardian* (19 February 2008), http://www.theguardian.com/film/2008/feb/19/iraq.

38. Mongrel, 'Standard Operating Procedure', p. 6.

39. Segrest, 'Career Achievement Award'.

40. Morris, 'Play It Again, Sam'.

41. Segrest, 'Career Achievement Award'.

42. Ibid.

43. Errol Morris, 'Interview with the Believer', *The Believer*, errolmorris.com/content/interview/believer0404.html, accessed 20 July 2013.

44. David Shields, *Reality Hunger: A Manifesto* (New York: Penguin Group, 2010).

45. Errol Morris, *Believer Magazine*, http://www.believermag.com/issues/200404/?read=interview_morris, accessed 20 July 2013.

46. Errol Morris, 'The Anti-Post-Modern Post-Modernist', http://www.errolmorris.com/content/lecture/theantipost.html, accessed 20 July 2013.

47. Elizabeth F. Loftus, *Eyewitness Testimony* (Cambridge: Harvard University Press, 1996).

48. 'The Morris Microscope'.

49. John Kusiak, 'John Kusiak – Film Composer for Errol Morris', Podcast, *PRX*, http://www.prx.org/pieces/67291-john-kusiak-film-composer-for-errol-morris, accessed 6 August 2013.

50. Kate Slininger, ' "There Are No Rules" – On Errol Morris', *Tumblr* (8 February 2012), http://kateslininger.tumblr.com/post/17305950016/there-are-no-rules-on-errol-morris.

51. Errol Morris, 'Which Came First? The Chicken or the Egg?', *The New York Times* (25 September 2007), http://opinionator.blogs.nytimes.com/2007/09/25/which-came-first-the-chicken-or-the-egg-part-one/.

52. 'In the Valley of the Shadow of Doubt', *Radiolab*, http://www.radiolab.org/2012/sep/24/in-the-valley-of-the-shadow-of-doubt/, accessed 13 January 2013.

53. Errol Morris, 'The Umbrella Man', *The New York Times* (21 November 2011), http://www.nytimes.com/2011/11/22/opinion/the-umbrella-man.html?_r=0.

54. Joshua Thompson, *Six Seconds in Dallas: A Micro-Study of the Kennedy Assassination* (New York: B. Geis, 1967).

55. *Stranger Than Paradise*, directed by Jim Jarmusch (1984; New York: Criterion, 2007), DVD.

56. *District 9*, directed by Neill Blomkamp (2009; Los Angeles: Sony Pictures, 2009), DVD.

57. See Kathryn Millard, 'Screenplay as Prototype' in *Analysing the Screenplay*, ed. Jill Nelmes (Abingdon: Routledge, 2011), pp. 142–57.

58. Jess Thorn, 'Errol Morris, Director of "Tabloid": Interview on The Sound of Young America', *Bullseye* (18 August 2011), http://www.maximumfun.org/sound-young-america/errol-morris-director-tabloid-interview-sound-young-america.

5 Adaptation: Writing as Rewriting and *The Lost Thing*

1. *The Lost Thing*, directed by Shaun Tan (2010; Richmond: Madman, 2010), DVD.

2. Raúl Ruiz, *Poetics of Cinema*, vol. 2 (Paris: Editions Dis Voir, 2007).

3. Salman Rushdie, *Haroun and the Sea of Stories* (London: Granta, 1991), p. 86.

4. *Random 8*, directed by Kathryn Millard (2012; Sydney: Ronin Films, 2013), DVD.

5. *Parklands*, directed by Kathryn Millard (1996; Sydney: Magnolia Pacific, 2003), DVD.

6. *Travelling Light*, directed by Kathryn Millard (2003; Sydney: Magna Pacific, 2003), DVD.

7. See Dotson Rader, 'Tennessee Williams, The Art of Theater No. 5', *The Paris Review* (Fall 1981), http://www.theparisreview.org/interviews/3209/the-art-of-theater-no-5-tennessee-williams.

8. Two sponsored documentaries produced for the South Australian Housing Trust in the 1960s. Clips appear in my 1996 film *Parklands*. Such productions are usually called ephemeral films.

9. Thomas Schatz, 'New Hollywood, New Millennium' in *Film Theory and Contemporary Hollywood Movies*, ed. Warren Buckland (New York: Taylor and Francis, 2009), p. 33.

10. Linda Hutcheon, *A Theory of Adaptation*, 2nd ed. (Abingdon: Routledge, 2012), p. 8.

11. Arthur W. Frank, *Letting Stories Breathe: A Socio-Narratology* (Chicago: University of Chicago Press, 2010), p. 9.

12. Keith Stuart, 'SuperMes and the Idea of Emergent Drama', *The Guardian* (7 February 2012), http://www.guardian.co.uk/technology/gamesblog/2012/feb/06/super-mes-and-emergent-drama.

13. Ted Hodgkinson, 'Interview: Ben Lerner', *Granta* (9 July 2012), http://www.granta.com/New-Writing/Interview-Ben-Lerner.

14. *Harishchandrachi Factory*, directed by Paresh Mokashi (2009; Los Angeles: Disney, 2010), DVD.

15. *Raja Harishchandra*, directed by Dadasaheb Phalke (1913; Pune: National Film Archive of India, 2012), DVD.

16. Bijoya Baruah Rajkhowa, 'Oral Tradition of the Ramayana in North East India' in *Critical Perspectives on the Ramayana*, ed. Jaydipsinh Dodiya (New Delhi: Sarup, 2001), p. 132.

17. Maksim Gorky cited in Emmanuelle Toulet, *Cinema is 100 Years Old* (London: New Horizons/Thames and Hudson, 1998), pp. 132–3.

18. K. Moti Gokulsing and Wimal Dissanayake, *Routledge Handbook of Indian Cinemas* (Abingdon: Routledge, 2013), p. 73.

19. Christopher Pinney, *'Photos of the Gods': The Printed Image and Political Struggle in India* (London: Reaktion, 2004), pp. 71–2.

20. See Roy Armes, *Third World Filmmaking and the West* (Berkeley: University of California Press, 1987), p. 106.

21. Moore quoted in Hutcheon, *A Theory of Adaptation*, p. xxv.

22. Christa Albrecht-Crane and Dennis Cutchins, *Adaptation Studies: New Approaches* (Madison: Fairleigh Dickinson University Press, 2010), p. 15.

23. Ibid., p. 18.

24. Pierre Bayard, *How to Talk About Books You Haven't Read* (New York: Bloomsbury, 2007), p. 73.

25. Victor Burgin, *The Remembered Film* (London: Reaktion, 2004), pp. 8–9.

26. The film no longer exists. Fragments can be seen on, *History of Australian Cinema: The Pictures That Moved, Part 1*, directed by Alan Anderson (1968; Collingwood: Artfilms, 2004), DVD. See also the NFSA collection note at http://www.nfsa.gov.au/collection/documents-artefacts/soldiers-cross/.

27. Frank Barrett, 'Coda: Creativity and Improvisation in Jazz and Organizations: Implications for Organizational learning', *Organization Science* 9, no. 5 (1998): p. 605.

28. *The Lost Thing*, directed by Shaun Tan (2010; Richmond: Madman, 2010), DVD.

29. Lillian Darmono, 'The Lost Thing: Interview with Shaun Tan', *Motionographer* (19 January 2011), http://motionographer.com/2011/01/19/the-lost-thing-interview-with-shaun-tan/.

30. Quoted by Karl Weick in 'Improvisation as a Mindset for Organizational Analysis' in *Organizational Improvisation*, ed. Miguel Pina e Cunha, João Vieira da Cunha and Ken Kamoche (London: Routledge, 2004), p. 53.

31. Shaun Tan, 'Picture Books: Who Are They For?', http://www.shauntan.net/essay1.html, accessed 7 August 2013.
32. Ibid.
33. Ibid.
34. Ralph Yarrow, *Indian Theatre: Theatre of Origin, Theatre of Freedom* (Richmond: Curzon, 2001), p. 69.
35. Tan, 'Picture Books'.
36. Karl Weick, *Sensemaking in Organizations* (Thousand Oaks: Sage, 1995), p. 64.
37. See 'About the Directors' section of the website for *The Lost Thing*, www.thelostthing.com, accessed 15 July 2013.
38. Darmono, 'The Lost Thing'.
39. Ibid.
40. Tan, 'Picture Books'.
41. Personal communication (2012).
42. Frank, *Letting Stories Breathe*, p. 37.
43. Personal communication (2012).
44. Cunha et al., *Organizational Improvisation*, p. 5.
45. Barrett, '*Coda:* Creativity and Improvisation', pp. 611–2.
46. Cunha et al., *Organizational Improvisation*, p. 120.
47. Personal communication (2012).
48. Keith Sawyer, *Group Genius: The Creative Power of Collaboration* (New York: Basic Books, 2007), pp. 62–3.
49. State Library of Victoria, 'Shaun Tan Tells Us About The Lost Thing', *YouTube*, http://www.youtube.com/watch?v=q5Ia-AHzxbM, accessed 12 July 2013.
50. Personal communication (2012).
51. Frank, *Letting Stories Breathe*, p. 37.

6   Degrees of Improvisation

1. Kathryn Millard, 'Writing for the Screen: Beyond the Gospel of Story', *Scan: Journal of Media Arts Culture* 3, no. 2 (2006).
2. J. J. Murphy, 'No Room for The Fun Stuff: The Question of the Screenplay in American Indie Cinema', *Journal of Screenwriting* 1, no. 1 (2010): p. 176.
3. Ibid.
4. See Dennis Lim, 'A Generation Finds Its Mumble', *The New York Times* (19 August 2007), http://www.nytimes.com/2007/08/19/movies/19lim.html?pagewanted=all&_r=0.
5. Damon Smith, 'Andrew Bujalski: Interview', *Sensesofcinema* (2007), http://sensesofcinema.com/2007/feature-articles/andrew-bujalski-interview/.
6. *Shoeshine*, directed by Vittorio De Sica (1946; Toronto: Entertainment One, 2011), DVD.
7. *Bicycle Thieves*, directed by Vittorio De Sica (1948; New York: Criterion, 2007), DVD.
8. *Putty Hill*, directed by Matthew Porterfield (2006; New York: Cinema Guild 2011), DVD.
9. *Man Push Cart*, directed by Ramin Bahrani (2005; New York: Noruz Films, 2007), DVD.

10. Hazel Smith and Roger Dean, *Improvisation, Hypermedia and the Arts since 1945* (Amsterdam: Harwood Academic Publishers, 1997), p. 276.
11. Ibid., p. 25.
12. Bruno Nettl as cited in Aaron Berkowitz, 'Introduction', in *The Improvising Mind: Cognition and Creativity in the Musical Moment*, ed. Gabriel Solis and Bruno Nettle (Oxford: Oxford University Press, 2010), p. 4.
13. Karl Weick, 'Improvisation as a Mindset for Organizational Analysis', *Organization Science* 9, no. 5 (1998): pp. 543–55.
14. Hamid Naficy, *A Social History of Iranian Cinema*, vol. 2 (Durham: Duke University Press, 2011), p. 213.
15. Ibid., pp. 213–4.
16. Bruno Nettl, 'On Learning the Radif and Improvisation in Iran' in *Musical Improvisation: Art, Education and Society*, eds. Gabriel Sollis and Bruno Nettl (Champaign: University of Illinois Press, 2009), p. 185.
17. David Shields, *Reality Hunger: A Manifesto* (London: Penguin, 2010), p. 1.
18. A. O. Scott, 'Neo-Neo Realism', *The New York Times* (17 March 2009), http://www.nytimes.com/2009/03/22/magazine/22neorealism-t.html?page wanted=all.
19. Ibid.
20. Ibid.
21. Richard Brody, 'About "Neo-Neo Realism"', *The New Yorker* (20 March 2009), http://www.newyorker.com/online/blogs/movies/2009/03/in-re-neoneorea.html.
22. David Bordwell, 'Neo-neo and All That', *David Bordwell's Website On Cinema*, http://www.davidbordwell.net/blog/2009/05/03/getting-real/, accessed 12 May 2013.
23. Michael Rowin, 'An Interview with Ramin Bahrani', *Reverse Shot* 24, http://www.reverseshot.com/article/interview_ramin_bahrani, accessed 12 May 2013.
24. Arthur W. Frank, *Letting Stories Breathe: A Socio-Narratology* (Chicago: University of Chicago Press, 2010), p. 22.
25. Robert McKee, *Story: Substance, Structure, Style, and the Principles of Screenwriting* (New York: HarperCollins, 1997), p. 62.
26. Ibid., p. 46.
27. Bert Cardullo, *Soundings on Cinema* (Albany: SUNY Press, 2011), p. 26.
28. Mikael Colville-Andersen, 'The Storytellers: Interview with Suso Cecchi-d'Amico, Screenwriter', *EuroScreenwriter*, http://zakka.dk/euroscreenwriters/screenwriters/suso_cecchi_damico.htm, accessed 12 May 2013.
29. Scott, 'Neo-Neo Realism'.
30. Robert Gordon, *Bicycle Thieves* (London: British Film Institute, 2008), p. 16.
31. Beno Weiss, *Italo Calvino* (Columbia: University of Southern Carolina Press, 1993), pp. 9–19.
32. Cesare Zavattini, 'Some Ideas on The Cinema', *Sight and Sound* 23, no. 2 (1953): pp. 64–9.
33. Cesare Zavattini, *Sequences from a Cinematic Life* (Upper Saddle River: Prentice Hall, 1970), pp. 9–10.
34. Ibid., p. 9.
35. *Shoeshine*, directed by Vittorio De Sica (1946; Toronto: Entertainment One, 2011), DVD.

36. Zavattini, 'Some Ideas', pp. 64–9.
37. Cardullo, *Soundings on Cinema*, p. 28.
38. *The Battle of The Rails*, directed by Rene Clement (1946; Chicago: Facets, 2006), DVD.
39. Luigi Bartolini, *Bicycle Thieves: The Story of a Stolen Bicycle in Rome* (London: MacMillan, 1952).
40. See P. Adams Sitney, *Vital Crises in Italian Cinema: Icongraphy, Stylistics, Politics* (New York: Oxford University Press, 2013), p. 83.
41. Gordon, *Bicycle Thieves*, p. 25.
42. Ibid., pp. 25–6.
43. Zavattini, 'Some Ideas', p. 6.
44. Cardullo, *Soundings on Cinema*, p. 29.
45. Karetnikova Inga, *How Scripts Are Made* (Carbondale: SIU Press, 1990), p. 125.
46. *The White Balloon*, directed by Jafar Panahi (1995; Los Angeles: PolyGram, 1996), DVD.
47. Gordon, *Bicycle Thieves*, p. 31.
48. See Walter J. Ong, *Orality and Literacy* (London: Routledge, 2002), p. 146 (emphasis added by author).
49. David Bordwell, 'The Art Cinema as a Mode of Film Practice' in *The European Cinema Reader*, ed. Catherine Fowler (London: Routledge, 2002), p. 96.
50. Frank Tomasulo, 'Re-reading Bicycle Thieves' in *Vittorio De Sica: Contemporary Perspectives*, ed. Stephen Synder and Howard Curle (Toronto: University of Toronto Press, 2000), p. 163.
51. Kristin Thompson, *Breaking the Glass Armor: Neoformalist Film Analysis* (Princeton: Princeton University Press, 1998), pp. 214–6.
52. Scott, 'Neo-neo Realism'.
53. Robert Stam and Randal Johnson, *Brazilian Cinema* (New York: Columbia University Press, 1997), p. 394.
54. Robert Stam, *Flagging Patriotism* (London: Routledge, 2007), p. 56.
55. Alberto Elena and Maria Diaz Lopez, *The Cinema of Latin America* (London: Wallflower Press, 2003), p. 90.
56. Kathryn Millard, 'A Screenwriter's Hunger Reality'. Presented at the Nonfiction Now Conference at RMIT, Melbourne, November 2012.
57. See Zavattini, 'Some Ideas', pp. 64–9.
58. See Mark Shiel, *Italian Neorealism: Rebuilding the Cinematic City* (London: Wallflower Press, 2006), p. 12.
59. Paul Berliner, *Thinking in Jazz* (Chicago: University of Chicago, 1997), p. 1.
60. Ibid., p. 15.
61. Colville-Andersen, 'The Storytellers'.
62. Berliner, *Thinking in Jazz*, p. 17.
63. Zavattini, 'Sequences from a Cinematic', p. 1.
64. Putty Hill Press Kit, 'Synopsis', http://puttyhillmovie.com, accessed 12 May 2013.
65. Personal communication (2013).
66. Ibid.
67. Personal communication, 2013 (For a history of the MacGuffin plot device, see *Screenonline.org*, http://www.screenonline.org.uk/tours/hitch/tour6.html).

68. *The Exiles*, directed by Kent MacKenzie (1961; New York: Milestone Films, 2009), DVD.
69. *The Exiles*, Press Kit, http://www.exilesfilm.com/ExilesPK.pdf, accessed 12 May 2013.
70. Ibid.
71. Ibid.
72. Personal communication (2013).
73. Hamilton Film Group, unpublished pitch document *Metal Gods*, 2008.
74. Ibid.
75. Personal communication (2013).
76. J. J. Murphy, 'Scripting on the Fly: Matthew Porterfield's Putty Hill'. Presented at the University Film and Video Conference Association, US, 2012.
77. Personal communication (2013).
78. Matthew Porterfield, unpublished scenario for *Putty Hill*, 2008.
79. Gaston Bachelard, *Poetics of Reverie* (Boston: Beacon Press, 1971).
80. Matthew Porterfield unpublished selling document for *Metal Gods*.
81. John Hopkins University, 'A Different Point of View', http://webapps.jhu.edu/jhuniverse/featured/matthew_porterfield/, accessed 12 May 2013.
82. Personal communication (2013).
83. David Bordwell, 'Art Is Not Reality; One of the Damned Things Is Enough', *David Bordwell's Website on Cinema* (3 May 2009), http://www.davidbordwell.net/blog/2009/05/03/getting-real/.
84. *Hamilton*, directed by Matthew Porterfield (2006; New York: Cinema Guild, 2011), DVD.
85. *I Used To Be Darker*, directed by Matthew Porterfield (2013).
86. Personal communication (2013).
87. *Man Push Cart* Press Kit, http://goodwithfilm.com/library/ambassadors/presskit_manpushcart_v2.pdf, accessed 12 May 2013.
88. *Man Push Cart* Press Kit.
89. Ibid.
90. Scott, 'Neo-Neo Realism'.
91. Richard Porton, 'A Sense of Place: An Interview with Ramin Bahrani', *Cineaste* (Spring 2008), http://www.cineaste.com/articles/an-interview-with-ramin-bahrani.htm.
92. Roberto Rossellini and Adriano Aprà, *My Method: Writings and Interviews* (New York: Marsilio Publishers, 1995), p. 19.
93. Porton, 'A Sense of Place'.
94. Jason Chan, 'Interview with Ramin Bahrani', *Flavorwire* (27 March 2009), http://flavorwire.com/15731/interview-with-goodbye-solo-director-ramin-bahrani.
95. Rossellini and Aprà, *My Method: Writings*, p. 14.
96. Ibid., p. xvi.
97. Ibid., p. 39.
98. Ibid., p. 35.
99. Bert Cardullo, *Michelangelo Antonioni: Interviews* (Jackson: University Press of Mississippi, 2008), p. 48.
100. Ed Templeton, *The Seconds Pass* (New York: Seems, 2010), Introduction.

101. A. O. Scott, 'A.O. Scott Responds to New Yorker Blog on the Value and Definition of Neo-Realism', *The New York Times* (23 March 2009), http://carpetbagger.blogs.nytimes.com/2009/03/23/ao-scott-responds-to-a-new-yorker-blogger-about-the-value-and-definition-of-neo-realism/.

7 Improvising Reality

1. *Ajami*, directed by Scandar Copti and Yaron Shani (2009; New York: Kino, 2010), DVD.
2. Scandar Copti and Yaron Shani, 'Ajami', Unpublished Screenplay, 1 January 2007.
3. *Ajami* Press Kit, http://www.kinolorber.com/data/presskit/ajami_pressbook.pdf, accessed 28 April 2012.
4. *Bicycle Thieves*, directed by Vittorio de Sica (1948; New York: Criterion, 2007), DVD.
5. *The Exiles*, directed by Kent Mackenzie (1961; London: British Film Institute, 2010), DVD.
6. *Kes*, directed by Ken Loach (1969; New York: Criterion, 2011), DVD.
7. *Nashville*, directed by Robert Altman (1975; Los Angeles: Paramount, 2000), DVD.
8. *Putty Hill*, directed by Matthew Porterfield (2006; New York: Cinema Guild, 2011), DVD.
9. *Man Push Cart*, directed by Ramin Bahrani (2005; New York: Noruz Films, 2007), DVD.
10. *Ajami* Press Kit.
11. Dan Heath and Chip Heath, *Made to Stick: Why Some Ideas Take Hold and Others Come Unstuck* (London: Random House, 2007), pp. 204–37.
12. See Jonathan Gottschall, *The Storytelling Animal: How Stories Make Us Human* (New York: Houghton Mifflin Harcourt, 2012).
13. Arthur W. Frank, 'Enacting Illness Stories' in *Stories and their Limits: Narrative Approaches to Bioethics'*, ed. Hilde Lindemann Nelson (London: Routledge, 1997), p. 43.
14. See Arthur W. Frank, *Letting Stories Breathe: A Socio-Narratology* (Chicago, Chicago University Press, 2010).
15. Cesare Zavattini, 'Some Ideas on the Cinema' in *Vittorio De Sica: Contemporary Perspectives*, eds. Stephen Snyder and Howard Curle (Toronto: University of Toronto Press, 2000), p. 224.
16. *Ajami* Press Kit.
17. See Yvette Biro, *Turbulence and Flow in Film: The Rhythmic Design* (Bloomington: Indiana University Press, 2008), p. 52.
18. Linda Aronson, *The 21st Century Screenplay: A Comprehensive Guide to Writing Tomorrow's Films* (Crows Nest: Allen &Unwin, 2010), p. 172.
19. Aronson, *The 21st Century*, p. 174.
20. Horace quoted by Walter J. Ong, *Orality and Literacy* (New York: Routledge, 2002), p. 139.
21. *Ajami*, directed by Scandar Copti and Yaron Shani (2009; New York: Kino, 2010), DVD.

22. *Ajami* Press Kit.
23. Personal communication (2012).
24. Ibid.
25. Dominic Radcliffe, 'Scandar Copti', *Little White Lies* (10 February 2011), http://www.littlewhitelies.co.uk/features/articles/scandar-copti-13791.
26. Scandar Copti and Rabih Boukhary, 'The Truth', *YouTube*, http://www.youtube.com/watch?v=VjQt11CcgwY, accessed 10 July 2013.
27. *Bus 174*, directed by Jose Padhila and Felipe Lacerda (2002; Albert Park: Accent, 2004), DVD.
28. *Ajami* Press Kit.
29. Bert Cardullo, 'A Cinema of Social Conscience: An Interview with Ken Loach', *The Minnesota Review*, http://minnesotareview.dukejournals.org/content/2011/76/81, accessed 7 August 2013.
30. Kira Cochrane, 'Ken Loach: "The ruling class are cracking the whip"', *The Guardian* (29 August 2011), http://www.theguardian.com/film/2011/aug/28/ken-loach-class-riots-interview.
31. Simon Hattenstone, 'Interview: Ken Loach', *The Guardian* (28 October 1998), http://www.industrycentral.net/director_interviews/KL01.HTM.
32. Barry Hines, *A Kestrel for a Knave* (London: Penguin, 2010).
33. Julia Hallam, *Realism and Popular Cinema* (Manchester: Manchester University Press, 2000), p. 109.
34. Jacob Leigh, *The Cinema of Ken Loach: Art in the Service of the People* (London: Wallflower Press, 2002), p. 68.
35. Bert Cardullo, *World Directors in Dialogue: Conversations on Cinema* (Plymouth: Scarecrow Press, 2011), p. 241.
36. Ian Buruma, 'The Way They Live Now', *New York Review of Books* (13 January 1994), p. 7.
37. Bert Cardullo, *Loach and Leigh, Ltd.: The Cinema of Social Conscience* (Newcastle upon Tyne: Cambridge Scholars Publishing, 2010), p. 18.
38. Personal communication (2012).
39. Ibid.
40. Ibid.
41. 'The Making of Ajami', documentary extra in *Ajami*, directed by Scandar Copti and Yaron Shani (2009; New York: Kino, 2010), DVD.
42. Adam Blatner, *Foundations of Psychodrama: History, Theory and Practice* (New York: Springer, 2000), pp. 15–16.
43. A. Paul Hare and June Hare, *J.L. Moreno* (London: SAGE, 1996), pp. 13–16.
44. See Jacob Moreno, 'Psychodrama and Therapeutic Motion Pictures', *Sociometry* 7, no. 2 (1944): pp. 230–44.
45. Jacob Moreno, 'Therapeutic Theater', *YouTube*, http://www.youtube.com/watch?v=ok9Hb5m4r7E, accessed 30 July 2013.
46. Adrian Martin, 'Kind of a Revolution, and Kind of Not: Digital Low-Budget Cinema in Australia Today', *Scan* 3, no. 2 (2006).
47. J. J. Murphy, 'No Room for The Fun Stuff: The Question of the Screenplay in American Indie Cinema', *Journal of Screenwriting* 1, no.1 (2010): p. 181.
48. J. J. Murphy, *The Black Hole of the Camera: The Films of Andy Warhol* (Berkeley: University of California Press, 2012), p. 6.
49. Murphy, 'No Room for the Fun Stuff', 2009, p. 181.

50. Ronald Tavel in J. J. Murphy, *The Black Hole of the Camera*, p. 6.
51. Anna Shternshis, *Soviet and Kosher Jewish Popular Culture in the Soviet Union 1923–1939* (Bloomington: Indiana University Press, 2006), p. 78.
52. See Gary Dawson, *Documentary Theatre in the United States* (Westport: Greenwood, 1999), pp. 20–1; William Stott, *Documentary Expression and 1930s America* (Chicago: University of Chicago Press, 1986), pp. 106–9.
53. Howard Schneider, 'In Israel, Shahir Kabaha Moonlights as a Movie Star', *The Washington Post* (21 February 2010), http://articles.washingtonpost.com/2010-02-21/news/36776055_1_israeli-soldiers-shahir-kabaha-movie-star.
54. Personal communication (2012).
55. Donald Schön, *The Reflective Practitioner: How Professionals Think in Action* (New York: Basic Books, 1983), p. 132.
56. Frank Barrett, 'Coda – Creativity and Improvisation in Jazz and Organizations', *Organization Science* 9, no. 5 (1998): pp. 606–7.
57. Zavattini, 'Some Ideas', p. 59.
58. Cardullo, *World Directors*, p. 219.
59. David MacDougall, *The Corporeal Image: Film, Ethnography and the Senses* (Princeton: Princeton University Press, 2006), p. 50.
60. Ibid., p. 37.

8 Composing the Digital Screenplay

1. Alex Stewart, *Making the Scene: Contemporary New York City Big Band Jazz* (Berkley: University of California Press, 2007), p. 17.
2. Stephen Bull, *Photography* (Abingdon: Routledge, 2009), pp. 28–9.
3. Quoted in Sarah Kember, *Virtual Anxiety: Photography, New Technology and Subjectivity* (Manchester: Manchester University Press, 1998), p. 20.
4. Henri Cartier-Bresson, *The Mind's Eye: Writings on Photography and Photographers* (New York: Aperture, 1999), e-book.
5. Hollis Frampton, *On the Camera Arts and Consecutive Matters* (Cambridge: MIT Press, 2009), p. 46.
6. Fred Ritchin, *After Photography* (New York: W. W. Norton, 2009), pp. 17–18.
7. See Neil Campbell and Alfredo Cramerotti, eds., *Photocinema: Working at the Creative Edges of Photography and Film* (Bristol: Intellect, 2013).
8. Ritchin, *After Photography*, p. 18.
9. Laszlo Moholy-Nagy, 'From Pigment to Light (1936)' in *Photography in Print: Writings from 1816 to the Present*, ed. Vicki Goldberg (Albuquerque: University of New Mexico Press: 1981), p. 339.
10. *Do Right and Fear No-one*, directed by Jutta Brückner (1975; Mainz: ZDF).
11. Marc Silberman, 'Interview with Jutta Brückner: Recognising Collective Gestures', *Jump Cut*, no. 27 (1982): pp. 46–7.
12. Silberman, 'Interview with Jutta'.
13. *Wings of Desire*, directed by Wim Wenders (1987; New York: Criterion, 2003), DVD.
14. Wim Wenders, 'In Defense of Places', *DGA* (November 2003), http://www.dga.org/Craft/DGAQ/All-Articles/0311-Nov-2003/In-Defense-of-Places.aspx.

15. Martin Brady and Joanne Leal, *Wim Wenders and Peter Handke: Collaboration, Adaptation, Recomposition* (Amsterdam: Rodopi, 2011), p. 247.
16. *La Pointe Courte*, directed by Agnès Varda (1955; New York: Criterion, 2008), DVD.
17. Richard Neupert, *A History of the French New Wave* (Madison: University of Wisconsin Press, 2007), p. 330.
18. Ibid., p. 299.
19. *The Gleaners and I*, directed by Agnès Varda (2000; London: Artificial Eye, 2011), DVD.
20. *The Gleaners and I: Two Years Later*, directed by Agnès Varda (2002; London: Artificial Eye, 2011), DVD.
21. *The Beaches of Agnès*, directed by Agnès Varda (2008; London: Artificial Eye, 2010), DVD.
22. Agnès Varda quoted in Jacqueline Levitin, Valerie Raoul and Judith Plessis, eds., *Women Filmmakers: Refocusing* (Vancouver: University of British Columbia Press, 2003), p. 35.
23. *The Beaches of Agnès*, directed by Agnès Varda (2008; London: Artificial Eye, 2010), DVD.
24. Nicolas Donin, 'Empirical and Historical Musicologies of Compositional Processes: Towards a Cross-Fertilisation' in *The Act of Musical Composition: Studies in the Creative Process*, ed. Dave Collins (Farnham: Ashgate, 2012).
25. *The Gleaners and I*, directed by Agnès Varda (2000; London: Artificial Eye, 2011), DVD.
26. *The Gleaners and I* Press Kit, http://www.zeitgeistfilms.com/films/gleaners andi/presskit.pdf, accessed 7 August 2013.
27. John Berger, *About Looking* (London: Bloomsbury, 2009), p. 76.
28. Fred Kleiner, *Gardner's Art Through the Ages: A Global History* (Boston: Wadsworth, 2010), p. 800.
29. Alexandra Murphy, *Jean-François Millet: Drawn Into The Light* (New Haven: Yale University Press, 1999), pp. 75–7.
30. *The Gleaners and I* Press Kit.
31. Andrea Meyer, 'Interview: Gleaning the Passion of Agnès Varda', *Indiewire* (8 March 2001), http://www.indiewire.com/article/interview_gleaning_the_passion_of_agnes_varda_agnes_varda.
32. See Donin, 'Empirical and Historical'.
33. See pg. 96 in ANR, 'La Création Acteurs, Objets, Contextes' (12 October 2012), http://www.agence-nationale-recherche.fr/Colloques/Creation2012/Booklet-Colloque-ANR-Creation-2012.pdf.
34. David Warwick, 'The Beaches of Agnès: Interview with Agnès Varda', *Electric Sheep* (2 October 2009), http://www.electricsheepmagazine.co.uk/features/2009/10/02/the-beaches-of-agnes-interview-with-agnes-varda/.
35. Chuck Sack, 'Joan Tewkesbury on Screenwriting: An Interview', *Literature-Film Quarterly* 6, no. 1 (1978): pp. 2–25.
36. Ibid., p. 9.
37. Joan Didion, 'To The Islands' in *Live and Learn*, ed. Joan Didion (London: Harper Perennial, 2005), p. 293.
38. Sack, 'Joan Tewkesbury', p. 10.
39. Gabriel Solis and Bruno Nettl, eds., *Musical Improvisation: Art, Education and Society* (Champaign: University of Illinois Press, 2009), p. 119.

40. Bruno Nettl, *Excursions in World Music* (Upper Saddle River: Prentice Hall, 1997), p. 61.
41. Bert Cardullo, ' "The Fruitful Tree Bends": Abbas Kiarostami' in *Action!: Interviews with Directors from Classical Hollywood to Contemporary Iran*, ed. Gary Morris (London: Anthem Press, 2008), p. 303.
42. Ibid., p. 301.
43. See AFP, 'Repressive Regimes Help Forge Great Cinema: Iranian Director', *Al Arabiya News* (8 October 2011), http://www.alarabiya.net/articles/2011/10/08/170781.html.
44. Cardullo, ' "The Fruitful Tree Bends" ', p. 307.
45. Abbas Kiarostami, 'With Borrowed Eyes', *Film Comment* 36, no. 4 (2000): pp. 20–5.
46. Mehrnaz Saeed-Vafa and Jonathan Rosenbaum, *Abbas Kiarostami* (Champaign: University of Illinois Press, 2003), p. 72.
47. *ABC Africa*, directed by Abbas Kiarostami (2001; New York: New Yorker, 2005), DVD.
48. Cardullo, ' "The Fruitful Tree Bends" ', p. 315.
49. *Five Dedicated to Ozu*, directed by Abbas Kiarostami (2004; New York: New Yorker, 2007), DVD.
50. Saeed-Vafa and Rosenbaum, *Abbas Kiarostami*, p. 120.
51. Kiarostami on Making of *Five*, YouTube, http://www.youtube.com/watch?v=xu9cbCJKLs8, accessed 7 August 2013.
52. *10 on Ten*, directed by Abbas Kiarostami (2004; London: Artificial Eye, 2011), DVD.
53. Ibid.
54. Ibid.
55. Cardullo, ' "The Fruitful Tree Bends" ', p. 309.
56. Umberto Eco, *The Open Work* (Cambridge: Harvard University Press, 1989).
57. Hans-Thies Lehmann, *Postdramatic Theatre* (Abingdon: Routledge, 2006), p. 46.
58. Alex Munt, 'Digital Kiarostami and the Open Screenplay', *Scan* 3, no. 2 (2006).
59. Bruno Nettl, *The Radif of Persian Music: Studies of Structure and Cultural Context* (Champaign: Elephant and Cat, 1987), p. 12.
60. Hamid Naficy, *A Social History of Iranian Cinema*, vol. 2 (Durham: Duke University Press, 2011), p. 214.
61. Keith Uhlich, 'Kiarostami at MoMA', *Slant* (7 March 2007), http://www.slantmagazine.com/house/2007/07/kiarostami-at-moma-day-2-conversing-with-kiarostami.
62. Ibid.
63. Abbas Kiarostami, 'Abbas Kiarostami's Best Shot', *The Guardian* (30 July 2009), http://www.guardian.co.uk/artanddesign/2009/jul/29/photography-abbas-kiarostami-best-shot.
64. See 'Kiarostami Exhibition', *Iran Heritage*, http://www.iranheritage.org/kiarostamiexhibition/, accessed 28 July 2013.
65. Ibid.
66. Xan Brooks, 'Cannes 2012: Abbas Kiarostami: "The World Is My Workshop" ', *The Guardian* (29 May 2012), http://www.theguardian.com/film/2012/may/28/cannes-abbas-kiarostami-interview.

67. *Journey to the End of Coal*, directed by Samuel Bollendorff and Abel Segretin (2008; Honkytonk Films), Web Documentary, http://www.honkytonk.fr/index.php/webdoc/.
68. Samuel Bollendorff, *The Forced March* (Paris: Textual, 2008).
69. Olivier Laurent, 'From Photography to Web-documentaries: Samuel Bollendorff's *Nowhere Safe*', *British Journal of Photography* (14 March 2012), http://www.bjp-online.com/british-journal-of-photography/interview/21593 50/photography-web-documentaries-samuel-bollendorffs-safe.
70. *Journey to the End of Coal*, directed by Samuel Bollendorff and Abel Segretin (2008; Honkytonk Films), Web Documentary, http://www.honkytonk.fr/index.php/webdoc/.
71. Laurent, 'From Photography'.
72. Ibid.
73. Medhi Ahoudig and Samuel Bollendorff, *Nowhere Safe: A Web Documentary on Housing for the Poor in France*, directed by Medhi Ahoudig and Samuel Bollendorff (2012; Textuel La Mine), Web Documentary, http://www.samuel-bollendorff.com/en/a-labri-de-rien/.
74. Gunther Kress, *Literacy in the New Media Age* (London: Routledge, 2003).
75. Stewart, *Making the Scene*, p. 17.
76. Cardullo, ' "The Fruitful Tree Bends" '.
77. Fred Ritchin, *Bending the Frame: Photojournalism, Documentary and the Citizen* (New York: Aperture, 2013), p. 3.

9 Collaboration: Writing the Possible

1. See Karl E. Weick and Kathleen M. Sutcliffe, *Managing the Unexpected: Resilient Performance in an Age of Uncertainty* (San Fransisco: John Wiley & Sons, 2007).
2. Sans Facon, 'Collaboration as a Place You Don't Expect' (2009), http://www.sansfacon.co.uk/texts/collab.html.
3. Julie Salamon, *The Devil's Candy: The Anatomy of a Hollywood Fiasco* (Cambridge: Perseus Books, 2002), p. 77.
4. Charles Musser, *The Emergence of Cinema: The American Screen to 1907*, vol. 1 (Berkeley: University of California Press, 1994), p. 6.
5. David Bordwell, Janet Steiger and Kristin Thompson, *The Classical Hollywood Cinema: Film Styles and Modes of Production to 1960* (Oxon: Routledge, 2006), pp. 85–141.
6. Ibid., p. 134.
7. Simon Griffiths and Anthony Giddens, *Sociology* (Cambridge: Polity, 2006), p. 745.
8. Bordwell et al., *The Classical Hollywood*, p. 146.
9. Ibid., p. 145.
10. Ibid., pp. 137–8.
11. Ibid., p. 141.
12. See Ben Kafka, *The Demons of Paperwork* (New York: Zone Books, 2012).
13. David Foster Wallace, *Consider the Lobster: Essays and Arguments* (New York: Hatchette, 2012), p. x1x.
14. See Bordwell et al., *The Classical Hollywood*, pp. 378–85.
15. See Ibid., p. 383.

16. J. J. Murphy, *Me and You and Memento and Fargo: How Independent Screenplays Work* (New York: Continuum, 2007), p. 163.
17. See Jon Elster, *Ulysses Unbound: Studies in Rationality, Precommitment and Constraints* (Cambridge: University of Cambridge Press, 2000).
18. Mette Hjort, *Lone Scherfig's Italian for Beginners* (Seattle: University of Washington Press, 2010), p. 44.
19. Ibid., pp. 44–5.
20. Ibid., p. 52.
21. Ibid.
22. Karl E. Weick, *Sensemaking in Organizations* (Thousand Oaks: Sage, 1995), p. 166.
23. George P. Huber and William H. Glick, eds., *Organizational Change and Redesign: Ideas and Insights for Improving Performance* (Oxford: Oxford University Press, 1995), p. 374.
24. Weick, *Sensemaking in Organizations*, p. 166.
25. Hilary Weston, 'Academy Award Nominated Director Benh Zeitlin Opens Up About "Beasts of the Southern Wild"', *BlackBook* (10 January 2013), http://www.blackbookmag.com/movies/academy-award-nominated-director-benh-zeitlin-opens-up-about-beasts-of-the-southern-wild-1.56771.
26. *Beasts of the Southern Wild* Press Kit, http://www.festival-cannes.fr/assets/Image/Direct/045640.pdf, accessed 8 August 2013.
27. Patrick Kenis, Martyna Janowicz and Bart Cambre, eds., *Temporary Organizations: Prevalence, Logic and Effectiveness* (Northampton: Edward Elgar, 2009), p. 171.
28. Lucy Alibar, *Juicy and Delicious* (New York: Diversion Books, 2012).
29. Hilary Weston, 'Lucy Alibar on Adapting Her Stage Play into Beasts of the Southern Wild', *BlackBook* (28 June 2012), http://www.blackbookmag.com/movies/lucy-alibar-on-adapting-her-stage-play-into-beasts-of-the-southern-wild-1.50249.
30. *Beasts of the Southern Wild* Press Kit.
31. Edward Douglas, 'Interview: Taming the Beasts of a Southern Wild', *Comingsoon* (27 June 2012), http://www.comingsoon.net/news/movienews.php?id=91670.
32. Rebecca Murray, 'Exclusive Interview with "Beasts of the Southern Wild" Director Benh Zeitlin', *About.com*, http://movies.about.com/od/directorinterviews/a/benh-zeitlin-beasts-interview.htm, accessed 8 August 2013.
33. Colin Colvert, 'Beasts is a Wild Success', *StarTribune* (9 January 2013), http://www.startribune.com/entertainment/movies/161501585.html.
34. Ibid.
35. Charles Jencks and Nathan Silver, *Adhocism: The Case for Improvisation* (Cambridge: MIT Press, 2013), p. vii.
36. '"Beasts of the Southern Wild" Director Benh Zeitlin on Creating a Creative Utopia', *Creativeplanetnetwork.com* (20 August 2012), http://www.creativeplanetnetwork.com/videography/news/beasts-southern-wild-director-benh-zeitlin-creating-creative-utopia/60185.
37. David Bordwell, 'Mad Detective: Doubling Down', *David Bordwell's Website on Cinema* (November 2010), http://www.davidbordwell.net/essays/maddetective.php.

38. 'Interview Johnnie To', *Cinemasie*, http://www.cinemasie.com/en/fiche/dossier/332/, accessed 8 August 2013.
39. Personal communication (2012).
40. Ibid.
41. Ibid.
42. Aaron Gerow, *Kitano Takeshi* (London: British Film Institute, 2007), p. 37.
43. Personal communication (2012).
44. David Bordwell, 'Truly Madly Cinematically', *David Bordwell's Website on Cinema* (3 April 2008), http://www.davidbordwell.net/blog/2008/04/03/truly-madly-cinematically/.
45. Nick Dawson, 'Johnnie To, "Mad Detective"', *Filmmaker Magazine* (18 July 2008), http://filmmakermagazine.com/1325-johnnie-to-mad-detective/.
46. Berys Gaut, *A Philosophy of Cinematic Art* (Cambridge: Cambridge University Press, 2010), p. 134.
47. Holly Willis, *New Digital Cinema: Reinventing the Moving Image* (London: Wallflower Press, 2005), p. 42.
48. Miguel Cunha and Ken Kamoche, *Organizational Improvisation* (London: Routledge, 2004), p. 96.
49. Michael Chanan, *The Dream That Kicks: The Early Years and Pre-History of Cinema in Britain* (London: Routledge, 1994), p. 40.
50. Karl Weick, 'Organizational Redesign as Improvisation' in *Organizational Change and Redesign: Ideas and Insights for Improving Performance*, ed. George P. Huber and William H. Glick (New York: Oxford University Press, 1995), pp. 352–3.
51. Philip Mosley, *The Cinema of the Dardenne Brothers: Responsible Realism* (New York: Columbia University Press, 2013), p. 10.
52. Joseph Mai, *Jean-Pierre and Luc Dardenne* (Champaign: University of Illinois Press, 2010), p. 63.
53. Phillip Mosley, *The Cinema of the Dardenne Brothers* (New York: Columbia University Press, 2010).
54. Joseph Mai, *Jean-Pierre and Luc Dardenne*, p. 63.
55. Doug Cummings, 'Armand Gatti and *L'Enclos (1961)'*, *Film Journey* (27 May 2009), http://filmjourney.org/2009/05/.
56. Dorothy Knowles, *Armand Gatti in the Theatre: Wild Duck Against the Wind* (London: Athlene Press, 1989), p. 13.
57. Jonathan Romney, 'Home Truths', *The Guardian* (25 February 2000), http://www.guardian.co.uk/film/2000/feb/25/3.
58. Geoff Andrews, 'Luc and Jean-Pierre Dardenne', *The Guardian* (12 February 2006), http://www.guardian.co.uk/film/2006/feb/11/features.
59. Ibid.
60. Ibid.
61. Mai, *Jean-Pierre and Luc*, p. 41.
62. Andrews, 'Luc and Jean-Pierre'.
63. Ibid.
64. Mai, *Jean-Pierre and Luc*, p. 42.
65. Ibid., p. 64.
66. Ariston Anderson, 'The Dardenne Brothers: On Hard Work, Patience & Mentors', *99U*, http://99u.com/articles/6987/the-dardenne-brothers-on-hard-work-patience-mentors, accessed 8 August 2013.

Conclusion

1. See Zygmunt Bauman, *Liquid Times: Living in an Age of Uncertainty* (Cambridge: Polity, 2007).
2. Ian Berkitt, *Social Selves: Theories of Self and Society* (London: Sage, 2008), p. 177.
3. Richard Sennett, *The Craftsman* (London: Allen Lane, 2008).
4. See Henry Jenkins, *Convergence Culture: Where Old and New Media Collide* (New York: NYU Press, 2006).
5. Brooke Barnes, 'Solving Equation of a Hit Film Script, With Data', *The New York Times* (5 May 2013), http://www.nytimes.com/2013/05/06/business/media/solving-equation-of-a-hit-film-script-with-data.html.
6. Howard Shalwitz, 'Theatrical Innovation: Whose Job Is It?', *TCG Conference* (21 June 2012), http://qawww.woollymammoth.net/wp-content/uploads/2012/08/TCG-Speech-for-Publication1.pdf.
7. Fred Ritchin, *After Photography* (New York: W. W. Norton, 2010), p. 17.
8. Steven Maras, *Screenwriting: History, Theory and Practice* (London: Wallflower Press, 2009), p. 115.
9. Daniel Simon, 'Afterword' in *Nonconformity: Writing on Writing*, ed. Nelson Algren (New York: Seven Stories, 1996), p. 81.
10. Nelson Algren, Brooke Hovath and Dan Simons, *Entrapment* (New York: Seven Stories Press, 2011), p. 89.
11. Richard Mabey, *Nature Cure* (London: Pimlico, 2005), p. 40.
12. Michel de Certeau, *Arts de Faire*, vol. 1 (Berkeley: University of California Press, 2011), pp. 115–30.
13. Zygmunt Bauman, *Living on Borrowed Time: Conversations with Citlali Rovirosa Madrazo* (Cambridge: Polity, 2010).
14. Sennett, *The Craftsman*.
15. Ibid., p. 161.
16. Ibid., p. 160.
17. Shaun Tan, 'Picture Books: Who Are They For?', http://www.shauntan.net/essay1.html, accessed 7 August 2013.
18. Miguel Pina Cunha and Ken Kamoche, *Organizational Improvisation* (London: Routledge, 2004), p. 139.
19. John Berger, 'Drawing is Discovery', *The New Statesman* (1 May 2013), http://www.newstatesman.com/culture/art-and-design/2013/05/drawing-discovery.

Select Bibliography

10 on Ten. Directed by Abbas Kiarostami. 2004. London: Artificial Eye, 2011. DVD.

ABC Africa. Directed by Abbas Kiarostami. 2001. New York: New Yorker, 2005. DVD.

Abel, Richard. *Encyclopedia of Early Cinema.* New York: Routledge, 2005.

Adorno, Theodor. 'The Essay as Form'. Translated by Shierry Weber Nicholsen, edited by Ed. Rolf Tiedemann. In *Notes to Literature.* New York: Columbia University Press, 1991.

Agrarian Utopia. Directed by Uruphong Raksasad. 2009. Bangkok: Extra Virgin, 2011. DVD.

Ajami. Directed by Scandar Copti and Yaron Shani. 2009. New York: Kino, 2010. DVD.

Albrecht-Crane, Christa, and Dennis Cutchins. *Adaptation Studies: New Approaches.* Madison: Fairleigh Dickinson University Press, 2010.

Algren, Nelson. *Nonconformity: Writing on Writing.* New York: Seven Stories, 1996.

Algren, Nelson, Brooke Hovath, and Dan Simons. *Entrapment.* New York: Seven Stories Press, 2011.

Alibar, Lucy. *Juicy and Delicious.* New York: Diversion Books, 2012.

Armes, Roy. *Third World Filmmaking and the West.* Berkeley: University of California Press, 1987.

Aronson, Linda. *The 21st Century Screenplay: A Comprehensive Guide to Writing Tomorrow's Films.* Crows Nest: Allen & Unwin, 2010.

Aufderheide, Patricia. *Documentary Film: A Very Short Introduction.* Oxford: Oxford University Press, 2007.

Bachelard, Gaston. *Poetics of Reverie.* Boston: Beacon Press, 1971.

——. *The Poetics of Space.* Translated by M. Jolas. Boston: Beacon Press, 1994.

Badawi, Muhammed. *A Critical Introduction to Modern Arabic Poetry.* Cambridge: Cambridge University Press, 1975.

Balio, Tino. *Grand Design: Hollywood as a Modern Business Enterprise 1930–1939.* Berkeley: University of California Press, 1995.

Barrett, Frank J. 'Coda: Creativity and Improvisation in Jazz and Organizations: Implications for Organizational Learning'. *Organization Science* 9, no. 5 (1998): pp. 605–22.

Barthes, Roland. *Image, Music, Text.* London: Fontana Press, 1977.

Bartolini, Luigi. *Bicycle Thieves: The Story of a Stolen Bicycle in Rome.* London: MacMillan, 1952.

Bauman, Zygmunt. *Liquid Times: Living in an Age of Uncertainty.* Cambridge: Polity, 2007.

——. *Living on Borrowed Time: Conversations with Citlali Rovirosa-Madrazo.* Cambridge: Polity Press, 2010.

Bayard, Pierre. *How to Talk About Books You Haven't Read.* New York: Bloomsbury, 2007.

Beard, William. *Into the Past: The Cinema of Guy Maddin*. Toronto: University of Toronto Press, 2010.

Beasts of the Southern Wild. Directed by Ben Zetlin. 2012. Los Angeles: Fox Searchlight, 2012. DVD.

Berger, John. *And Our Faces, My Heart, Brief as Photos*. London: Bloomsbury, 2005.

———. *About Looking*. London: Bloomsbury, 2009.

Berkitt, Ian. *Social Selves: Theories of Self and Society*. London: Sage, 2008.

Berkowitz, Aaron. *The Improvising Mind: Cognition and Creativity in the Musical Moment*. Oxford: Oxford University Press, 2010.

Berliner, Paul. *Thinking in Jazz*. Chicago: University of Chicago Press, 1997.

Bicycle Thieves. Directed by Vittorio De Sica. 1948. New York: Criterion, 2007. DVD.

Biesecker, Barbara A., and John Louis Lucaites, eds. *Rhetoric, Materiality, and Politics*. Vol. 13. New York: Peter Lang, 2009.

Biro, Yvette. *Turbulence and Flow in Film: The Rhythmic Design*. Bloomington: Indiana University Press, 2008.

Blatner, Adam. *Foundations of Psychodrama: History, Theory and Practice*. New York: Springer, 2000.

Bollendorff, Samuel. *The Forced March*. Paris: Textual, 2008.

Bolter, Jay David. *Writing Space: Computers, Hypertext, and the Remediation of Print*. Hillsdale: Lawrence Erlbaum, 1991.

Boon, Kevin Alexander. *Script Culture and the American Screenplay*. Detroit: Wayne State University Press, 2008.

Bordwell, David. 'The Art Cinema as a Mode of Film Practice'. In *The European Cinema Reader*, edited by Catherine Fowler. London: Routledge, 2002.

Bordwell, David, Janet Steiger, and Kristin Thompson. *The Classical Hollywood Cinema: Film Styles and Modes of Production to 1960*. Oxon: Routledge, 2006.

Brady, Martin, Joanne Leal, Wim Wenders, and Peter Handke. *Collaboration, Adaptation, Recomposition*. Amsterdam: Rodopi, 2011.

Brink, Joram Ten. *Building Bridges: The Cinema of Jean Rouch*. London: Wallflower, 2007.

Bull, Stephen. *Photography*. Abingdon: Routledge, 2009.

Burgin, Victor. *The Remembered Film*. London: Reaktion, 2004.

Bus 174. Directed by Jose Padhila and Felipe Lacerda. 2002. Albert Park: Accent, 2004. DVD.

Campbell, Neil, and Alfredo Cramerotti, eds. *Photocinema: Working at the Creative Edges of Photography and Film*. Bristol: Intellect, 2013.

Cardullo, Bert. *Michelangelo Antonioni: Interviews*. Jackson: University Press of Mississippi, 2008.

———. ' "The Fruitful Tree Bends": Abbas Kiarostami'. In *Action!: Interviews with Directors from Classical Hollywood to Contemporary Iran*, edited by Gary Morris. London: Anthem Press, 2008.

———. *Loach and Leigh, Ltd.: The Cinema of Social Conscience*. Newcastle upon Tyne: Cambridge Scholars Publishing, 2010.

———. *Soundings on Cinema*. Albany: State University of New York Press, 2011.

———. *World Directors in Dialogue: Conversations on Cinema*. Plymouth: Scarecrow Press, 2011.

Carrière, Jean-Claude. *The Secret Language of Film*. New York: Pantheon, 1994.

Carruthers, Mary. *The Book of Memory: A Study of Memory in Medieval Culture.* Cambridge: Cambridge University Press, 1990.

Cartier-Bresson, Henri. *The Mind's Eye: Writings on Photography and Photographers.* New York: Aperture, 1999.

Certeau, Michel de. *Arts De Faire.* Vol. 1. Berkeley: University of California Press, 2011.

Chanan, Michael. *The Dream That Kicks: The Early Years and Pre-History of Cinema in Britain.* London: Routledge, 1994.

Christin, Anne-Marie. *A History of Writing.* 2nd ed. Paris: Flammarion, 2002.

Corrigan, Timothy. *The Essay Film: From Montaigne, after Marker.* Oxford: Oxford University Press, 2011.

Cunha, Miguel, and Ken Kamoche. *Organizational Improvisation.* London: Routledge, 2004.

Dancyger, Ken, and Jeff Rush. *Alternative Scriptwriting: Successfully Breaking the Rules.* Burlington: Focal Press, 2007.

Dawson, Gary. *Documentary Theatre in the United States.* Westport: Greenwood, 1999.

Didion, Joan. 'To the Islands'. In *Live and Learn.* London: Harper Perennial, 2005.

District 9. Directed by Neill Blomkamp. 2009. Los Angeles: Sony Pictures, 2009. DVD.

Do Right and Fear No-one. Directed by Jutta Brückner. 1975. Mainz: ZDF,

Donin, Nicolas. 'Empirical and Historical Musicologies of Compositional Processes: Towards a Cross-Fertilisation'. In *The Act of Musical Composition: Studies in the Creative Process,* edited by Dave Collins. Farnham: Ashgate, 2012.

Donmez-Colin, Gonul, ed. *The Cinema of North Africa and the Middle East.* London: Wallflower, 2007.

Eco, Umberto. *The Open Work.* Cambridge: Harvard University Press, 1989.

Elder, Bruce. *Harmony and Dissent: Film and Avant-Garde Art Movements in the Early Twentieth Century.* Vol. 3. Waterloo: Wilfred Laurier University Press, 2008.

Elena, Alberto, and Maria Diaz Lopez. *The Cinema of Latin America.* London: Wallflower Press, 2003.

Elster, Jon. *Ulysses Unbound: Studies in Rationality, Precommitment and Constraints.* Cambridge: University of Cambridge Press, 2000.

Five Dedicated to Ozu. Directed by Abbas Kiarostami. 2004. New York: New Yorker, 2007. DVD.

Follow the Fleet. Directed by Mark Sandrich. 1936. Los Angeles: Universal Pictures, 2005. DVD.

Frampton, Hollis. *On the Camera Arts and Consecutive Matters.* Cambridge: MIT Press, 2009.

Frank, Arthur W. 'Enacting Illness Stories'. In *Stories and Their Limits: Narrative Approaches to Bioethics,* edited by Hilde Lindemann Nelson. London: Routledge, 1997.

——. *Letting Stories Breathe: A Socio-Narratology.* Chicago: University of Chicago Press, 2010.

Ganz, Adam. 'Time, Space and Movement: Screenplay as Oral Narrative'. *Journal of Screenwriting* 1, no. 2 (2010): pp. 225–36.

——. ' "Leaping Broken Narration": Ballads, Oral Storytelling and the Cinema'. *Storytelling in World Cinemas* 1: Forms, Vol. 1 (2012): pp. 71–89.

——. 'Play from Slide Show: PowerPoint, Screenwriting, and Writing on Screen'. Presented at Screenwriting in a Global and Digital World, 6th Screenwriting Research Network International Conference, Madison, 2013.

Garga, Bhagwan Das. *So Many Cinemas: The Motion Picture in India*. Mumbai: Eminence Designs, 1996.

Gassner, John, and Edward Quinn, eds. *The Reader's Encyclopedia of World Drama*. Mineola: Dover, 2002.

Gates of Heaven. Directed by Errol Morris. 1978. Los Angeles: MGM, 2005. DVD.

Gaut, Berys. *A Philosophy of Cinematic Art*. Cambridge: Cambridge University Press, 2010.

Gerow, Aaron. *Kitano Takeshi*. London: British Film Institute, 2007.

Geuens, Jean-Pierre. *Film Production Theory*. Albany: State University of New York Press, 2000.

——. 'The Space of Production'. *Quarterly Review of Film and Video* 24, no. 5 (2007): p. 413.

Ginsberg, Terri, and Chris Lippard. *Historical Dictionary of Middle-Eastern Cinema*. Lanham: Scarecrow Press, 2010.

Ginzburg, Carlo. 'Clues: Roots of an Evidential Paradigm'. Translated by John Tedeschi and Anne C. Tedeschi. In *Clues, Myths, and the Historical Method*. Baltimore: Johns Hopkins University Press, 1989.

Gokulsing, K. Moti, and Wimal Dissanayake. *Routledge Handbook of Indian Cinemas*. Abingdon: Routledge, 2013.

Gordon, Robert. *Bicycle Thieves*. London: British Film Institute, 2008.

Gottschall, Jonathan. *The Storytelling Animal: How Stories Make Us Human*. New York: Houghton Mifflin Harcourt, 2012.

Griffiths, Simon, and Anthony Giddens. *Sociology*. Cambridge: Polity, 2006.

Grimshaw, Anna, and Amanda Ravetz. *Observational Cinema: Anthropology, Film, and the Exploration of Social Life*. Bloomington: University of Indiana Press, 2009.

Gruber, Howard. 'The Evolving Systems Approach to Creative Work'. In *Creative People at Work: Twelve Cognitive Case Studies*, edited by Howard Gruber and Doris Wallace. Oxford: Oxford University Press, 1989.

——. 'Network of Enterprise in Creative Scientific Work'. In *Creativity, Psychology and the History of Science*, edited by Howard E. Gruber and Katja Bödeker. Dordrecht: Springer, 2005.

Grundmann, Roy, and Cynthia Rockwell. 'Truth Is Not Subjective: An Interview with Errol Morris'. *Cineaste* 25, no. 3 (2000): p. 4.

Gulzar, Govind Nihalani, and Saibal Chatterjee, eds. *Encyclopaedia of Hindi Cinema*. New Delhi: Encyclopaedia Britannica (India), 2003.

Guo, Li. *The Performing Arts in Medieval Islam: Shadow Play and Popular Poetry in Ibn Daniyal's Mamluk Cairo*. Vol. 93. Leiden: Brill, 2011.

Hallam, Julia. *Realism and Popular Cinema*. Manchester: Manchester University Press, 2000.

Hamilton. Directed by Matthew Porterfield. 2006. New York: Cinema Guild, 2011. DVD.

Hare, A. Paul, and June Hare. *J.L. Moreno*. London: SAGE Publications, 1996.

Harishchandrachi Factory. Directed by Paresh Mokashi. 2009. Los Angeles: Disney, 2010. DVD.

Hazel, Smith, and Roger Dean. *Improvisation, Hypermedia and the Arts since 1945*. Amsterdam: Harwood Academic Publishers, 1997.

Heath, Dan, and Chip Heath. *Made to Stick: Why Some Ideas Take Hold and Others Come Unstuck*. London: Random House, 2007.

Henley, Paul. *The Adventure of the Real: Jean Rouch and the Craft of Ethnographic Filmmaking*. Chicago: University of Chicago Press, 2009.

Hines, Barry. *A Kestrel for a Knave*. London: Penguin Group, 2010.

History of Australian Cinema: The Pictures That Moved, Part 1. Directed by Alan Anderson. 1968. Collingwood: Artfilms, 2004. DVD.

Hjort, Mette. *Lone Scherfig's Italian for Beginners*. Seattle: University of Washington Press, 2010.

Hochman, Stanley. *Mcgraw-Hill Encyclopedia of World Drama*. Vol. 1. New York: McGraw Hill, 1984.

Hu, Jubin. *Projecting a Nation: Chinese National Cinema before 1949*. Hong Kong: Hong Kong University Press, 2003.

Hu, Tze-Yue G. *Frames of Anime: Culture and Image-Building*. Hong Kong: Hong Kong University Press, 2010.

Huber, George P., and William H. Glick, eds. *Organizational Change and Redesign: Ideas and Insights for Improving Performance*. Oxford: Oxford University Press, 1995.

Huhtamo, Erkki. 'Natural Magic: A Short Cultural History of Moving Images'. In *The Routledge Companion to Film History*, edited by William Guynn. Abingdon: Routledge, 2011.

——. 'Screen Tests: Why Do We Need an Archeology of the Screen?' *Cinema Journal* 51, no. 2 (2012): pp. 144–8.

Hutcheon, Linda. *A Theory of Adaptation*. 2nd ed. Abingdon: Routledge, 2012.

Hyde, Lewis. *The Gift: Creativity and the Artist in the Modern World*. London: Vintage, 2007.

I Used To Be Darker. Directed by Matthew Porterfield. 2013. Park City: Sundance Film Festival, Hamilton Film Group.

Inga, Karetnikova. *How Scripts Are Made*. Carbondale: Southern Illinois University Press, 1990.

Ings, Simon. *The Eye: A Natural History*. London: Bloomsbury, 2008.

Jencks, Charles, and Nathan Silver. *Adhocism: The Case for Improvisation*. Cambridge: MIT Press, 2013.

Jenkins, Henry. *Convergence Culture: Where Old and New Media Collide*. New York: New York University Press, 2006.

Jenkins, Henry, and David Thorburn, eds. *Rethinking Media Change: The Aesthetics of Transition*. Cambridge: MIT Press, 2003.

John-Steiner, Vera. *Notebooks of the Mind: Explorations of Thinking*. 2nd ed. Oxford: Oxford University Press, 1997.

Joshi, Om Prakash. *Painted Folklore and Folklore Painters of India: A Study with Reference to Rajasthan*. New Delhi: Concept Publishers, 1976.

Kafka, Ben. *The Demons of Paperwork*. New York: Zone Books, 2012.

Kaminishi, Ikumi. *Explaining Pictures*. Honolulu: University of Hawaii Press, 2006.

Kember, Sarah. *Virtual Anxiety: Photography, New Technology and Subjectivity*. Manchester: Manchester University Press, 1998.

Kenis, Patrick, Martyna Janowicz, and Bart Cambre, eds. *Temporary Organizations: Prevalence, Logic and Effectiveness*. Northampton: Edward Elgar, 2009.

Kes. Directed by Ken Loach. 1969. New York: Criterion, 2011. DVD.

Keyhole. Directed by Guy Maddin. 2011. Thousand Oaks: Monterey Media, 2012. DVD.

Kiarostami, Abbas. 'With Borrowed Eyes'. *Film Comment* 36, no. 4 (2000): pp. 20–5.

Kleiner, Fred. *Gardner's Art through the Ages: A Global History.* Boston: Wadsworth, 2010.

Knowles, Dorothy. *Armand Gatti in the Theatre: Wild Duck against the Wind.* London: Athlene Press, 1989.

Kress, Gunther. *Learning to Write.* 2nd ed. London: Routledge, 1994.

——. *Literacy in the New Media Age.* London: Routledge, 2003.

Kress, Gunther, and Theo van Leeuwen. *Reading Images: The Grammar of Visual Design.* Abingdon: Routledge, 2006.

La Pointe Courte. Directed by Agnès Varda. 1955. New York: Criterion, 2008. DVD.

Land Without Bread. Directed by Luis Bunuel. 1928. New York: Kino, 2000. DVD.

Laurent, Olivier. 'From Photography to Web-Documentaries: Samuel Bollendorff's *Nowhere Safe'. British Journal of Photography* (2012).

Lehmann, Hans-Thies. *Postdramatic Theatre.* Abingdon: Routledge, 2006.

Leigh, Jacob. *The Cinema of Ken Loach: Art in the Service of the People.* London: Wallflower Press, 2002.

Lessig, Lawrence. *Remix: Making Art and Commerce Thrive in the Hybrid Economy.* New York: Penguin Group, 2008.

Leviathan. Directed by Lucian Castaing-Taylor and Verena Paravel. 2012. New York: Cinema Guild, 2013. DVD.

Levitin, Jacqueline, Valerie Raoul, and Judith Plessis, eds. *Women Filmmakers: Refocusing.* Vancouver: University of British Columbia Press, 2003.

Loftus, Elizabeth F. *Eyewitness Testimony.* Cambridge: Harvard University Press, 1996.

Lopate, Phillip. 'In Search of the Centaur: The Essay-Film'. In *Beyond Document: Essays on Non-Fiction Film,* edited by Charles Warren. Middletown: Wesleyan University Press, 1996.

Mabey, Richard. *Nature Cure.* London: Pimlico, 2005.

Macdonald, Ian. 'Disentangling the Screen Idea'. *Journal of Media Practice* 5, no. 2 (2004): pp. 89–100.

MacDougall, David. *The Corporeal Image: Film, Ethnography and the Senses.* Princeton: Princeton University Press, 2006.

Maddin, Guy. *My Winnipeg.* Toronto: Coach House Books, 2009.

Mahoney, Charles, ed. *A Companion to Romantic Poetry.* Vol. 73. Chichester: Wiley Blackwell, 2011.

Mai, Joseph. *Jean-Pierre and Luc Dardenne.* Champaign: University of Illinois Press, 2010.

Mair, Victor H. *Painting and Performance: Chinese Picture Recitation and Its Indian Genesis.* Honolulu: University of Hawaii Press, 1988.

Man Push Cart. Directed by Ramin Bahrani. 2005. New York: Noruz Films, 2007. DVD.

Man with a Movie Camera. Directed by Dziga Vertov. 1929. London: BFI, 2000. DVD.

Maras, Steven. *Screenwriting: History, Theory and Practice.* London: Wallflower Press, 2009.

Martin, Adrian. 'Kind of a Revolution, and Kind of Not: Digital Low-Budget Cinema in Australia Today'. *Scan* 3, no. 2 (2006).

——. 'Where Do Cinematic Ideas Come From?' *Journal Of Screenwriting* (forthcoming).

Maslow, Abraham. *Religion, Values, and Peak-Experiences*. New York: Viking, 1970.

Mason, William, and Sandra Martin. *The Art of Oman Khayyam*. London: I.B. Tauris, 2007.

McKee, Robert. *Story: Substance, Structure, Style, and the Principles of Screenwriting*. New York: HarperCollins, 1997.

Millard, Kathryn. 'Writing for the Screen: Beyond the Gospel of Story'. *Scan* 3, no. 2 (2006).

——. 'The Screenplay as Prototype'. In *Analysing the Screenplay*, edited by Jill Nelmes. Abingdon: Routledge, 2011.

——. 'A Screenwriter's Hunger Reality'. Paper presented at the Nonfiction Now Conference, RMIT, Melbourne, November 2012.

Moholy-Nagy, Laszlo. 'From Pigment to Light (1936)'. In *Photography in Print: Writings from 1816 to the Present*, edited by Vicki Goldberg. Albuquerque: University of New Mexico Press, 1981.

Moreno, Jacob. 'Psychodrama and Therapeutic Motion Pictures'. *Sociometry* 7, no. 2 (1944): pp. 230–44.

Morris, Errol. 'Truth Not Guaranteed: An Interview with Errol Morris'. *Cineaste* 17, no. 1 (1989): pp. 16–17.

Mosley, Philip. *The Cinema of the Dardenne Brothers: Responsible Realism*. New York: Columbia University Press, 2013.

Munt, Alex. 'Digital Kiarostami and the Open Screenplay'. *Scan* 3, no. 2 (2006).

Murphy, Alexandra. *Jean-François Millet: Drawn into the Light*. New Haven: Yale University Press, 1999.

Murphy, J.J. *Me and You and Memento and Fargo: How Independent Screenplays Work*. New York: Continuum, 2007.

——. 'No Room for the Fun Stuff: The Question of the Screenplay in American Indie Cinema'. *Journal of Screenwriting* 1, no. 1 (2010): pp. 175–96.

——. *The Black Hole of the Camera: The Films of Andy Warhol*. Berkeley: University of California Press, 2012.

Musser, Charles. *The Emergence of Cinema: The American Screen to 1907*. Vol. 1. Berkeley: University of California Press, 1994.

Muth, Jon J. *M: A Graphic Novel Based on the Film by Fritz Lang*. New York: Harry N. Abrams, 2008.

My Winnipeg. Directed by Guy Maddin. 2007. Montreal: Seville Pictures, 2008. DVD.

Naficy, Hamid. *A Social History of Iranian Cinema*. Vol. 2. Durham: Duke University Press, 2011.

Nanook of the North. Directed by Robert J. Flaherty. 1922. New York: Criterion, 1999. DVD.

Narayan, Kirin. *Storytellers, Saints and Scoundrels: Folk Narrative in Hindu Religious Teaching*. Philadelphia: University of Pennsylvania Press, 1989.

Nash, Eric. *Manga Kamishibai: The Art of Japanese Paper Theatre*. New York: Abrams, 2009.

Nashville. Directed by Robert Altman. 1975. Los Angeles: Paramount, 2000. DVD.

Nettl, Bruno. *The Radif of Persian Music: Studies of Structure and Cultural Context.* Champaign: Elephant and Cat, 1987.

——. *Excursions in World Music.* Upper Saddle River: Prentice Hall, 1997.

——. 'On Learning the Radif and Improvisation in Iran'. In *Musical Improvisation: Art, Education and Society,* edited by Gabriel Solis and Bruno Nettl. Champaign: University of Illinois Press, 2009.

Neupert, Richard. *A History of the French New Wave.* Madison: University of Wisconsin Press, 2007.

Norman, Marc. *What Happens Next: A History of American Screenwriting.* London: Aurum, 2008.

Ong, Walter J. *Orality and Literacy.* New York: Routledge, 2002.

Parklands. Directed by Kathryn Millard. 1996. Sydney: Magnolia Pacific, 2003. DVD.

Patience (After Sebald). Directed by Grant Gee 2012. New York: Cinema Guild, 2012. DVD.

Pavis, Patrice. *Dictionary of the Theatre: Terms, Concepts and Analysis.* Toronto: University of Toronto Press, 1998.

Peterson, Robert S. *Comics, Manga and Graphic Novels: A History of Graphic Narratives.* Santa Barbara: ABC-CLIO, 2011.

Pinney, Christopher. *'Photos of the Gods': The Printed Image and Political Struggle in India.* London: Reaktion, 2004.

Pratt, Lise, and Christel Dillbohner, eds. *Searching for Sebald: Photography after W.G. Sebald.* Los Angeles: Institute of Cultural Inquiry, 2007.

Psycho. Directed by Alfred Hitchcock. 1960. Los Angeles: Universal Pictures, 2003. DVD.

Putty Hill. Directed by Matthew Porterfield. 2006. New York: Cinema Guild, 2011. DVD.

Quigley, Austin E. *The Modern Stage and Other Worlds.* London: Methuen, 1985.

Raja Harishchandra. Directed by Dadasaheb Phalke. 1913. Pune: National Film Archive of India, 2012. DVD.

Rajadhyaksha, Ashish, and Paul Willemen. *Encyclopedia of Indian Cinema.* New Delhi: BFI and Oxford University Press, 1994.

Rajkhowa, Bijoya Baruah. 'Oral Tradition of the Ramayana in North East India'. In *Critical Perspectives on the Ramayana,* edited by Jaydipsinh Dodiya. New Delhi: Sarup, 2001.

Ranade, Ashoka Da. *Hindi Film Song: Music Beyond Boundaries.* New Delhi: Promilla & Co., 2006.

Random 8. Directed by Kathryn Millard. 2012. Sydney: Ronin Films, 2013. DVD.

Reiniger, Lotte. *Shadow Theatre and Shadow Plays.* London: Batsford, 1970.

Ritchin, Fred. *After Photography.* New York: W. W. Norton, 2009.

——. *Bending the Frame: Photojournalism, Documentary and the Citizen.* New York: Aperture, 2013.

Rorty, Richard, ed. *The Linguistic Turn: Essays in Philosophical Method.* Chicago: University of Chicago Press, 1992.

Rossellini, Roberto, and Adriano Aprà. *My Method: Writings and Interviews.* New York: Marsilio Publishers, 1995.

Rouch, Jean. *Ciné-Ethnography.* Vol. 13. Minneapolis: University of Minnesota Press, 2003.

Ruiz, Raúl. *Poetics of Cinema*. Vol. 2. Paris: Editions Dis Voir, 2007.

Rushdie, Salman. *Haroun and the Sea of Stories*. London: Granta, 1991.

Sack, Chuck. 'Joan Tewkesbury on Screenwriting: An Interview'. *Literature-Film Quarterly* 6, no. 1 (1978): pp. 2–25.

Saeed-Vafa, Mehrnaz, and Jonathan Rosenbaum. *Abbas Kiarostami*. Champaign: University of Illinois Press, 2003.

Salamon, Julie. *The Devil's Candy: The Anatomy of a Hollywood Fiasco*. Cambridge: Perseus Books, 2002.

Sanjog. Directed by Abdul Rashid Kardar. 1942. Concord: Samrat International, 2000. DVD.

Sawyer, Keith. *Group Genius: The Creative Power of Collaboration*. New York: Basic Books, 2007.

Schatz, Thomas. 'New Hollywood, New Millennium'. In *Film Theory and Contemporary Hollywood Movies*, edited by Warren Buckland. New York: Taylor and Francis, 2009.

Schön, Donald. *The Reflective Practitioner: How Professionals Think in Action*. New York: Basic Books, 1983.

Sebald, W.G. *The Rings of Saturn*. London: Random House, 1998.

Semsel, George Stephen, Hong Xia, and Jianping Hou, eds. *Chinese Film Theory: A Guide to the New Era*. New York: Praeger, 1990.

Sengupta, Amitabh. *Scroll Paintings of Bengal: Art in the Village*. Bloomington: AuthorHouse, 2012.

Sennett, Richard. *The Craftsman*. London: Allen Lane, 2008.

Shalwitz, Howard. 'Theatrical Innovation: Whose Job Is It?' Paper presented at the TCG Conference, 21 June 2012.

Shiel, Mark. *Italian Neorealism: Rebuilding the Cinematic City*. London: Wallflower Press, 2006.

Shields, David. *Reality Hunger: A Manifesto*. New York: Penguin Group, 2010.

Shklovsky, Victor. *Literature and Cinematography*. Translated by Irina Masinovsky. Champaign: Dalkey Archive Press, 2008.

Shoeshine. Directed by Vittorio De Sica. 1946. Toronto: Entertainment One, 2011. DVD.

Shternshis, Anna. *Soviet and Kosher Jewish Popular Culture in the Soviet Union 1923–1939*. Bloomington: Indiana University Press, 2006.

Silberman, Marc. 'Interview with Jutta Brückner: Recognising Collective Gestures'. *Jump Cut*, no. 27 (1982): pp. 46–7.

Sitney, P. Adams. *Vital Crises in Italian Cinema: Iconography, Stylistics, Politics*. New York: Oxford University Press, 2013.

Solis, Gabriel, and Bruno Nettl, eds. *Musical Improvisation: Art, Education and Society*. Champaign: University of Illinois Press, 2009.

Stam, Robert. *Flagging Patriotism*. London: Routledge, 2007.

Stam, Robert, and Randal Johnson. *Brazilian Cinema*. New York: Columbia University Press, 1997.

Standard Operating Procedure. Directed by Errol Morris. 2008. Los Angeles: Sony Pictures, 2008. DVD.

Steiner, Vera John. *Notebooks of the Mind: Explorations of Thinking*. Oxford: Oxford University Press, 1997.

Stewart, Alex. *Making the Scene: Contemporary New York City Big Band Jazz*. Berkley: University of California Press, 2007.

Stories from the North. Directed by Uruphong Raksasad. 2006. Bangkok: Extra Virgin, 2010. DVD.

Stott, William. *Documentary Expression and 1930s America.* Chicago: University of Chicago Press, 1986.

Stranger Than Paradise. Directed by Jim Jarmusch. 1984. New York: Criterion, 2007. DVD.

Straw, Will. 'Reinhabiting Lost Languages: Guy Maddin's Careful'. In *Canada's Best Features: Critical Essays on 15 Canadian Films,* edited by Eugene P. Walz. Amsterdam: Rodopi, 2002.

Sunrise: A Song of Two Humans Photoplay. Directed by F.W. Murnau. 1927. Los Angeles: Fox Films, 2009. DVD.

Sweetgrass. Directed by Lucien Castaing-Taylor and Ilisa Barbash. 2009. New York: Cinema Guild, 2010. DVD.

Temple, Michael, and James Williams, eds. *The Cinema Alone: Essays on the Work of Jean-Luc Godard 1985–2000.* Amsterdam: University of Amsterdam Press, 2010.

Templeton, Ed. *The Seconds Pass.* New York: Seems, 2010.

The Battle of The Rails. Directed by Rene Clement. 1946. Chicago: Facets, 2006. DVD.

The Beaches of Agnès. Directed by Agnès Varda. 2008. London: Artificial Eye, 2010. DVD.

The Boot Cake. Directed by Kathryn Millard. 2008. Sydney: Ronin Films, 2009.

The Exiles. Directed by Kent Mackenzie. 1961. New York: Milestone Films, 2009. DVD.

The First National Collection. Directed by Charles Chaplin. 1923. Los Angeles: Image, 2000. DVD.

The Fog of War: Eleven Lessons from the Life of Robert S. McNamara. Directed by Errol Morris. 2009. Los Angeles: Sony Pictures, 2004. DVD.

The Gleaners and I. Directed by Agnès Varda. 2000. London: Artificial Eye, 2011. DVD.

The Gleaners and I: Two Years Later. Directed by Agnès Varda. 2002. London: Artificial Eye, 2011. DVD.

The Gold Rush. Directed by Charles Chaplin. 1926. New York: Criterion, 2012. DVD.

The Great Dictator. Directed by Charles Chaplin. 1940. New York: Criterion, 2011. DVD.

The Lost Thing. Directed by Shaun Tan. 2010. Richmond: Madman, 2010. DVD.

The Thin Blue Line. Directed by Errol Morris. 1988. Los Angeles: MGM, 2005. DVD.

The White Balloon. Directed by Jafar Panahi. 1995. Los Angeles: PolyGram, 1996. DVD.

Thompson, Joshua. *Six Seconds in Dallas: A Micro-Study of the Kennedy Assassination.* New York: B. Geis, 1967.

Thompson, Kristin. *Breaking the Glass Armor: Neoformalist Film Analysis.* Princeton: Princeton University Press, 1998.

Three Songs of Lenin. Directed by Dziga Vertov. 1934. Los Angeles: Image Entertainment, 2000. DVD.

Tomasulo, Frank. 'Re-Reading Bicycle Thieves'. In *Vittorio De Sica: Contemporary Perspectives,* edited by Stephen Synder and Howard Curle. Toronto: University of Toronto Press, 2000.

Top Hat. Directed by Mark Sandrich. 1935. Los Angeles: Universal Pictures, 2005. DVD.

Toulet, Emmanuelle. *Cinema Is 100 Years Old*. London: New Horizons/Thames and Hudson, 1998.

Travelling Light. Directed by Kathryn Millard. 2003. Sydney: Magna Pacific, 2003. DVD.

Trend, David. *The End of Reading: From Gutenberg to Grand Theft Auto*. New York: Peter Lang, 2010.

Tulving, Endel. *Elements of Episodic Memory*. Oxford: Oxford University Press, 1985.

Tunbridge, Laura. *The Song Cycle*. Cambridge: Cambridge University Press, 2010.

Varadpande, Manohar Laxman. *History of the Indian Theatre: Panorama of Folk Theatre*. Vol. 2. New Delhi: Abhinav, 1992.

——. *History of the Indian Theatre: Classical Theatre*. Vol. 3. New Delhi: Abhinav, 2005.

Vernon, Florida. Directed by Errol Morris. 1981. Los Angeles: MGM, 2005. DVD.

Versaci, Rocco. *This Book Contains Graphic Language: Comics as Literature*. New York: Continuum, 2007.

Vertov, Dziga. *Kino-Eye: The Writings of Dziga Vertov*. Translated by Kevin O'Brien. Berkeley: University of California Press, 1984.

Walking from Munich to Berlin. Directed by Oskar Fischinger. 1927. Los Angeles: CVM, 2006. DVD.

Wallace, David Foster. *Consider the Lobster: Essays and Arguments*. New York: Hatchette, 2012.

Ware, Mike. 'John Herschel's Cyanotype: Invention or Discovery?' *History of Photography* 22, no. 4 (1998): pp. 371–9.

Weick, Karl. 'Organizational Redesign as Improvisation'. In *Organizational Change and Redesign: Ideas and Insights for Improving Performance*, edited by George P. Huber and William H. Glick. New York: Oxford University Press, 1995.

——. *Sensemaking in Organizations*. Thousand Oaks: Sage, 1995.

——. 'Improvisation as a Mindset for Organizational Analysis'. *Organization Science* 9, no. 5 (1998): pp. 543–55.

——. 'Improvisation as a Mindset for Organizational Analysis'. In *Organizational Improvisation*, edited by Miguel Pina e Cunha, João Vieira da Cunha and Ken Kamoche. London: Routledge, 2004.

Weick, Karl E., and Kathleen M. Sutcliffe. *Managing the Unexpected: Resilient Performance in an Age of Uncertainty*. San Fransisco: John Wiley & Sons, 2007.

Weiss, Beno. *Italo Calvino*. Columbia: University of Southern Carolina Press, 1993.

Wells, Paul. *Basics Animation 01: Scriptwriting*. Lausanne: AVA Publishing, 2007.

Willis, Holly. *New Digital Cinema: Reinventing the Moving Image*. London: Wallflower Press, 2005.

Wings of Desire. Directed by Wim Wenders. 1987. New York: Criterion, 2003. DVD.

Woolf, Virginia. 'A Sketch of the Past'. In *Moments of Being: Unpublished Autobiographical Writings*, edited by Jeanne Schulkind. London: Chatto and Windus for Sussex University Press, 1976.

Yarrow, Ralph. *Indian Theatre: Theatre of Origin, Theatre of Freedom*. Richmond: Curzon, 2001.

Zarhy-Levo, Yael. *The Making of Theatrical Reputations*. Iowa City: University of Iowa Press, 2008.

Zavattini, Cesare. 'Some Ideas on the Cinema'. *Sight and Sound* 23, no. 2 (1953): pp. 64–9.

———. *Sequences from a Cinematic Life*. Upper Saddle River: Prentice Hall, 1970.

Zhang, Yingjin. *Chinese National Cinema*. New York: Routledge, 2004.

Zhen, Zhang. *An Amorous History of the Silver Screen: Shanghai Cinema 1896–1937*. Chicago: University of Chicago Press, 2005.

Zielinski, Siegfried. *Deep Time of the Media: Toward an Archaeology of Hearing and Seeing by Technical Means*. Translated by Gloria Custance. Cambridge: MIT Press, 2008.

Index

Note: The letter 'n' following locators refers to notes.

Lightning Source UK Ltd.
Milton Keynes UK
UKOW01f1552231216
290763UK00001B/33/P